FLASH FORESIGHT

TESTIMONIALS

"I love this book! It's as much fun to read as it is inspiring to learn from. Buy it, read it, and put it to use—in a flash!"

—**Alan M. Webber,** co-founder, *Fast Company* magazine

"With the increasing pressure to innovate and gain competitive advantages, leaders from start-ups to multi-national organizations will find deep insights from the seven principles of *Flash Foresight*. It will change the way you think about your current obstacles and open your mind to limitless opportunities.

—**Terry Jones,** founder of Travelocity and chairman of Kayak.com

"Fascinating! A powerful competitive weapon that cuts through the clutter, *Flash Foresight* shows you what you need to do to survive and thrive in the challenging times that lie ahead."

—**Rear Admiral David Bill III,** USN

"Full of provocative insights and powerful strategies from a veteran entrepreneur. The 'Take Your Biggest Problem—and Skip It' chapter alone is worth the price of admission."

—**Steve Forbes,** editor in chief of *Forbes* and CEO of Forbes Inc.

"After reading *Flash Foresight* and applying the principles to our business, in less than a year we have been able to double our revenues and increase the value of our company by a factor of four."

—**Arnie Bellini,** former CEO of ConnectWise

"For a quarter century Daniel Burrus has made a science out of showing individuals, companies, and organizations how to discover the limitless potential of their own future. *Flash Foresight* is an outstanding blueprint for innovation and success!"

—**Anthony Robbins,** author, entrepreneur, and peak performance strategist

"*Flash Foresight* is a revolutionary book that offers the insights and strategies leaders will need to profit from the transformational times ahead."

—**Marshall Goldsmith,** author of *Mojo* and *What Got You Here Won't Get You There*

"*Flash Foresight* is all about accelerating business and personal growth, showing you how to see major hidden opportunities, skip over the most difficult problems, and using the power of certainty to transform your business and your life. I highly recommend it!"

—**Jack Canfield,** co-author of *The Success Principles* and bestselling *Chicken Soup for the Soul®* series

"What if you could predict the future? Reinvent the way you solve problems? Skip over an obstacle and get right to the finish line? Read *Flash Foresight* and let Daniel Burrus show you how. The possibilities are infinite. This book doesn't just think outside the box—it's nowhere *near* the box."

—**Ken Blanchard,** co-author of *The One Minute Manager®* and *Leading at a Higher Level*

"Superbly written and thoroughly researched, *Flash Foresight* equips the reader with seven valuable principles that provide uniquely effective strategies to grow personally as well as professionally."

—**Stephen R. Covey,** author, *The 7 Habits of Highly Effective People* and *The Leader in Me*

"*Flash Foresight* provides a flight plan through turbulence and a provocative window to the future that will stimulate a great amount of innovation and positive change."

—**Howard Putnam,** former CEO of Southwest Airlines

"In uncertain times, foresight needs to be 20/20. Daniel Burrus' visionary concepts shed new light on the strategies that will keep your business looking bright."

—**Harvey Mackay,** author of *Swim with The Sharks Without Being Eaten Alive*

"*Flash Foresight* is filled with powerful stories that teach readers how to get bursts of insight about the future that reveal hidden opportunities and provide real solutions to what were seemingly impossible problems. I highly recommend it!"

—**Peter Guber,** chairman and CEO of Mandalay Entertainment Group; producer of *The Color Purple, Rain Man,* and *Gorillas in the Mist*

"*Flash Foresight* is full of powerful, useful, easy-to-understand-and-apply principles for discovering and inventing the future . . . When you are finished, you'll never see the future in the same way again."

—**Joel Barker,** author of *Paradigms: The Business of Discovering the Future*

"A must-read for leaders in both business and education, *Flash Foresight* provides provocative insights that will intrigue and inspire your professional and personal life."

—**Dr. Nido Qubein,** president of High Point University; chairman of Great Harvest Bread Co.

"This book is nothing short of a revelation. A must-read for any thought leader and all those who aspire to be."

—**Joe Calloway,** author of *Becoming a Category of One*

"I always get great insights from Daniel Burrus, and his new book, *Flash Foresight,* does not disappoint! Not only will it help you create a brighter future, but it will also give you tools and ideas for living better today. I highly recommend it."

—**Mark Sanborn,** author of *The Fred Factor* and *You Don't Need a Title to be a Leader*

"This book is extraordinary! A brilliant must-read for any executive who chooses to play big and not settle for incremental improvement. This book could create a worldwide transformation."

—**Roxanne Emmerich,** author of *Thank God It's Monday! How to Create a Workplace You and Your Customers Love*

"If people had understood and applied the strategies in *Flash Foresight,* we might have avoided some of the trials and tribulations of recent times. Here's to a brighter future for everyone who reads and uses Daniel's book."

—**Tom Hopkins,** author of *Selling in Tough Times*

"*Flash Foresight* is chock-full of examples showing how organizations of all sizes have applied Burrus's seven powerful principles to do seemingly impossible things. A fast read that will prime the pump for any entrepreneur or organization ready to transform their product or service."

—**Dianna Booher,** author of *The Voice of Authority* and *Communicate with Confidence*

FLASH FORESIGHT

ALSO BY DANIEL BURRUS

Technotrends

The Anticipatory Organization

FLASH FORESIGHT

How to See the Invisible and Do the Impossible

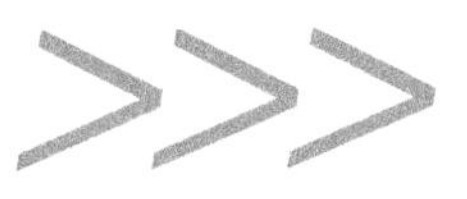

SEVEN RADICAL PRINCIPLES THAT WILL TRANSFORM YOUR BUSINESS

DANIEL BURRUS

with John David Mann

RIVER GROVE BOOKS

This publication is designed to provide accurate and authoritative information in regard to the subject matter covered. It is sold with the understanding that the publisher and author are not engaged in rendering legal, accounting, or other professional services. Nothing herein shall create an attorney-client relationship, and nothing herein shall constitute legal advice or a solicitation to offer legal advice. If legal advice or other expert assistance is required, the services of a competent professional should be sought.

Published by River Grove Books
Austin, TX
www.rivergrovebooks.com

Distributed by River Grove Books

Design and composition by Jaime Putorti
Cover design by Jaime Putorti

Publisher's Cataloging-in-Publication data is available.

Print ISBN: 978-1-966629-17-7

eBook ISBN: 9780062036551

First Edition

To my wife, my soul mate, my best friend, and biggest fan, Sharon: you are a constant source of love and inspiration.

And to the millions of people around the world who have been in my audiences, read my books, and taken action on the ideas I sparked in their minds. It is your positive actions that fuel my passion for continuing to inspire you to shape a better tomorrow.

FLASH

n. 1. a sudden burst of light or glint from a reflective surface. 2. an insight that occurs suddenly and unexpectedly: *a flash of inspiration.*

FORESIGHT

n. 1. knowledge or insight gained by looking into the future. 2. perception of the nature of events before they occur.

FLASH FORESIGHT

n. a sudden burst of insight about the future that produces a new and radically different way of doing something that will open up invisible opportunities and solve seemingly impossible problems before they happen.

>>> CONTENTS

>>> INTRODUCTION

Something gave Dale Morgen a big idea.

Like most of us, Dale was concerned about the rising cost of energy, the problems of environmental pollution and climate change, and the politics of petroleum. Like most of us, he also knew that the nuclear-power alternative creates its own problems, including radioactive waste and the nagging threat of a catastrophic accident, not to mention the possibility of theft and nuclear terrorism.

However, unlike most of us, Dale is an accomplished inventor with more than thirty wildly successful patents under his belt.[1] In the course of his work he has honed a certain skill, and that skill is the *something* that gave him his big idea. I call it *flash foresight,* and the purpose of this book is to show you how it works so you can use it, too, in your career and in your life.

Flash foresight uses the data of your five senses, as well as that intuitive sixth sense we all have that some call a *gut feeling* or *hunch*. But flash foresight goes further, because in using it you synthesize those sensory and intuitive faculties and project them forward through the dimension of *time.* A *flash foresight* is a blinding flash of the future obvious. It is an intuitive grasp of the foreseeable future that, once you see it, reveals hidden opportunities and allows you to solve your biggest problems—*before* they happen. Flash foresight will allow *anyone* to both see and shape his or her future.

I'm not telling you anything you don't already know instinctively. You've had flash foresights; we all have. They are those fleeting glimpses we sometimes have of where things might be heading. Have you ever said, "I *knew* I should have done that," or "I *knew* that would happen"? That's hindsight, and it happens because you don't typically know ahead of time when your hunch is accurate and when it's not. Learning how to make that distinction—between glimpses of the future that are reliable foresight, and those that are simply hunches—is what this book is about. Flash foresight is a sensibility, a skill you can develop, refine, and strengthen. I'll show you how it works and how you can make it work for you on a regular basis.

Through the pages of *Flash Foresight,* we'll look at real people with real problems who have discovered how to find real solutions. We'll see how hundreds of overworked critical care nurses were able to add more than three hours of free time into their impossibly busy days; how a struggling urban school district found a way to generate the income to pay for its own endangered programs—without having to spend a dime; and how a phone company is transforming the social and economic landscape of Africa by doing something its American competitors never thought of. We'll look at dozens of examples of how people just like you have used flash foresight to see the invisible and do the impossible.

Let's start with our inventor Dale and see how he used this powerful principle to arrive at his great idea.

Dale knew that there is another approach to our worsening energy crisis that does *not* use fossil fuels, does *not* produce greenhouse gases or any other pollution, does *not* create radioactive waste or pose any other environmental dangers. It's called *nuclear fusion,* and many scientists believe it could become the energy source of the twenty-first century and beyond.

"Let's say you burn a certain amount of hydrogen and oxygen in today's most efficient fuel cell," explains Morgen, "and you get ten electron volts. Take two hydrogen isotopes and *fuse* them, now you get 16.7 *million* electron volts. Fusing the hydrogen from a bathtub's worth of water would produce the same amount of energy you'd get from burning forty trainloads of coal. A relatively tiny amount of ocean water would provide everyone on the planet with all the energy we could ever use for the next 50,000 years. And the only by-product is harmless, nonradioactive helium."

Understandably, this prospect has a lot of major international players hot on the fusion trail. For example, a consortium of twenty countries, including the United States, China, Japan, Korea, Russia, and a half-dozen European countries, is building a massive, multibillion-dollar facility in southern France. The International Thermonuclear Experimental Reactor (ITER) is the most expensive project ever mounted in pursuit of this holy grail. At California's famous Lawrence Livermore lab, another fusion facility is under construction that will span three football fields to blast its millimeter-sized hydrogen-fuel pellets with massive lasers.

However, there's a problem. So far, even with these massive and astronomically costly facilities, the fusion reaction requires more energy going in than it yields in output. Like an investment that keeps losing money, today's fusion reactors produce a net energy *loss*. The largest functioning fusion reactor in the world is the U.K.'s Joint European Torus (JET), yet even that facility has been able to reach a maximum output of barely two-thirds the input required—like investing $100 to get back a total return of less than $65.

And that's where Dale's idea comes into the picture. His flash foresight was this: *Instead of making these facilities bigger and bigger, why not make them radically smaller?* In fact, why not make a fusion reactor so small you can't even see it—so small it would be built out of single molecules? In a word: *nanofusion.*

Dale is not alone in this idea; he is one of a handful of early innovators who are exploring the emerging field of nanofusion. Dale's model is similar to the Lawrence Livermore reactor in concept, only instead of firing mile-long lasers at small glass pellets, his reactor would fire a nanolaser made from a single carbon molecule—called a *nanotube*—at hydrogen isotopes wrapped inside another type of carbon molecule called a *buckyball.* This material has a much higher purity and density—and lo and behold, it produces a *net positive yield*: more energy coming out than it takes to make the reaction. Potentially, says Dale, *vastly* more.

Imagine the impact such a technology would have on the world. For all practical purposes, there would be no more energy crisis. Oil-producing nations would become just nations like any other—still producing oil, but no longer supplying the bulk of our energy needs. We would have enough energy to fuel our global economy for centuries—conceivably, forever—and without producing any greenhouse gases or radioactive waste.

"A lot of the other guys in fusion didn't even want to hear about this idea, at first," says Dale. "They thought we were crazy—but they said that about my other inventions, too." The long list of "crazy" inventions in whose development Dale's keen sense of flash foresight has played a key role includes the personal digital assistant (PDA) and matrix control for LCD and plasma TVs.

"Most people in the scientific community think practical fusion is fifty to a hundred years away," Dale adds. "We don't think it will take that long."

There are still considerable technological barriers to realizing this radical idea. For one thing, the nanofusion pioneers need to find a way to create a viable nano-based superconductor. "That's a formidable challenge," says Dale. How long does he think it will take to surmount the various challenges and actually have a working model of the process? "I'd say, oh, ten to fifteen years. Maybe less."

This book is not about nanofusion, or predicting that nanofusion will be the answer, or even about solving the energy crisis. It's about the *something* that gave Dale his big idea. What was that *something*? Was it a hunch, a gut instinct? A feeling? Intuition? No—it was something far more powerful than any of these. It was *flash foresight*.

Dale's insight is a classic *eureka!* moment, one of those legendary leaps of informed intuition, like Newton's discovery of gravity after watching an apple fall from a tree, or Kekulé's dream of a ring of snakes that prompted his discovery of the carbon ring, the foundation of organic chemistry. We think of such flashes of insight as the hallmark of unfathomable genius—a kind of inspired epiphany that defies explanation or logic. Yet Dale's intuitive leap was actually triggered by the application of one simple principle.

Before we pull away the curtain and reveal exactly what that principle is, let's look at one more example—this one from a very different side of the energy equation.

In early 2006 I happened to speak at a conference of international insurance underwriters, where a series of oil executives described the extent of the devastation wrought during the previous hurricane season in the Gulf of Mexico.

This 800-mile basin is currently the source of nearly one-third of America's domestic oil supply and one-quarter of our natural gas. It is also one of the most hurricane-prone bodies of water on the planet, making the environmentally dicey business of oil extraction even more challenging.

Like most of us, these executives were also concerned about the rising costs of energy—in their case, on an especially vast scale. Sea-based oil platforms are among the largest mobile structures in the world. One platform, aptly named Thunder Horse, cost $5 billion to build and put out on the gulf. Another, with the modest name of Mars, sports a drilling rig that alone weighs 1,000 tons. Housing thousands of people, such a *flotel* (as these facilities are called) is really a miniature city perched out on the ocean's surface.

These superstructures are designed to withstand "100-year conditions," that is, to survive a hurricane so powerful it should occur only once every century or so. Unfortunately, those once-per-century storms have been happening a lot lately. In the fall of 2004 Hurricane Ivan ripped through the gulf, generating the highest waves ever recorded in the region. Wrecking seven platforms and crippling production for the next six months, Ivan was rated a *2,500*-year storm.

A year later, Katrina happened. There are about 800 manned, U.S.-owned oil platforms in the gulf, employing more than 50,000 people; the bulk of production is concentrated in about two dozen of them, each costing at least a billion or two to put into the water.

Katrina destroyed or sank fifty platforms and shut down 95 percent of production.

Now, the conference speakers explained, engineers faced the challenge of figuring out how to redesign these billion-dollar "hurricane-proof" giants to be twenty-five times *more* hurricane-proof.

"And that's not the worst of it," whispered the man sitting next to me, an executive with an oil company. "As bad as they are, hurricanes may not be our biggest problem. It hasn't happened yet, but we need to be prepared for the possibility of a terrorist attack. But how? It's hard enough to protect our guys from the elements out there. How the heck do you create top-level security out on the open sea?"

It was a thorny question, and while nobody asked it from the stage, it was on everyone's mind. Whoever spoke next would have to address it somehow. That next person turned out to be me: I was about to give the event's keynote address.

As a technology forecaster and strategist, I've tracked innovations in science and technology for more than twenty-five years, helping businesses and other organizations around the globe craft creative and productive strategies for the future based on technology-driven trends.

I took the stage, looked out at the group, and said, "Okay, we've clearly got a problem. Here's what we might do to deal with it—we could take the rigs off the water's surface and put them down on the ocean floor."

It wasn't hard to read their faces: *Impossible!* And who could blame them? It certainly *sounds* like science fiction, and ten years ago, it would have been. But technology allows us to make the impossible possible. We already use robotics for sophisticated vehicle repair in outer space and delicate surgery deep inside the human body. In fact, we already use robots on the ocean floor for exploration, equipment repair, and other tasks. We can certainly manage the tasks involved in robotic undersea oil extraction—and with far more efficiency, safety, and environmental integrity than we're doing now.

Here's the basic plan I quickly sketched out for the group.

"We put our platform on the water's surface, connected to the ocean floor, just as we presently do—only instead, we design the structure so that the drilling facility can disengage and move on, something like the segments of a rocket ship, leaving the platform behind. Once the drilling is done, we disengage the drill, submerge the platform, and let it descend to the ocean floor. All the people move on with the drill and head for their next drilling location or for port, leaving behind a pumping platform on the ocean floor with robotics performing all the necessary tasks for operations and maintenance.

"Of course, it would make the most sense to implement this at first in shallower water, where the majority of our wells are anyway, that is, to walk before we run. Once we've perfected the process, we can look at moving it out into deeper water—if we even need deepwater operations by that point.

"At present, most of the personnel on our oil rigs are there purely to support those few who do the actual work on the rigs, spending months away from their families in a harsh, punishing environment. Hundreds of lives have been lost in ocean rig disasters over the years. The cost of maintaining these flotels, in both economic and human terms, is staggering. Manage the task robotically, and you almost eliminate the need for staffing, which means a huge reduction in both the economic costs *and* the risk of casualties.

"And it would be far safer for the environment as well.

"During Katrina, we lost eight or nine million gallons of oil—nearly as much as we lost in the *Exxon Valdez* disaster. Even with all the catastrophic damage on the gulf's surface, the most vulnerable piece of the whole puzzle is the elaborate network of underwater pipelines. There's some 33,000 miles of piping down there that was badly damaged by Hurricane Ivan in 2004, causing a large invisible underwater spill. The way we're set up right now, it's difficult and expensive to do an effective job of repairing that network—but once we invest in the advanced robotics and underwater electronics to run the submerged facilities, it'll be a small step to extend our reach and maintain a far safer piping network."

Four years later this idea took on an entirely new significance when another disaster happened in the gulf, this one caused not by hurricanes or terrorism but by that deadliest of foes, human fallibility. On April 20, 2010, an oil well blowout led to an explosion on the Deepwater Horizon, an oil platform on the gulf's surface. The fire burned out of control and two days later the platform sank to the ocean floor, creating a swath of entangled cables, broken pipes, and snapped valves—and an oil spill even worse than that of the *Exxon Valdez*.

Suddenly the operators and designers of the platform were rushing to come up with technological solutions to an underwater disaster happening at nearly one mile deep. It was a classic and tragic case of hindsight: being forced to act in reaction to a crisis rather than with the calm deliberation of foresight.

Investigations later revealed that the rig's operators, BP, had cut significant corners in the Deepwater Horizon operation and, furthermore, that the federal government had issued waivers granting BP categorical exclusion from conducting the usual environmental-impact studies because, as BP put it, "a catastrophic blowout was impossible." But nothing is impossible. Obviously, as hindsight tells us, these cost-cutting steps were a series of calamitous errors. But let's take a closer look at the context of the disaster.

The catastrophic explosion and fire on the Deepwater Horizon could only have happened on the water's surface, not underwater, on the ocean floor. In fact, the great majority of all oil spills have started with problems that occurred on the surface.

Imagine for a moment that the Deepwater Horizon had been designed to submerge and operate on the ocean floor. If that were true, the explosion and resulting mass of broken piping would have been an unlikely scenario. And if we had been investing significant efforts and resources in advanced oil-spill containment and cleanup as well as the underseas application of advanced robotics (as we have, for example, with applications in surgery and space vehicle repair), the chances are excellent that, even if such an accident did occur, we would have been able to mobilize the necessary technology to stop the leak within days, before it became serious, instead of months.

I'm not necessarily forecasting that this idea represents the future of oil extraction, but it certainly suggests interesting possibilities.

It's too late now to prevent the Deepwater Horizon disaster, but that 2006 flash foresight has since borne fruit. Some in the industry have begun working in earnest on the concept, and in the foreseeable future we will see a far safer, more economical, and more environmentally sound approach to oil extraction.

Have you guessed what the simple flash foresight principle is underlying both Dale Morgen's nanofusion and this ocean-floor oil rig concept? It's this: *Go opposite.* While everyone else in fusion was focusing on building gigantic reactors that filled football fields, Dale and his colleagues went in the opposite direction, designing one so small it would easily fit onto the point of a pin.

The conventional design for oil rigs puts them on the surface of the ocean. Our solution was to *do the opposite,* and place them on the ocean floor.

The reason this principle works is as simple as the principle itself: when you look in the opposite direction from where everyone else is looking, you see things nobody else is seeing. It opens up hidden opportunities, unnoticed resources, and overlooked possibilities, acting as a spark that ignites a flash foresight. Practicing *go opposite* lets you see things that up until that moment were invisible—and therefore impossible—to almost everyone.

At my company, we track the very latest developments in every imaginable aspect of technology—lasers, robotics, genetics, fiber optics, everything. We look at these developments globally and have been doing so for more than a quarter century. Having spent most of my time over those years looking into the visible future, here is something I've noticed: *The more you look, the more you see.* The question is, where are you looking? The key to the power of *go opposite* is that it puts you looking where no one else is looking. Do that long enough, and you'll start seeing what no one else is seeing—which will give you the ability to do what no one else is doing.

Here are some examples of successes in diverse areas that arose from flash foresights that were triggered by the *go opposite* idea, whether or not their creators were consciously aware of it (and if it isn't immediately obvious why each of these is an example of *go opposite,* don't worry, we'll revisit them all, one by one, in Chapter 5).

- Amazon.com
- Crocs
- Dell
- JetBlue and Southwest Airlines
- Kiva
- Netflix
- Starbucks
- Volkswagen
- Zappos

Warren Buffett, the famed investor, has explained his uncanny knack for making successful investments with just twelve words: "Be greedy when others are fearful, and fearful when others are greedy." A beautifully simple expression of *go opposite,* and one that has earned him billions.

So, is it really that simple? Just do the opposite of what everyone else is doing, and you'll solve the problem nobody else is solving? Of course not. But it's *nearly* that simple. *Go opposite* is only one flash foresight trigger. Over the twenty-five years I've been studying and systematically applying flash foresight, I've discovered *seven* such triggers.

1. *Start with certainty* (use hard trends to see what's coming).
2. *Anticipate* (base your strategies on what you know about the future).
3. *Transform* (use technology-driven change to your advantage).
4. *Take your biggest problem and skip it* (it's not the real problem anyway).
5. *Go opposite* (look where no one else is looking to see what no one else is seeing and do what no one else is doing).
6. *Redefine and reinvent* (identify and leverage your uniqueness in new and powerful ways).

7. *Direct your future* (or someone else will direct it for you).

Not every flash foresight uses every one of these triggers, but most will use at least several. You can think of it as something like the seven notes of the musical scale. Not all melodies use all seven notes. But if you want to know how to write music, you'd better know all seven, because you're going to need them sooner or later.

If you were to freeze-frame Dale Morgen's thought process and examine each thread, you would actually find a number of these triggers interacting to spark his flash foresight, and the same holds true with the oil rig concept. In fact, let's track a few of these. Of course, Dale is an inventor, and I'm a technology forecaster—but if you follow what we both did here, you'll find you can use these same principles just as easily in your life, too.

As mentioned, my company has been tracking cutting-edge innovations in all areas of technology for over twenty-five years. This has made us familiar with the facts and particulars of oil drilling (Chevron, ExxonMobil, and Shell are on my client list), and also with the current state of the art in robotics and the other technical issues involved. So this example of flash foresight began with trigger 1: *Start with certainty.*

This familiarity with trends in technology also allows me to know what technology can and can't do today, how it's changing, and—most important—what will be possible tomorrow. In other words, to *anticipate,* trigger 2. Knowing the extraordinary leaps technology will be taking in just a few short years allows me to look at doing things in completely new and seemingly impossible ways, rather than just doing them in the same ways we currently do them but with incremental improvements: in other words, to completely *transform,* trigger 3.

The big problem here was "how to protect rigs on the water's surface." Instead of trying to solve that problem, we decided to *skip* it altogether—trigger 4—by taking the rigs *off* the water's surface. And put them where? *Go opposite,* trigger 5: go to the ocean floor.

How do we do this? By using trigger 6, *redefine and reinvent,* redeploying the type of technology we're already using for prostate surgery and EVA (extravehicular activity) repairs on spaceflights to completely reinvent the oceanic oil-extraction process.

Do you see what just happened there? In rapid sequence, we just used six of the seven flash foresight triggers. It looks quite methodical and sequential when we reverse-engineer the whole process; in those few moments before it was my turn to speak, the actual flash foresight came rather more intuitively and immediately. But that's simply a matter of practice.

Using these flash foresight triggers is very much like walking. When you break down the act of walking into its component parts, it's quite complex: shifting your balance from ball to toe and then left to right, compensating the shift with a swing of your arms—if you had to think about every muscular element, you'd be overwhelmed. And so you were, when as an infant you took your first halting steps. Yet today you stride without a thought.

That's what flash foresight is like. At first you consciously exercise all seven mental processes, one at a time, carefully and perhaps haltingly. In time, it comes more naturally, and eventually it becomes fluid and virtually effortless.

Sometimes flash foresight is about using an amazing new technology, as with the oil rigs. But just as often, it's not about technology at all, but simply about using your eyes to look at things in a different way.

Years ago a young friend opened a brand-new pediatric dental practice in the Chicago area. We had lunch one day, not long after her grand opening. She had been very excited about opening her new office, and I asked her how it was going.

"Not as well as I'd like," she confessed. She had a modest clientele, but her few patients were not generating the referrals she had hoped for. She needed word about her practice to spread, but it wasn't happening. She wondered, would I mind coming in and taking a look, to see what I might notice? So we got up from our lunch and went right up to her office. I spent five or ten minutes looking around, and then asked her to come back out with me to the entrance for a moment.

"This is a children's practice, right?" I said. "So let's start by approaching it from a child's point of view."

This time, we got down on our knees, shuffled into the waiting room, and looked around. "What do you see?" I asked my friend.

She glanced at me with surprise. "Not much of anything!"

It was true. Everything in the room was set at eye level—*adult* eye level. The receptionist was a wonderfully sweet and friendly person, but because she sat way up there behind an adult-scale desk, if you were a kid coming into the place you wouldn't even see her face.

"For starters," I suggested, "what if we lowered that reception desk so we can make eye contact with your nice receptionist? Then, what about our sense of hearing? When you first come into the room, what does it sound like?"

We both listened. It sounded like someone evil was torturing mice in the next room. Not the kind of sound you want to hear when you're a child coming in to see the dentist. I suggested we put in some one-beat-per-second music to evoke the sense of a heartbeat. It would be calming and soothing, and cover up all that noise from the drills and other equipment. A bit of sound-deadening material in the treatment rooms wouldn't hurt, either.

Then I asked my friend, "What does it smell like?"

Almost as soon as I said the words, she wrinkled her nose. Frankly, it smelled just like a doctor's office. To a child, that smell equals *panic*. The moment a kid walks in that door he's thinking about the last time he got a shot, and he doesn't like it.

My friend looked at me. "We need to change that, don't we?" she said.

"It sure seems so," I agreed.

My friend's problem was that she was thinking like a dentist, not like a kid. It was a matter of perspective—and once again, a case of using the *go opposite* trigger: instead of thinking like a grown, tall adult, think like a young, short kid.

The next time I visited her office, she had transformed the place. In fact, she had implemented every one of the ideas we'd discovered. Her practice was thriving.

Flash foresight is what you get when you combine that shift of perspective, that willingness to get down on your hands and knees and look at things from a fresh point of view, with a grasp of where current trends of change are taking us in the future. It's about transforming the impossible with a glimpse of the possible.

You may not be personally concerned with protecting oil rigs from hurricanes or single-handedly solving the energy crisis. You've got your own life, with its own unique challenges. Like my pediatric dentist friend, maybe you're trying to figure out how to make your business work, how to keep your company's head above water, or how to further your career when all the best jobs are drying up. The problems you're facing are probably a lot less dramatic than protecting an oil rig in a hurricane—but to you, they may feel just as urgent, and just as impossible. Maybe it's a time crunch or a financial squeeze, a disappearing market, an impossible workload, or an unsolvable situation. Whatever it is, there is an elegant solution; all we need to do is make it visible.

In the past, flash foresight was useful, but not essential. Things changed so gradually, we could get by without it. Today, as the pace of technological change accelerates almost beyond the point of comprehension, it's essential.

There was a time when only a select few—the priests, scribes, and accountants—knew how to read. There was a time when only a few dozen people had ever driven a car, even fewer who cared. There was a time when only a handful of academic researchers and military strategists knew what the Internet was or how to use it.

Up to now, only a handful have known how to use flash foresight. It's time *everyone* knew.

FLASH FORESIGHT

>> CHAPTER ONE

Start with Certainty

On March 10, 1986, I walked onto the shop room floor of a vast, open manufacturing plant on the edge of Kansas City, stepped to a microphone, cleared my throat, and looked out at the several thousand men and women who sat silently waiting to hear what this visiting speaker had to say. They were not happy; in fact, they were furious.

We were standing at ground zero of a labor-management dispute at the Folgers Coffee Company that had led to a deadlock in negotiations. For the first time in the facility's seventy-eight-year history, they had shut down the entire plant to have a companywide meeting.

Some weeks beforehand, one of the executives had heard me speak and approached me afterward to ask if I would come talk to their employees, who were locked in a contract clash. I pointed out that he was talking to a futurist, not a mediator; labor disputes were not exactly my area. He said he understood that, but in one of my talks, he'd heard me speak about the principle of *starting with certainty,* and he had a sense that idea might help break the logjam. In any case, he wanted me to come give it a shot.

And now, here it was, the big moment. I licked my lips, and the microphone crackled.

"My name is Dan Burrus," I began, "and your bosses invited me here to speak with you. But I want you to know that I've already been paid—so frankly, now that I'm here, I can say whatever I want."

A tense laugh rippled through the crowd.

"Before we go any further," I continued, "maybe we can agree on a few things. Can we all agree that you would all like to stay employed?"

A few dozen heads nodded grimly, and I jotted down a check-mark by the first item of a list I'd written on a blank pad that morning: STAY EMPLOYED.

"Can we all agree that you'd rather not have to relocate your families to other cities?"

This time a few hundred heads nodded, and a handful of voices muttered, "Hell yes!" and "Damn straight!" I checked off another item: STAY IN KANSAS CITY.

"Let's see, what else . . . Can we agree that we'd rather see this company stay in business than go belly-up?"

It went on like this for a while, and by the time we were finished, we'd worked our way through forty different points of alignment. I read the list out loud, glanced up at the assembly of workers and then at the smaller cluster of management sitting nearby, and said, "That's forty things you agree on. Seems to me, the only thing you have to work out is how you're going to make these forty things happen."

And the amazing thing was, *they did*. Before they knew it, the workers settled their grievances with the Folgers management and the plant was rolling again.

What happened here? After all, I didn't bring them any new information. By asking questions, all I did was to bring out of them what they *already knew*. Yet that was enough to break through the impasse, forge a new contract, and get their company back to production. The workers at Folgers already had everything they needed to find the solutions they sought. The problem was that they had been focusing on what they did *not* agree on instead of what they *did*.

Nations often do this, too; so do married couples. We all do it. It's so easy to focus on the *can't*: what we *can't* resolve, where we *don't* see eye-to-eye, what we *don't* know. But with that as our focus, coming to any kind of common understanding is just about impossible.

The same thing is true about the future. Doesn't it seem like the times we live in are full of uncertainty? In fact, more uncertain than ever before? Like everything is changing so much and so fast, there's just no way to know what's coming at us?

Not true. No matter how much it may seem like that, that's not how it really is. In fact, there's more certainty about our future today than ever before. We know a great deal more about the future than we think we know. We just need to understand where to look. Like the striking workers at Folgers, we can easily be overwhelmed by how much we think is impossible to predict. But the more we focus our attention on what seems uncertain—on what we *don't* know—the more we incapacitate our ability to take successful action.

For example, take the American automobile.

In the fall of 2004, at an evening event for the American Public Transportation Association, I had the opportunity to sit next to Rick Wagoner, then chairman and CEO of General Motors.

As the evening relaxed into informal socializing, Rick made a few comments to our group about the future of the auto industry and the U.S. economy that echoed statements I've heard from presidents, prime ministers, and leaders of organizations around the world.

> *Well, we just don't know . . . We give it our best guess, but who really knows where it'll all go? . . . The truth is, it's impossible to say—no matter how much data you gather and project, the future is flat-out unpredictable.*

If this were true, the future would indeed be a fearsome and forbidding place, fraught with impossible dangers. If it were true, frankly, our situation would be pretty hopeless. And if it were true, there would be no point in writing this book.

Fortunately, it *isn't* true. There is plenty about the future that is entirely predictable. But it's certainly understandable why Rick should have been so steeped in doubt and uncertainty. Just look at what his company, his industry, and his country had been going through.

At the dawn of the twentieth century, no nation was brimming with more potential than America, and no invention had a brighter future than the American automobile. The motor car represented the best of American ingenuity and innovation, and in the course of the century it changed forever the way we lived and thought, shopped and courted, made war and spread the peace. In 1953, at the century's midpoint, the president of GM made a declaration that echoed for decades: "What's good for GM is good for the country." A variation of that assertion became one of the American century's most pervasive slogans: "As GM goes, so goes the nation."

So, how was GM going? By the time I sat at dinner with Rick Wagoner, not so well. General Motors, which for decades had reigned supreme as the largest industrial company in the world, had lost billions of dollars, shut down more than a dozen plants, and laid off tens of thousands of employees. It would get worse. In the first quarter of 2007, for the first time in over seventy-five years, GM lost its title as the world's leading automaker—to Toyota. By the summer of 2009 Rick was forced to resign (along with hundreds of other executives) and the company, now a recipient of an astronomical federal bailout, was struggling to emerge from bankruptcy. Once the largest company in the world, GM had become the largest corporate business failure in history.

The American automobile started out as a brilliant example of flash foresight. What happened? The industry fell prey to the natural human tendency to protect and defend the status quo. It stopped looking to the future and asking, "What do we know—for sure?"

As GM goes, so goes the nation. Where is the American automobile going—or for that matter, where is America itself going? What I heard Rick saying in 2004 was: "We don't really know." But we *do* know—or at least, we know a great deal more than we realize.

In speeches I often say, "Wouldn't it be great if you could predict the future—and be right?" and the audience always laughs. It never fails. Perhaps this is because they know on a gut level that whenever someone says he's going to predict the future, the chances are excellent that he'll be *wrong*. (How often do you read the headline "Noted Psychic Wins Lottery"?) But perhaps they also laugh out of a sense of delight, because they know that if it *were* possible, it would be amazing. Imagine, if you could predict the future *and be right*? What an advantage you'd have! And that's exactly the point of this book.

Here is the next point I usually make in my talks: "You *can* predict the future accurately. All you have to do is leave out the parts you could be wrong about."

That, too, always gets a laugh—but I'm serious. And the amazing thing is, when you do leave out the parts you could be wrong about, there's enough left that you can be right about to make all the difference. The question is, how do you know which is which? That is the first of our seven flash foresight triggers, and it's what this chapter is about.

>>>Cyclic Change

In the book of Ecclesiastes, King Solomon wrote, "Vanity of vanities; all is vanity," and his words are echoed in the teachings of the ancient Greek thinker Heraclitus, who said, "*Panta rhei*," which means "Everything changes." Lao Tzu agreed, writing in the Tao Te Ching, "The only thing that is permanent is change."

It does seem true: the only thing that *never* changes is the fact that everything *always* changes. The only permanent thing about our world is that all is in a state of constant flux. Which is pretty disturbing, isn't it? After all, if we're looking for certainty, that doesn't give us much to go on . . . does it?

Actually, it does. In fact, it gives us *everything we need*. Because there are certain patterns in how things change that are as dependable as clockwork.

There are two distinct kinds of change we can use to find certainty; the first is *cyclic change.*

Cyclic change provides us with all sorts of certainty. Right now it's autumn here in the Northern Hemisphere, and I can confidently predict that within six months, it will be spring. Nature is brimming with examples of cyclic change; understanding the cycles of seasons, weather, crop development, animal migration, tidal fluctuations, and other such cycles helped create the first civilizations. In fact, the history of civilization is to some extent the story of humanity getting a grip on cyclic change and using it to increase our chances for survival.

There are also cycles in our economy and body politic, of boom times and lean times, expansive and defensive behaviors. Shakespeare wrote, "There is a tide in the affairs of men which, taken at the flood, leads on to fortune," and that tide appears in every aspect of our lives. Prices and interest rates rise and fall; Democrats rule Congress, then Republicans. There is a push toward the apparent safety of totalitarianism, and then a counter-push toward the greater personal freedoms of liberalism. Social standards grow more permissive, then more restrictive, and then back toward more permissive. The pendulum swings until it can swing no further, then reverses course and backtracks.

Politically, economically, socially, in every channel of human expression, we manifest with a tide that perennially ebbs and flows. Like a great social heartbeat, the mood of the people expands and contracts, now progressive and gregarious, now more conservative and protectionist. Moods cycle, reflected in fashions, politics, and even international relations, as well as personal relationships. In fact, humanity has identified over *three hundred* distinct cycles that allow us to accurately predict the future to some extent.

EXAMPLES OF CYCLIC CHANGE

planting and harvest
birth and death
day and night

tides and phases of the moon
seasons
migrations
stock prices
economic recessions
building and real estate activity
seasonal sales
interest rates

Keeping a sober eye on the truth of cyclic change lies at the heart of Warren Buffett's uncanny success as an investor; he is a master of those "tides in the affairs of men." In our introduction we mentioned Buffett's famous investment philosophy, "Be fearful when others are greedy, and greedy when others are fearful." In addition to being a good example of the *go opposite* principle, it is also a perfect example of understanding cyclic change. Buffett's simple philosophy illustrates the dictum *start with certainty.* If the market is contracting, then what can we know for certain? That before long, it will expand again. And if the market is going through a robust expansion, what does certainty tell us? Get ready for a contraction.

In 2008 the U.S. economy slipped into its worst crisis since the Great Depression of the 1930s. In this sophisticated, postmodern world, how could such a thing have possibly happened? Because we ignored the simple truth of cyclic change. Did we really think the real estate market would rapidly expand forever? That housing values would just go up, up, up, in some cases doubling in a year, and never come back down? Based on our actions, evidently that is exactly what we thought.

Of course, we knew this wouldn't *really* happen; we knew that property values can't dramatically increase forever because, as any schoolchild could tell us, "What goes up, must come down." But we got caught up in all the flurry of the moment, of possibilities and exhilaration. We got confused by our own hopes that the market would rise and rise and keep on rising without cyclical corrections happening. We ignored what we knew and got distracted by what we didn't. We forgot to *start with certainty.*

"Yes," you might be thinking, "but nobody could have predicted with any certainty exactly *when* this would all come crashing down . . . could they?"

Actually, they could. In a 2005 radio interview, Yale economics professor Robert J. Shiller, author of *Irrational Exuberance* and *The Subprime Solution*, pointed out that U.S. real estate prices were "out of touch with economic reality" and called the market "a bubble" that would burst before long. This, added Shiller, was a *certainty*: "The only question is when."

In fact, you didn't need to be a professor of economics to see this; you just needed to look. Most of the subprime mortgages that precipitated this crisis were interest-only adjustable-rate mortgages (ARMs) set to start ballooning at either the five-year or seven-year mark. The real estate boom got under way in 2000 and was roaring by 2002 and 2003. If you start with 2002 to 2003 and add five years, you get 2007 to 2008—which was exactly when it all started to melt down. As homeowners began defaulting on mortgages and rushing to sell, real estate prices that were already falling began plummeting. And a large number of seven-year ARMs would reset in 2009 and 2010, driving the foreclosure trend even further. Obviously, this was not the only factor in this complex crisis, but this is nevertheless a perfect example of how cyclic change can yield predictability.

The truth is, a lot of people sensed this crash coming. They just hoped it wouldn't. But hope is not a strategy. Certainty is.

The same thing happened with the high-tech bubble of 1998 to 2000. In March 2000, the month the NASDAQ reached its high point, savvy investors were already following the Buffett dictum, pulling out of tech stocks and taking a more cautious position. Likewise, as the stock market came crashing down in the fall of 2008, while most were panicking and selling off their imploding stock portfolios, savvy investors were wading into the fray and quietly buying those financial stocks that were hit worst.

Why? Because they knew that cyclic change is inevitable. And this was not a guess: they knew this with *certainty*.

>>>Linear Change

However, cyclic change is not the whole story. Having a clear grasp of cyclic change is an important element of flash foresight, but it's not the core of the matter. Developing a keen sense of flash foresight depends more on the certainty that comes from understanding another pattern of change, one that is quite different from cyclic change. This second pattern is *acyclic* and *progressive*—that is, it does not cycle back on itself but progresses forward in one direction only. In other words, within this second type of change, what goes up does *not* necessarily come down. I call this *linear change*.

A simple example of linear change is your age. Your life progresses in one direction; no matter how well you take care of your health, you are not going to start aging backward. Actually, there *is* a cyclic nature to human aging, too, in that after you go through your teenage years, before long your children will start going through those same phases, and then your grandchildren, and so forth. And there is yet another cyclic overlay to the human journey, in that we begin as helpless babies, then mature and become autonomous adults, and then in our later years progressively lose our strength and faculties and become more dependent again, almost like a second infancy.

Still, in the absolute sense, *aging itself is linear*. Your children will grow up to become adults, but they will not then "de-age" back to become young again.

Or take a larger example, that of social and governmental change. As we have already noted, society's moods ebb and flow in a variety of cycles, including a pendulum swing within each individual society between a more liberal, open culture and a more restrictive, defensive, and reactionary one.

At the same time, as you look back over the full sweep of global history, you cannot help seeing a larger pattern of unidirectional, linear change. Despite the localized ebbs and flows, there has been an overall consistent trend toward more and more freedom for more and more people. There is something going on here that is not cyclic. Despite its many setbacks and temporary defeats, the march of freedom has moved throughout history in one linear direction.

EXAMPLES OF LINEAR CHANGE

aging (of individual)
growth in the earth's population
increase in data, information, and knowledge
increase in worldwide literacy
increasing number of patents and inventions
acceleration of computer processing speed
convergence of features and functions
globalization

The varieties of cyclic change are endless; some cycles rise and fall sharply, like the EKG of a heartbeat, while others arc more smoothly, like the gradual flux of the seasons. Some, such as brain waves, cycle in fractions of a second, while others take place over eons, like the ice ages. But no matter what their shape or speed, they are all cyclic.

Linear change, too, takes place in many forms, from the sudden, logarithmic burst of a population explosion to the gradual accumulation of interest on a CD, yet they all share in common the trait that they curve in one direction only, and do not cycle back on themselves as cyclic change does.

The following diagrams illustrate examples of these two types of change.

Cyclic and Linear Change

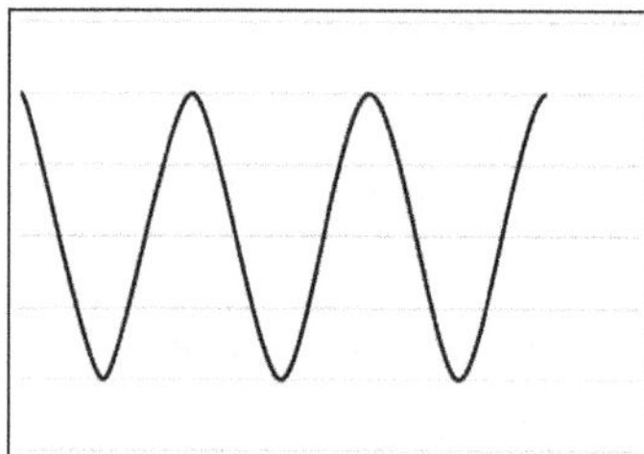

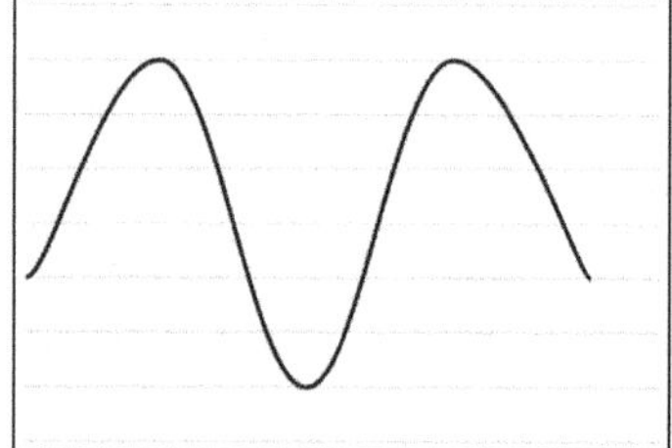

Examples of cyclic change

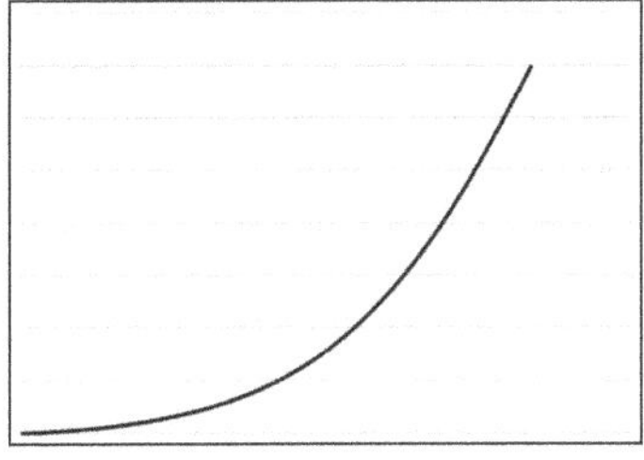
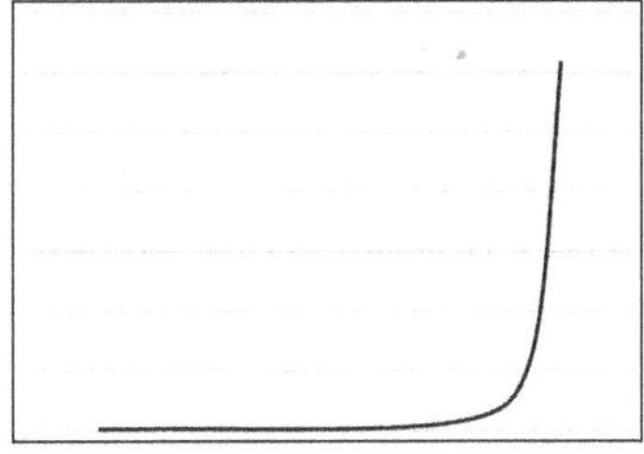

Examples of linear change

All the examples from our list of cyclic changes—the seasons, tides, stock prices, and so forth—belong to the first set of graphs. But it's the second set of graphs where things get really interesting. Linear change is where the real action is, precisely because it is *not* a repeating pattern and therefore creates entirely new and unique circumstances and opportunities. Linear change is what makes the future fundamentally new, and grasping this type of change is what allows you to begin making the invisible future become visible.

To a significant extent, developing your sense of flash foresight means being able to recognize linear change and its interplay with cyclic change. However, this is not always as easy as it might at first seem. Some changes are nothing but temporary blips on the radar of time, and contain no reliable information about the future. Other changes are so substantial and reliable that they offer very clear glimpses into the future. How do you know the difference? Because if you have no reliable way of knowing, you can end up with some pretty strange predictions, as the following example illustrates.

On August 16, 1977, one of the greatest recording artists of all time died at the tender age of forty-two. During his lifetime, Elvis Aaron Presley sold more than a billion recordings and achieved a level of star status unique among musicians. But if no one could equal him, many could certainly imitate. By the time the King died, there were a little over one hundred professional Elvis impersonators, and after his death that number quickly skyrocketed. An entire new profession had been born. How prevalent would it become?

Five years after the singer's death, as an exercise in trend analysis (albeit an admittedly whimsical one), I constructed a careful scientific study on the growing number of Elvis impersonators. Examining the statistics from the years 1977 to 1982, the findings projected that by the year 2000, one out of every three Americans would be a professional Elvis impersonator.

Given the cold, hard numbers at the time, this may have *looked* like a reasonable assumption, but obviously it wasn't. Why not? Because while those may have been "cold hard numbers," the trend they implied was as soft as the peanut butter and banana sandwiches the king of rock 'n' roll loved so much.

Of course, nobody *really* expected that we would all become Elvis impersonators. But the trend analysis nonetheless made a point: we make *and believe* faulty projections like that all the time, both in our own lives and on the massive scale of corporate and governmental policy decisions. We base trends on accurate, factual numbers, yet the trends don't turn out to be accurate.

In 1999 the United States government told us we were going to have a trillion-dollar surplus over the following decade. This projection was based on numbers that seemed just as sound as the Elvis numbers—and proved to have about the same level of reliability. According to the projections, we *should* be a nation of financially secure Elvis impersonators. Oops.

And this was not an error committed by only the federal government: of the fifty American states, forty-seven made similar projections of whopping budgetary windfalls. State governments got used to those rapidly increasing property tax revenues and spent that income as if there were no end in sight. They bet the farm on those projections—and came close to losing that farm. What happened? They bet on trends that looked solid, but weren't: the Elvis fallacy. It's a recipe for disaster, and it gets us in trouble over and over—trouble that could have been avoided if we knew the difference between *hard trends* and *soft trends*.

>>>Hard Trends and Soft Trends

People typically don't believe forecasts because forecasts are based on trends, and people don't trust trends. We think trends are like fads: here today, but who knows for how long? The word *trendy* means "fashionable," and everyone knows what happens to fashions: they go, well, in and out of fashion. "Trends," we say with a shrug. "Hey, sometimes they work out, sometimes they don't. It's a crapshoot."

But science means something different by the word *trend*. It means "a general direction in which something is developing or changing." And one of the principal findings of my twenty-five years of research is that there are two distinct kinds of trends, which I call *soft trends,* like the Elvis prediction and the trillion-dollar surplus that never materialized, and *hard trends.*

A hard trend is a projection based on measurable, tangible, and fully predictable facts, events, or objects. A soft trend is a projection based on statistics that have the *appearance* of being tangible, fully predictable facts. A hard trend is something that *will* happen: a future *fact.* A soft trend is something that *might* happen: a future *maybe.*

This distinction completely changes how we view the future. Understanding the difference between hard and soft trends allows us to know *which parts of the future we can be right about.* It gives us the insight we need to start with certainty, because it shows us where we are dealing with future *fact* and where we are dealing with hypothetical outcomes—future *maybes.* The reason we typically don't trust trends is that we haven't learned how to make the distinction between hard trends and soft trends. The Elvis fallacy is treating a soft trend as if it were a hard trend. Once we know the difference, we know where to find certainty—and the future suddenly becomes visible.

That trillion-dollar surplus the government predicted at the end of the nineties was a soft trend, only we treated it like a hard trend. We were not only expecting it to happen, we were acting on it as if it had already happened: we were spending like crazy. So much money was coming in during '99, we were going nuts. We were gazing at the soft trend like a rabbit hypnotized by a snake. The Elvis fallacy.

"Hard numbers" don't necessarily mean a hard trend. My Elvis projection was based on "hard numbers," in the sense that they were *accurate,* but it was obviously not a hard trend. Why not? *Because it was soft*—in other words, the numbers it was based on could easily change in the future. Making a choice to become Elvis impersonators is purely that—a choice, and one that could easily flip the next day. Using an increase in Elvis impersonators as a basis for predicting the future is no more secure than saying that because we had a few days of rain lately, it will continue raining forever, or that because the number of hula hoops or Beanie Babies sold this year was twice that of last year, it will be twice as big again next year. These were fads, subject to the whims of fashion—not trends driven by immutable forces that could be counted on to continue.

The distinction between hard and soft trend is not always quite so obvious. To many observers, that trillion-dollar surplus looked quite believable. That's the problem with soft trends. Sometimes they look ridiculous, like my Elvis impersonator model—and sometimes they have the appearance of being credible. Still, soft is soft, and unless the trend is based on a direction of change that is clearly fixed, there is nothing certain about that trend. Saying something *could* happen is very different from saying it *will* happen, and that difference makes all the difference.

A hard trend can be either cyclic or linear in nature; both types of change yield hard trends. For example, if the stock market is falling today, we know that in the future, it will go back up again—and we know that *with certainty.* The rise and fall of the stock market is a cyclic change, and a hard trend.

Exactly when will it turn and start going up again, and how high will it go when it does? We don't know. The exact timing and extent of the market's behavior is a soft trend, because our behavior and choices can influence it. What we know is that after it falls, it will rise, and after it rises, it will fall. That may sound like a fairly simplistic hard trend, but it has been reliable enough to make Warren Buffett a very rich man.

On the other hand, if the rate at which our laptop computers can process an audio or video clip has gotten a lot faster in the last few decades, what can we know about the future? They'll be even faster. The increasing speed and capacity of computer processors is not cyclic, it is linear—and a hard trend.

Exactly which manufacturers will be introducing the newest, breakthrough models five years from now? We don't know. The acceleration of the technology is a hard trend—but who takes advantage of that technological advancement and brings it to market, that's a soft trend.

To get a clearer sense of what a hard trend looks like, let's revisit the American landscape at the close of World War II, when the American suburbs were poised to explode across the nation and GM still ruled the world. As American GIs returned victorious from their overseas tours of duty, millions of families were reunited—and nine months later, something happened that was 100 percent predictable: *a lot* of babies started appearing. Today there are about 78 million Americans who were born during the eighteen-year population boom lasting from 1946 through 1964, and there are similarly large groups in Japan, Europe, and the other developed nations of the post-WWII era.

Demographics is one of the primary generators of tangible, measurable hard trends, and the post-WWII baby boom is one of the clearest and most dramatic examples. This postwar population boom is a physical fact: those millions of people were born and they're going to stay born. What's more, they're going to consistently and progressively get older, creating a *fully predictable* set of consequences as they age.

"Right, the baby boom," you may be saying, "that's old news." You already know about the baby boom. Everyone does. And that's what makes it such a great example—because even though we think we know all about it, *we keep missing it.* This hard trend has been clearly visible for over half a century—and yet, amazingly, this population bump has continued to catch us by surprise at every stage of the boomers' lives.

In 1945 we might have predicted that when all those soldiers came home, something big was going to happen. But we didn't, and when the wave of births started happening in 1946, we didn't have enough hospitals.

Okay, so we missed the hospitals; but surely we could learn from our mistakes. We had a good five years before all these newborns would be ready for kindergarten, so we had plenty of time to prepare, right? Wrong. After five years of headlines screaming that there weren't enough hospitals to have all these babies, all of a sudden we didn't have enough kindergartens. About seven years later, what do you know: suddenly we didn't have enough junior high schools. A few years after that, we discovered that there were not enough high schools. And you'll never guess what happened next: suddenly we found that we had not built enough colleges.

Who could have possibly seen all this coming? Anyone could—if they had developed the habit of looking at hard trends.

Recently my company consulted to a major insurance company. As we talked about hard trends and soft trends, about certainty and the fact that demographics was a good hard trend generator, one gentleman interrupted: "Yes, yes, we know all about demographics and baby boomers. We understand all that."

"Great!" I replied, "then we don't have to cover all that ground. So, let me just ask you a few quick questions. Roughly how many salespeople do you have driving your total sales around the globe?"

They knew this number right off the bat, and it was huge.

"Okay," I ventured, "let's see . . . Could you tell me, of those salespeople who generate 80 percent or more of your global sales, how many are within three years of retirement?"

There was an awkward silence. They could not tell me that number. They'd never thought to ask the question.

One executive went onto his laptop to access the information. They knew who their top salespeople were, so it wasn't hard to pull the answer from their database. Once we'd queried the system and gotten back our answer, the awkward silence turned to a shocked silence.

Sixty percent.

In the following three years, three out of five of their top salespeople would be gone, and all that know-how and experience would be gone with them. The executives were thunderstruck. An important piece of information had just become visible. Why hadn't they seen this coming? Because they hadn't looked. They had not developed the habit of *starting with what they knew.*

At about the same time, I happened to be consulting with leaders from the Social Security Administration. As we began our session, the man who'd brought me in to speak introduced me to their head of training, and we began talking about the situation facing Social Security.

At one second past midnight on January 1, 2008, the first baby boomer turned sixty-two, making her eligible for early Social Security benefits.[1] During 2008, about 3.2 million baby boomers turned sixty-two—that's about 365 *per hour.* Today, the Social Security caseload is about 50 million people; by 2030, it will be 84 million people. Medicare will go from 44 million beneficiaries to 79 million. At that point, we'll have about two workers contributing to the system for each retired beneficiary. Back in 1945, that ratio was *forty-two* to one.[2]

As with the insurance company, I asked them if they had looked at the effects of retirement on their own organization. "For example," I said, "how many of you are retiring within the next few years?" It was a fairly large group of senior leaders, and quite a few hands went up. Much to their shock, a major percentage of their key senior people—again, the ones with the bulk of experience and know-how—were on their way out the door.

I once heard the CEO of Sony say, "If we only knew what we know!" He was talking about the data stored in their computers, but the comment applies here, too: we all *think* we know that a lot of baby boomers are about to retire—but do we?

Two months later, we had a vivid demonstration of the trend we were looking at: the man who had brought me in to consult to the agency was gone; a month later, so was the head of training. Both had retired. The exodus of retiring boomers had begun. Or to put it more accurately, they weren't really *gone*: they were still part of the Social Security system, only now they were its *customers.*

>>>Why We Keep Falling for the Elvis Fallacy

Despite all that has been said and written about the baby boom, we continue not to see it coming. Those 78 million boomers who were flooding America's ill-prepared kindergartens in the 1950s and America's ill-prepared colleges in the late 1960s are now flooding our ill-prepared health care system. If our trend blindness persists, in another ten years we won't have even a fraction of the doctors and nurses we'll need to care for this boom generation. Meanwhile, America's pension plans, along with Medicare, Medicaid, and Social Security, are catastrophically underfunded. Where's the money going to come from?

Nearly 80 million baby boomers are going to need greatly increased health care in the United States alone, with tens of millions more around the globe: that's a hard trend. Are we going to be able to provide that care or not? And if we are, then who will be doing the providing, and how? The answers to those questions are soft trends.

Again, notice where the hard trend is—and where it is *not*. The increasing numbers of boomers who will need medical care as they get older and their bodies need more repair is a hard trend, because those numbers are fixed and cannot be changed. But that projected lack of sufficient numbers of doctors and nurses to provide that care is a *soft* trend, because it is something we *can* change if we see it and elect to act on it.

Here is an example of the difference between a hard trend and a soft trend. Ten years from now (assuming you are still living), you are going to be ten years older than you are today. That's a hard trend. Why? Because there's nothing you or anyone can do to change that fact.

What will your state of health be like then—worse? Much worse? Better? About the same? I don't know; neither do you, and neither does anyone else. It is not definitively knowable, because that is a soft trend. Why? Because you can do things to affect it.

While we're on the subject of health, this is a point especially worth noting: a doctor's prognosis, no matter how clear or definitive it may seem, is *never* a hard trend. We often see it as such: when the man in the white coat intones, "I'm so sorry—you have six months to live," it's pretty easy to feel grim. But plenty of people have defied their doctors' predictions by months, even by years.

How is that possible? By changing. Whether through a change in diet or exercise, in breathing and posture, in attitude and strength of will, nutritional supplementation or other unconventional health approaches, people have the ability to take actions that change their state of health—which means it is always a soft trend.

This is, in a nutshell, the power of flash foresight: knowing how to identify hard trends gives us the ability to *see* the future. Knowing how to identify soft trends gives us the ability to *shape* the future.

Recently, a colleague of mine who lives in Washington, D.C., told me that a car parked in a neighbor's driveway down the street had been vandalized. The next day it had happened again, this time to a neighbor just a few houses away. The following day it happened again, this time to his next-door neighbor's car.

"Hey," I said, "things aren't looking good for your car tonight!"

But was that a hard trend? No, it was soft—because he could do something about it. And he did. He got his car into a garage.

A soft trend may have a good chance of happening, even an excellent chance—but no matter how likely it looks, it's not carved in stone. There is an opportunity to do something about it. For years everyone seemed to accept that Toyota would eventually outsell GM. American automakers have been struggling ever since the seventies and eighties, when they lost the quality edge to their Japanese competitors, and they've been in catch-up mode ever since, missing the hard trends for decades.

For example, the rise of India, China, and the price of gas.

Strangely enough, while we often treat the cyclic change of real estate and stock prices as if they are linear and their values will go up forever, we also make the opposite mistake: we often treat a linear change as if it's cyclic. For decades, the Big Three automakers have been building cars as if cheap gasoline would continue forever. It won't.

Actually, the price of gas is affected by both kinds of change, cyclic *and* linear, as are many things in our world; the key is to sort them out and see which is which. The linear change patterns are the ones that tend to disrupt the status quo and change the direction of the future, and are therefore especially powerful. Seasonal consumption patterns, economic upticks and downturns, events in geopolitics, and other cyclic influences do cause fuel prices to rise and fall. But these smaller cyclic influences pale beside the long-term hard trend that is inexorably driving up the price of gas overall: the continuously increasing global demand caused by an explosive growth in the middle-class populations of emerging nations. It's not Saudi Arabia, Iraq, and Venezuela that are the overarching factor here: it's China and India. By the time you hold this book in your hands, there will probably be more cars being manufactured in China than in any other country in the world. And these newly auto-owning populations will *not* be going back to relying on bicycles.

So yes, gas prices will fluctuate somewhat from week to week and season to season, and the impact of events such as a global recession will temporarily bring down demand and prices. But recessions will always pass, and global demand will go back up again, taking prices with it. The larger trend is following a broad path of linear change, and that trend is *upward.*

For years the hard trends made it utterly predictable that the market for automobiles would trend toward smaller and more fuel-efficient cars, cars with lower emissions, and, ultimately, cars that run on something other than exclusively petroleum fuel. It made no sense whatsoever to base a manufacturing strategy on large, gas-hungry vehicles, with relatively little effort devoted to alternative-fuel vehicles, in hopes that gasoline would eventually become more affordable again. Yet American automakers continued to spend millions fighting proposed new emissions standards and billions in advertising and manufacturing costs to keep turning out large and inefficient gas guzzlers.

The automakers were not alone: the government colluded in that fixated rearview-mirror stare by creating economic incentives that made it more lucrative to continue churning out more of that dying breed.

When I sat with Rick Wagoner at that dinner in 2004, GM had just shifted its production focus from sedans to SUVs. SUVs were soaring in popularity, and it must have looked for all the world like the demand would keep going and going. It was one of those things that certainly *seemed* like the smart thing to do at the time. It's just that it wasn't. It was a classic example of the Elvis fallacy. I'm sure that Rick never imagined at the time that five years later, with him no longer at the helm, a bankrupt GM would sell off its ultimate gas-gulping muscle car, the Hummer—to a Chinese construction company with no automobile manufacturing experience. Yet that is what happened.

The growing market demand for more fuel-efficient vehicles was a hard trend. GM losing its market dominance to Toyota was *not* a hard trend, because GM could have stopped it from happening. But they didn't.

"As GM goes, so goes the nation. . . . ," yet while that may have been true for the past half century, it's not necessarily going to *stay* true. It is a soft trend, not a hard trend. Just because things have been going a certain way, you cannot count on them to continue going that way *unless they're based on a fixed, clearly measurable hard trend.* In fact, if they are not clearly and causally linked to a hard trend, what you *can* count on is that they *are* going to change. The question is, in what direction is the change going to happen?

To make sure we're clear on this, let's look for a moment at two other auto companies: Toyota and Hyundai. With GM's sales shrinking and Toyota's continuing to rise, it was clear to all that Toyota would take the title of number one automaker worldwide. But by early 2010 Toyota was suddenly embroiled in a crisis of its own, and it was Toyota's CEO, not GM's, now sitting in the congressional hot seat answering pointed questions about his own performance. This is the beauty of knowing how to recognize soft trends as well as hard trends: knowing hard trends will tell you, for example, where technology is going and what capabilities we can expect to have in the future. But soft trends point to where the opportunity lies. If Toyota's market supremacy were a hard trend, there would be no point in having any competitive car companies. But it's not. The advances in technology are a certainty; *who implements* those advances is soft.

There may be no better example than Hyundai. For years the icon of automotive cheapness, Hyundai was often viewed as sort of the joke of the industry. In the midst of the economic hard times of 2009, someone at Hyundai got creative: they started running television ads saying, "Buy a car from us, and if you lose your job, we'll let you return it, no problem." Their sales took off like crazy. By 2010 Hyundai was making a credible bid for taking the lead in luxury autos, with models going head-to-head with BMW, Lexus, and Mercedes-Benz.

We can predict with certainty many things about what kinds of vehicles we'll be buying five years from now. For example, we will still need trucks and larger cars, because there will still be stuff to haul and we'll still want to have a way to fit whole families into vehicles, so the cars of the future will not all be tiny. But we also know they *will* be more fuel-efficient and green, because of the hard trends of China's and India's demographics, and the realities of environmental impact. All these things, we can know for sure. But as to who we'll be buying them from—that is an aspect of the future that is up for grabs.

Not long ago, I spoke with a group of representatives from a large real estate company in Michigan about the difference between hard trends and soft trends. We had just gone through a definition of *hard trend*, and one man said:

"Okay, I think I have an example. In Detroit, the auto manufacturers have been taking a real beating, and people are moving out in droves. In fact, they've been moving out for over a decade. And since the auto manufacturers are just doing worse and worse, it's a hard trend that people are going to continue moving out of Detroit for the foreseeable future—right?"

Wrong. That's a soft trend. A very credible one, certainly, and one with a high degree of likelihood. But *likelihood* is not the same as *certainty*. What if Toyota (or Hyundai!) bought GM?

The key to opening the window that looks out onto the visible future is knowing how to distinguish a soft trend from a hard trend. It is knowing how to avoid falling for the Elvis fallacy. It is knowing how to recognize certainty.

>>> Finding the Fortune in Hard Trends

Demographics is only one major source of hard trends; another, which we'll devote much of this book to exploring, is the forward thrust of technological advancement.

In 1993 I was invited to address a convention of the National Booksellers' Association, attended by a crowd of some 10,000 bookstore owners. My keynote address included these remarks.

"Within the next two to three years, you're going to see a huge, successful *virtual bookstore* opening up online, and it's going to transform the way people shop for books. It could be one of you here in this room who does this—but chances are, it will be someone from the outside, someone who is not already invested in the present way of doing things. Someone who will look at things with fresh eyes and have a flash foresight."

No one in the room took my comments too seriously; after all, this was 1993, and hardly anyone even knew the World Wide Web existed, much less what it was. Mosaic, the first graphical-interface Web browser, had just been released that April, and the first widely used browser (Netscape Navigator) would not appear until the end of the following year. The concept of e-commerce as we know it today did not yet even exist.

And you already know what happened next. A year later, a thirty-year-old entrepreneur incorporated a brand-new company called Cadabra.com. A year after that, Cadabra launched an online bookselling portal, which its founder eventually renamed Amazon. That entrepreneur was Jeff Bezos, and four years later he was *Time* magazine's Man of the Year cover story. Bezos saw the hard trend; today he is one of the richest men in America.

Back in 1993, of course, none of this had happened yet, but

given the state of development of the World Wide Web and the increasing capabilities of home computers and modems, I was certain that it would—certain enough to risk my reputation by going on record with that prediction to an audience of thousands. It wasn't a lucky guess, and it had nothing to do with being psychic: given the hard trends, it was fully predictable.

That Amazon prediction was not an isolated event; over the past twenty-five years I've made hundreds of accurate predictions about the future of technology and how it will change every aspect of our lives. Here is a small sampling of my early predictions, including the year they were published; note that they were all made publicly, in speeches, articles, interviews, and books, and have not been edited in hindsight.

DATE OF PUBLICATION	***PREDICTION* / FULFILLMENT**
1983	*The 1990s will see a digital revolution.*
	In 1983 we lived in an analog world and the word *digital* was seldom used in business or education. During the 1990s a global conversion from analog to digital technology sparked multiple predictable revolutions in such fields as cell phones, photography, and e-mail, to name just a few.
1983	*Fiber optics will soon become the medium of choice for broadband data transmission.*
	Fiber optics was still an emerging technology in 1983 and only a few were experimenting with it. By the end of the 1980s fiber optics had become the backbone of broadband communications globally, and in the late 1990s it created the worldwide explosion of the Internet in virtually every area of human enterprise.
1983	*There will be computers in every classroom by the mid-1990s.*
	In 1983 only a relatively few people were using computers and in order to use one, you needed to learn a programming language such as BASIC. In 1995 *USA Today* reported that every classroom in America had at least one computer.

DATE OF PUBLICATION	*PREDICTION* / FULFILLMENT
1984	*We will sequence the human gene code by the year 2000.*
	The Human Genome Project was begun six years later, in 1990; a "rough draft" of the complete human gene code was announced jointly by U.S. president Bill Clinton and U.K. prime minister Tony Blair on June 26, 2000.
1984	*By 1990 all computers will use an icon interface.*
	When Apple introduced the first Macintosh in 1984, the business world regarded it as an irrelevant toy. Microsoft introduced the first edition of its Windows operating system a year later, in 1985, to lukewarm response. The first edition to achieve widespread popularity was Windows 3.0, which was released in 1990 and sold two million copies within six months. Virtually all computers have used an icon-based interface ever since.
1986	*By the late 1990s we will use GPS to pinpoint location with applications ranging from agriculture to trucking.*
	In 1986 GPS was being used only by the military, and few saw a nonmilitary use. By the late nineties farmers were using GPS to plow their fields, and trucking companies were using it to track each truck on the road.
1988	*By the end of the 1990s e-mail will outpace paper mail.*
	In 1988 only scientists and technologists were using e-mail. By 1998 the number of e-mails sent over the Internet exceeded the number of physical letters sent through the postal service.
1988	*From the mid-1990s on, businesses will widely use and profit from the Internet.*
	In 1988 using the Internet required a working knowledge of computer programming, and the idea of a widespread business application seemed like science fiction. With the introduction of the first graphical-interface Web browsers in 1993 and 1994, this barrier was demolished, and the migration of the business community onto Web sites followed over the next several years.
1988	*There are more software programmers in India than in the United States; once they get networked, sometime in the late nineties, a revolution will be born.*
	In 1988 few were aware that India had more programmers than the United States; fewer still could see the impact on India's economy and the global service revolution that would result.

DATE OF PUBLICATION	*PREDICTION* / FULFILLMENT
1993	*Within another two to three years, someone will create a successful online bookstore.*
	As described above, Amazon.com was founded in 1994.
1996	*Between 2000 and 2005 we will see the rapid growth of wireless Web access.*
	In 1996 the Netscape and Microsoft Web browsers were barely one year old, and virtually every computer's Web access was through a slow wired connection. In mid-1999 Apple introduced its first AirPort (WiFi hub), and the wireless Web was born.
1996	*In less than ten years, people will have Web browsers on their smartphones.*
	In 1996 Nokia released the Nokia 9000, the earliest palmtop computer–style smartphone; it was expensive, huge, and weighed close to a pound. By 2006 nearly one hundred million Web-capable smartphones were shipping worldwide per year.
1997	*By the early 2000s the next generation of Web architecture (XML) will usher in a social networking revolution.*
	By 2004 the terms *Web 2.0* and *social networking* had come into widespread use to describe the new types of Web experience made possible by XML technology.
2006	*Starting in 2008 we will begin to see record defaults on mortgages due to the large number of speculative home purchases with zero-interest ARMs that will reset, driving foreclosures up and home values down.*
	In 2006 few were seeing the visible triggers that would send the United States and the rest of the world into an economic crisis.
2008	*Social media and social-media marketing will go mobile and will be standard on smartphones by 2010.*
	In 2008 the business world was just discovering social media; few were taking it seriously, and fewer still were seeing the possibility of it going mobile.

How could one possibly see these things happen before they happened? It's not guesswork or psychic acuity. It's purely a question of knowing how and where to look, and taking the time to do the looking. In my case, it was possible to make all these predictions and hundreds more, even down to specific timelines many years ahead of time, simply because I'd spent a good deal of time studying hard trends in technology.

Hard trends make the future visible. Once you see the distinction of hard trends, you start opening all sorts of doors to new possibilities.

In the late 1980s, while working with executives at the Mayo Clinic, I asked them to take a look at their visible future. When they did, what they saw was a world of decreasing Medicare and Medicaid reimbursements, increasing losses in their emergency rooms, and a generally depressing economic scenario. The future they saw, based on what seemed to them the likely demographic and economic trends, looked bleak.

But most of what they saw represented soft trends. The aging of the population itself was a hard trend—but that didn't necessarily have to translate into economic losses for the Mayo Clinic.

I directed their attention to a few key hard trends they hadn't been looking at: the increasing presence of computers in consumers' homes and the increasing speed and power of those computers, along with the introduction of CD-ROM technology. A steady increase in processing power and storage capacity (two hard trends) and the progressive miniaturization of components (another hard trend) were making it easier and easier to store, distribute, and search huge amounts of information, making it possible to access certain types of knowledge tools that had hitherto been impossible.

The world, in other words, was moving rapidly toward a *knowledge-based economy*. So I came up with this simple suggestion: why not take advantage of that hard trend and turn the Mayo Clinic into an organization that derived income not only from treating people who came to their facilities, but also from selling their *knowledge*?

From our vantage point today, this advice looks rather obvious, but it was a radical idea at the time. Remember, this was the late 1980s. The concept of CD-ROM was barely a few years old; Microsoft would not release Encarta, the first commercial CD-based encyclopedia, for another half a decade. Yet to Mayo's credit, they leaped at the idea. The result was a CD that consumers could use anytime, day or night, to determine whether their child's rash and fever required a trip to the emergency room or could be treated with aspirin, or to get top-notch professional help in any one of thousands of other medical situations.

To some, this project seemed a long shot when they started spending time and money on it. "After all," many wondered at the time, "who would want access to medical guidance using a computer in their home?"

But the long shot paid off, and paid off in a big way. The clinic put a $100 price tag on this product; in its first year, it sold 670,000 copies. That's $67 million in gross sales in just one year—a very profitable flash foresight.

In fact, the benefits went even beyond sales of the immediate product. By expanding its services to offer a knowledge-based product, the Mayo Clinic began developing a new and powerful twenty-first-century brand in the marketplace. They not only created new value and new revenue, but with the subsequent rise of the Internet, their name recognition became international.

Today, when you visit MayoClinic.com, you'll see their slogan: "Tools for healthier lives." Their Web site lets you "manage your health with information and tools that reflect the expertise of Mayo's 2,500 physicians and scientists . . ." In other words, Mayo transformed itself from an organization that delivers on-site health care to an organization that delivers expertise and knowledge, anytime, anywhere.

Let's look at another example of using a hard trend to win in the marketplace, this one involving Dale Morgen, the inventor we met earlier.

As the nineties got under way, researchers had been working hard to develop a type of liquid crystal display screen for commercial application. However, there was a technical challenge they could not seem to overcome: the frustratingly slow refresh rate of the LCD's individual pixels, which, while fast enough to provide a readable picture, was nowhere near fast enough to meet the demands of a commercial television screen.

Around 1989, Dale Morgen had another of his big ideas: why not add a bit of memory to each pixel? The memory would act as an image buffer, managing the flow of information to each pixel. As you watched the screen you'd actually be about one second behind the broadcast, but no one would notice.

Everyone told Dale he was crazy. Memory was far too expensive to make the idea even remotely feasible: adding memory individually to each pixel would vault the cost of the average television set up into the tens of thousands of dollars! But Dale was not deterred. He knew a hard trend: the price of memory would fall dramatically.

And so it has. After languishing quietly for a decade and a half, Dale's patent was ready when the hard trend caught up with it. Today LCD screens claim more than 50 percent of market share, which means companies are shipping more than 100 million television sets around the world per year—and his matrix control technology is being used in plasma TVs as well. Dale is sitting on a modest fortune. His LCD patent became an idea whose time had come, as he knew it would, because of the hard trend of technological advancement.

>>>Some Million-Dollar Flash Foresights

Now let's be inventors ourselves for a moment. Let's say we want to take advantage of the certainty provided by the baby boom to create a successful business that will thrive in the years ahead. In fact, let's say we want to create a new million-dollar company. Where do we look? You might start by looking no further than your own family.

At age seventy-five, my mother used to say that climbing up and down her three flights of stairs "keeps me young." She passed away at the age of eighty-two—but if she had lived much longer, it's clear that she would have had to move. She knew this, but she didn't *want* to move. She loved living where she was. But because of the layout of the staircases in her house, electric chair lifts would have been out of the question. And as she became frailer, getting herself up and down through those floors would have become impossible.

She was not alone. There are millions of people living in two-story homes who want to stay there, but who will soon face the same problem my mother faced. And that's nothing compared to her children's generation. When you pour the 78 million–strong baby boom into this future situation, the problem becomes enormous. And so does the opportunity.

One flash foresight solution: retrofit these homes with *personal elevators*.

The highest of high-end homes have had these for years; why not bring the feature to the average home? Installing an elevator inside the home would be complicated, expensive, and in many cases not practical. So let's do what some hotels have done and *go opposite*: put the elevator on the *outside*. It's inexpensive and practical, it gets your parents up and down, and it gives them a good view of the neighborhood to boot.

So you develop an inexpensive, lightweight, durable elevator that retrofits on the outside of the house and goes up just one story. Would there be a market for that? There sure would. Baby boomers have parents just like my mom, so they need them *now*—and they'll need them even more in the future when they are in the same situation themselves.

Throughout this book, we'll explore entrepreneurial ideas that tap a range of technological hard trends. For now, let's stay with this hard trend of baby boom demographics, and use it to come up with a handful of other ideas you could flesh out to become full-fledged million-dollar entrepreneurial enterprises.

BOOMER VIDEO GAMES

We have immersive, participatory video games for kids that place the user right into the action in wars, science fiction worlds, and all sorts of other settings. What about video games for baby boomers that place you at Woodstock, the 1968 Democratic Convention, or the trial of the Chicago Seven, and let you interact with your friends within those events?

LATE-LIFE FINANCIAL PLANNING

In past generations, financial planners helped you make money, accumulate money, and then plan how to give it away. Today, because we're living much longer, that strategy is undergoing a radical change. Unlike their parents and grandparents, those of the baby boom generation plan on doing something different after retiring instead of dying after a few years: *living, and for a long time.* The focus in senior financial planning is now shifting from accumulating and transferring wealth to making one's money last—in many cases, for decades.

Today more than 80 percent of the wealth in the United States is controlled by people over the age of fifty. Ten years from now that mass of wealth will be in the hands of people preparing for retirement—or at least, their version of retirement. They'll be getting conservative with their money, looking for stocks with a dividend, and they're going to stay that way, because they know they won't have another lifetime to make up the shortfall if they're *not* conservative.

Will that have an impact on the stock market? It certainly will. Is that bad news? Only if you didn't know about it ahead of time. How can you find ways as a financial services company to serve that emerging market?

UNRETIREMENT HOMES

The entire concept of nursing homes is ripe for revolution. The majority of baby boomers do not expect to fully retire, but will stay engaged in some sort of gainful employment, often different from the work of their past career. Volunteerism, social involvement, entrepreneurialism, and collaborative new ventures will be commonplace career-shift choices—and because of advances in health care, wellness, and life extension, boomers are going to live a lot longer. There will be a huge market for living facilities that combine the health-care resources of nursing homes with more upscale styling and site design that better suits this sort of second-life career lifestyle. Let's call them *unretirement* homes.

And what about specially themed unretirement homes? A

commune-style home would focus on gardening, energy self-sufficiency, and other sorts of back-to-the-land endeavors. How about an unretirement home where everyone played music? Or you could create an unretirement home that focused on fine cuisine, or arts and letters, or theater, or electronics.

Or, here's another thought: why don't we create an eHarmony for elders? Not for dating, but so we can match roommates in nursing homes. I recently heard in the news that an elderly person was charged with murder: she couldn't stand her nursing home roommate and strangled her.

GREEN FUNERAL HOMES AND BOOMER CEMETERIES

Baby boomers are on average going to live a lot longer than their parents—but we all die eventually. When that population swell hits dying age the nation will probably be no better prepared with cemeteries than we were with nursery schools, grade schools, or colleges. The burial industry, macabre though it sounds to say it, will become an enormously profitable growth niche. And not everyone wants to be buried; cremation centers will boom, too.

This is not purely a matter of available land, but also one of approach. What does a twenty-first-century, environmentally conscious cemetery look like? As boomers approach their final chapter in life and focus on leaving a legacy, what kind of funeral service do they want? How can we evolve the entire funeral-burial-farewell process so that it becomes more than a one-time ceremony and makes more of an ongoing impact and contribution to the world—because if you can find a way to design *that* experience, this generation will want to buy it.

>>>You, the American Automaker

Now let's take that same perspective, only this time you're not an entrepreneur brainstorming a start-up. This time you are an American automaker. You have decided to keep your eye on the hard trends, to steer clear of the Elvis fallacy, and to drive your company straight into the visible future. What do you do now?

You might start by asking, where's your market? Today GM sells more cars and trucks to China than any other company in the world. If you're GM, you already know something Rick Wagoner evidently didn't know in 2004 (though he should have and easily could have): unless you make some radical shifts in the kinds of vehicles you're manufacturing, someone else will be outselling you in China within ten years at most, and probably a lot sooner than that. And that's not a maybe, you know that *for certain.*

How do you know that? Because petroleum fuels, over the long term, are going to continue to become more and more costly, both economically and environmentally.

In parts of China today there are already new emission standards that are equivalent to the targets set for ten years from now in California, our most environmentally progressive state. In other words, in terms of environmental impact, America *at its most progressive* is a good decade behind China's market demand. China has been choking on its own fumes, and they're starting to make the tough decisions that the United States is still avoiding. American automakers have been complaining that they can't meet more stringent emission standards and better mpg ratings, because it would cost them billions. That's rearview-mirror thinking. Unless they start producing the vehicles the world of the future will need, those billions won't be there anyway.

As an American automaker, what will *you* do? With your eyes firmly on the visible future, you won't grudgingly try to *meet* those numbers—you'll immediately look for ways you can leap ahead and *exceed* them.

There are roughly one billion kids today in emerging nations who are going to enter the consumer market over the next five to eight years. Add to them the hundreds of millions of adults in these emerging nations who want cars *now.* This demographic group will be in the market for close to a *billion* new cars over the next decade. That's a hard trend: it *will* happen. Who's going to make and sell them? That's a soft trend; we can't be certain about the answer to that one, and in fact, we can *change* the answer to that one. To do that, we need to ask a different question, one we *can* be certain about: *What kind of cars will they be?*

They're going to be eco-friendly cars that are inexpensive and have a small profile, so they can fit on the narrower streets of those emerging economies. They are going to be a combination of electric vehicles and hybrids running on multiple fuels. Why? Again, a hard trend: we're going to reduce our exclusive reliance on oil as our primary automotive fuel. That's a whole different kind of car. Someone is going to make an absolute fortune selling those cars in Africa, the Middle East, India, China, and the rest of Asia.

If you don't serve this emerging market, someone else will. In India, where the streets are quite narrow, the Indian automobile manufacturer Tata is already designing very small cars for use there—and they have announced their intention to market a hybrid version of their tiny car, making the world's smallest (and cheapest) hybrid. Tata's auto is named, appropriately enough, the Nano. And look out, Europe and America: Tata now owns Jaguar and Land Rover.

What if, instead of leaving innovation to the newcomers (as the booksellers did with Amazon), you decided to refocus the resources of your American auto company onto designing cars for these emerging markets? In fact, what if you put your focus on becoming the *best automaker on the planet* by doing that? You would be going with the tide, instead of against it. The financial profits would be immense, as would the goodwill and brand power you would generate. Imagine the shot in the arm you would engender, not only for your own beleaguered industry but for American industry as a whole.

"But we've got major manufacture-cost problems," you point out. "How can we possibly compete with Toyota's approach to manufacture?"

Well, why not go with a model like Dell's? Today, in hindsight, everyone can readily see how brilliant the Dell model was. But when Michael Dell set out to have other manufacturers make its computers according to Dell's customer specs, to have people pay for the computer they wanted, not from a showroom but sight unseen, and then take their money and go manufacture it out of parts from their "just in time" supply chain, people thought he was a fool. He was no fool: he had a flash foresight and acted on it. Dell later lost its way, because they grew big and sought to milk their cash cow instead of continuing to pioneer and innovate—but the model of "just in time" inventory, a highly responsive supply chain, and customer-custom design is even more practical today than it was when Dell first explored it.

Early in Ford's history, founder Henry Ford made a famous remark about his Model T: "Customers can have it any color they like, so long as it's black." Ford's greatest contribution to technology was the concept of assembly-line mass production, a process that derives its power from the uniformity of its product. At the time, Ford's insight was itself a flash foresight. Yet a century later, that is still the approach of American automakers today. We still haggle over our limited options on the shop floor and pay through the nose for extra features. Meanwhile, the truth of today's manufacturing technology is that it is now possible to produce 100 uniquely different items at nearly the same profitability as producing 100 exact replicas of the same item. "Have it your way" is not just a fast-food slogan: it's an accurate distillation of twenty-first-century consumer expectation.

So why not give your customers preordered, custom-designed automobiles? Instead of keeping all that massive investment in manufacturing capacity, outsource all the manufacturing. Let your customers go online, choose the features they want, and design the car they want, make a down payment, and then go have it made. Cash up front. Instead of tying up billions in manufacturing capacity, you're using the customer's money.

Dell computers are made in Taiwan; so are IBM's, so are Apple's. Where it's made isn't the point: it's still a Dell or a Mac, because it's manufactured to Dell's or Apple's brand and quality specs. We could just as easily manufacture our GM cars overseas.

Or here's a thought: instead of outsourcing your labor, why not *insource* it: have it done right here in the United States, as Toyota is doing. Toyota makes most of the cars for the American market here in the United States, and they're hiring American workers to do it. In fact, why not talk with Toyota and explore the possibility of them being your manufacturing arm? Why don't you have U.S. workers build your cars according to Toyota specs, with your company name on it? With your highly customizable, fluid-design Dell model, you're going to need to hire a lot more engineers. And with the popularity of your new on-demand customizable autos, soon your plants are going to be *hiring*, not laying off.

Even before doing any of the above, there's one sweeping change you might make as an American auto company: stop thinking of yourself as an American auto company, and start seeing yourself instead as a global auto company, building cars all over the world, using employees all over the world, to serve markets all over the world. Could you perhaps form a strategic alliance with Tata? Or if you'd rather, set up your own manufacturing facility over there? China has already realized it can't continue building conventional, polluting, twentieth-century cars, and has now set a goal of becoming the number one hybrid-car manufacturer on the planet. Why not build your own facility over there and build for them?

And while you're becoming a global car company, why not also become a *green* car company? Instead of building cars in China and shipping them to the United States (which GM is doing), build your autos all over the world, manufacturing them locally for the markets they're going to serve—so you stop all the polluting involved in all that shipping, and at the same time start employing the local populations to build their own cars.

Of course, you haven't solved all your problems. You've got some major issues with labor and health care to deal with. You're going to need to show your labor unions how to look at the visible future, because you're going to need twenty-first-century unions that are focused on retraining their workers for the visible future, instead of protecting and defending the turf of bygone years—that is, unions that understand the need to shift from lifelong employment to lifelong *employability*. And you'll need to completely redesign your approach to health care. We'll talk more about both issues in later chapters. But in the pursuit of your car company's makeover, you're well on your way.

Strategy based on certainty has low risk and high reward. Base your strategies on certainty, on the known future visible in hard trends and the soft trends that you can manipulate, knowing which is which and acting accordingly, and you will build something that will not only survive but even thrive in the years ahead.

Hope is not a strategy: certainty is.

>>>History May Be Bunk—but the Future Is Real

They say we can learn from history, and that's true—to an extent. But there may have been more insight than wisecrack in Henry Ford's remark, "History is bunk," because, in fact, hindsight does not necessarily bring wisdom. If it did, everyone would have lots of wisdom. Yet we still keep making the same mistakes.

No, too often what hindsight brings is not wisdom but *lament.* "I should have bought Google stock when it first hit $100 a share. We should have sold our house when the market was up. I should have realized our marriage was in trouble. I should have known. . . ."

The universal lament: *I should have seen it coming.* But if we're operating out of hindsight, we *never* see it coming.

Why does it always seem that we learn about something too late to take advantage of it? The answer is so simple it's shocking: we didn't see it coming because we weren't looking.

In 2008, as GM began its final downward spiral toward insolvency, Rick Wagoner expressed regret that he had not moved faster on developing an alternative-fuel car. He said he wished he hadn't pulled the plug on the EV1, GM's earlier electric-car prototype, and he acknowledged "underestimating how the emergence of consumer societies in China and India would help put a $100 floor under oil prices."[3]

Lament—the eternal expression of hindsight.

In another announcement, just before GM's annual meeting in June 2008, Rick declared that the soaring price of gas had forced a "structural shift" by American consumers, away from larger vehicles and toward smaller, more fuel-efficient cars. "These prices are changing consumer behavior, and changing it rapidly," he said, adding, "we don't believe it's a spike or temporary shift. We believe it is permanent."[4] In other words, as we had said in our brief conversation four years earlier: *This is not a cyclic change but a linear change—and it's a hard trend.*

So why did it take 2008's $4-a-gallon gasoline to finally bring this point home, when it was fully and wholly predictable years earlier? This is a sobering question, and one that every captain of industry would do well to ask. Because GM is only one example among thousands. The leaders of the American auto industry are in the same boat as every other CEO, every other manager, every other employer, and in fact, every other person in America—and everywhere else in the world. We're all too busy reacting to the present, putting out fires, to look at and act on the opportunities the future holds.

But looking into the visible future is no longer a luxury. In an era of rapid, epic change, it has become a survival necessity. When we buy into the myth that "we live in an uncertain world," and indeed, that in the twenty-first century, the world is becoming "more uncertain than ever," we do so at our peril. It simply isn't true.

Is the world changing faster than ever before? Absolutely. But within that bewildering maelstrom of change, there are always vast currents of certainty—currents that allow us not only to predict the future but to positively *shape* it. We just have to know where to look.

If we don't make this shift today, it will be far more difficult tomorrow. Because as dizzying as the pace of change has been these past few years, this has been only a warm-up. Things are about to start changing a *lot* faster.

>>>CHAPTER 1 ACTION STEPS

Typically we limit ourselves by looking at all the things we don't know and all the things we can't do. Instead, create the habit of starting with a list of things you ***can*** *know and do. Don't let yourself get boxed in by the word* ***can't****. Every time you bump into something you aren't certain about, put that to the side and keep focusing on the things you are certain about.*

- *Make a list of all the* ***cyclic changes*** *that are affecting you, your life, and your business.*
- *Make a list of all the* ***linear changes*** *that will have an impact on your life.*
- *Make a list of all the* ***hard trends*** *that are taking place in your industry, so you know what you can be certain about. Eliminate from this list anything you are not certain is a hard trend.*
- *Make a list of all the* ***soft trends*** *taking place in your industry, so you can see what you can change or influence.*
- *Instead of being blocked by the uncertainties around you, ask yourself: "****What can I be certain about?*** *What do I* ***know*** *will happen in the next few weeks, months, and years? And how can I innovate to take advantage of what I now* ***know for certain*** *about the future?"*
- ***Business plans on certainty have low risk.*** *Does your business plan take advantage of certainty?*
- ***Involve others*** *from your business, business partners, even your customers, in the process of identifying what* ***will*** *happen versus what* ***might*** *happen. Use the results to* ***cocreate the future****.*
- ***Question your assumptions****. Examine each item on your list to see if it is a truly a hard trend or a soft trend, a certainty or only a possibility.*

>>> CHAPTER TWO

Anticipate

On the morning of December 26, 2004, the earth was rocked by one of the most powerful earthquakes ever recorded. With a ferocity that caused the entire planet to vibrate measurably, the quake spawned a series of catastrophic tsunamis in the Indian Ocean that slammed into the shores of fifteen countries and killed nearly a quarter of a million people. It was then the deadliest natural disaster in recorded history, and nobody saw it coming.

Or at least, almost nobody.

Surprisingly, a group of villagers on the Indonesian island of Simeulue, about a hundred miles off the western coast of Sumatra, survived because, unlike the hundreds of thousands of others living around the westernmost curve of the Ring of Fire, they evacuated before the killing water reached land. So did a Scottish biology teacher named John Chroston, who was vacationing with his family at Kamala Bay on Phuket Island, Thailand. And so did a ten-year-old British schoolgirl named Tilly Smith.

Chroston happened to be out in the ocean swimming that morning, when he saw something that made him get out of the water, grab his wife and daughter, and persuade a hotel shuttle bus to turn around and take its passengers to high ground, picking up a handful of Thai women and children on the way.

Tilly Smith was vacationing at Mai Khao Beach, some fifteen miles to the north, when she saw the same thing Chroston saw. The girl told her parents, who passed the warning on to others. As a result of Tilly's insight, the beach was completely evacuated by the time the tsunami reached shore—one of the very few beaches on the island with no reported casualties.

More than a thousand miles away, the residents of Simeulue saw the same thing John Chroston and Tilly Smith saw, and they, too, immediately fled inland. Of the 83,000 people on the island, only 7 died.

What did these people see that everyone else missed? *They saw the ocean recede.*

One of the telltale signs of an impending tsunami (as Tilly had learned in her geography class back in England a few weeks before) is a sudden pulling back of the water's edge—the ocean's version of sucking in a breath before exploding with a blast of destruction. In some areas of Southeast Asia, children observed this receding of the ocean and saw it innocently as an opportunity to go out onto these freshly exposed stretches of beach to collect shells. Tragically, nobody knew to tell them any different.

Another tiny group who escaped the destruction were the members of several aboriginal tribes of the Andaman Islands in the Bay of Bengal, to the northwest of Phuket. Of the six extant tribes, the only one who suffered significant losses was that in the Nicobar district, whose members had converted to modern ways—in other words, had let go of their traditional cultural and spiritual traditions and hunter-gatherer lifestyle. Tribespeople of the Onge tribe, who had retained the traditional wisdom of their forebears, say they've always known that the sea and land tend to fight over boundaries, and when they saw the signs of a brewing argument, they knew it was time to evacuate inland.

They might have used different terminology to describe it, but like John Chroston, Tilly Smith, and the people of Simeulue, the Andaman aborigines knew a hard trend when they saw one.

We're using the metaphor of tsunami for the forces of technological transformation about to deluge our world—but there is a crucial difference. In the path of the Indian Ocean devastation, the most one could hope to do would be to evacuate and survive. In the face of tomorrow's onrush of technological metamorphosis, we can do far more than survive. With the perspective and the tools of flash foresight, we can not only survive that wave but clamber up on top and ride it into a bright and profitable future.

In the years ahead, there will be only two kinds of people: those who see the waters receding as the giant prepares to blow—and those who don't. Those who don't will experience massive chaos and dislocation. Those who do will find unprecedented opportunity.

>>>Change from the Inside Out

Agility has been quite a buzzword lately in corporate circles. "Customer needs are changing so fast," goes the conventional wisdom, "the competition and the marketplace are changing so fast, *everything's* changing so fast, that if you want to survive, you need to be incredibly agile."

Maybe twenty years ago; not anymore. Agility was a reasonable survival strategy during a time of rapid change like the 1980s, 1990s, and perhaps even the 2000s—but today the pace of technological change has gone beyond rapid. Change has become simply too fast for even the best reaction time to be fast enough. By the time the wave arrives, it's too late. It's certainly better to be agile than sluggish—but no amount of agility would have saved anyone from the Indian Ocean on December 26, 2004. It was not agility that saved John Chroston, or Tilly Smith, or the Andaman aborigines. It was *anticipation*.

Another popular buzzword in the nineties was *proactive*, the quality of taking responsibility for what happens in one's life as opposed to letting oneself be at the mercy of external influences or circumstances. It wasn't a bad concept for the late twentieth century; it's certainly more effective to be proactive than to be reactive. But in the twenty-first century, being proactive has outlived its usefulness. It's too late to be proactive: we need to become *preactive.*

The dictionary defines *proactive* as being "take-charge, energetic, driven, bold, dynamic." Those were fine leadership traits—for the last few decades. In practice, being proactive typically looks like this: "Don't wait, do something *now*—take action!" But do what? How do you know the action you're taking is the right action? Being proactive is the attempt to solve today's problems before they grow worse. And that's not good enough: we need to solve *tomorrow's* predictable problems, and we need to solve them before they happen. We don't just need to take positive action: we need to take positive action that anticipates future known events. To be preactive.

Being proactive is agile; being preactive is anticipatory.

The shift from proactive to preactive, from reaction to anticipation, also creates a shift in the nature of our relationship to change. We tend to think of change as disruptive, but this is generally true only when change comes *from the outside in.* For example, when a new law is passed, we have to make changes to ensure that our company complies. When a competitor comes into town offering lower prices, we are forced to change some aspect of how we do business. When a new technology comes out that changes customer behavior, or when the boss changes strategy, or when a competing marketplace opens up overseas, we scramble to adapt.

This happens to us personally, as well. When gas prices escalate, we change our driving habits. When the economy contracts, we are forced to change our spending habits, possibly even change how we make a living, where we live, and how we live. If you or your spouse is laid off, your family is forced to adapt.

Speaking with audiences around the world, I find that everyone shares this experience in common: from schoolteachers to nurses to managers to CEOs, when we explore what their typical day really looks like, everyone acknowledges that they spend most of their time in crisis management. Whenever change comes at us from the outside in, we are forced into a position of reaction, of putting out the latest fires. And those fires are coming at us faster and faster, which is why the idea of agility has become so compelling. But no matter how agile you become, dodging bullets becomes pretty exhausting—especially when those bullets keep coming at an accelerating pace.

There is an alternative to living as a constant crisis manager: taking the initiative to become an *opportunity manager.*

You know what they say about problems: a problem is "an opportunity in disguise." But that is typically not true, because by the time we know we have the problem, it's too late to turn it into any kind of opportunity. The wave is traveling too fast. A problem is only an opportunity if you *see* it before you *have* it.

Being preactive means putting yourself into opportunity mode, looking at problems before they occur, and then preventing them from happening in the first place. It means, instead of *reacting* to change that happens from the outside in, *creating* change from the inside out.

Change from the outside in is typically disruptive. Change from the inside out is purposeful and constructive. Inside-out change, preactive change, opportunity-managing change is where growth comes from, both personal growth and organizational growth. This is the kind of change that allows you to direct your future and seize your destiny. And the only possible way to operate in that kind of change is by becoming anticipatory.

Not far from where I live, there is a railroad crossing with an old wooden sign with three words on it. You've probably seen one like it. It says:

STOP
LOOK
LISTEN

That's excellent advice. As change accelerates around us and the pressure to keep up intensifies, our natural tendency is to try and speed up with it. But that strategy won't work. Rather than try to speed up even more, we need to slow down, stop, and think.

STOP: For a moment, put all your current problems aside and make the decision that you are going to devote a little time, on a regular basis, to becoming an anticipatory individual. If you work within a company or other organization, decide that you are going to become an anticipatory organization.

Once you have stopped the action, gotten clear on the need to be preactive, and made your decision to become anticipatory, then

LOOK: Take a look into the visible future and ask yourself this question: "What are the problems I'm about to have?"

What problems are you not having today but will have in the next three to six months? The next one to three years? The next decade? *Those* are the problems you need to solve. Shift your focus from solving only today's problems. The only way you can possibly get ahead of the curve is to solve tomorrow's problems today—in other words, solve them before they happen, so that you never have them in the first place.

And once you have taken your long look into the visible future, then

LISTEN: Listen to what your intuition is telling you about those future problems and ways you might approach them. Listen to clues that might be lying just outside your range of vision. As you learn more about how to see the visible future and your sense of flash foresight gets keener, you will pick up more and more of these clues, and in time, solutions will start to appear to you almost the moment you look for them.

When I talk with clients about becoming anticipatory, they often respond, "That sounds fascinating, and I wish we could do that—but we just don't have time to sit around thinking about three years from now. We're too busy dealing with what's on our plates right now!"

Of course they're too busy. We're all too busy. The executive team at GM were busy for the decade leading up to bankruptcy. Being busy didn't help them, and it won't help you, either. There will never be a time when we're not too busy—which is exactly why the visible future continues being invisible to nearly everyone. Here is the question you need to ask yourself: "In order to speed up, am I willing to slow down?"

One example of this approach is a tactic I call *future benchmarking.*

Benchmarking is a popular technique of strategic management that involves tracking and imitating the best practices of the leader in your field. But there is an inherent problem here: we're benchmarking the best practices of the *present.* By the time we reverse-engineer it, copy it, and implement it, it will be obsolete. Because change is moving forward so rapidly, we'll always be playing catch-up, and in the accelerating environment of the twenty-first century, catch-up is a fool's game.

There is no advantage to keeping up. What we really want to do is jump ahead. How? By skipping over today's best practices and benchmarking what the best practices *will* be in the visible future, based on hard trends and future certainties.

Let's say you're a manufacturer. You look around and see that Toyota's "lean manufacturing" approach is the best model around right now, so you say, "Let's copy that." But it may take you four or five years to successfully copy what Toyota is doing, and by the time you get there, you'll be four or five years behind—and these days, four or five years is a lifetime. So what do you do?

Instead of looking at what Toyota is doing today, let's ask ourselves, "Based on the hard trends, what is our best projection of what Toyota will be doing four or five years from now?"

Then we can base our entire strategy on emulating *those* best practices so we can become the leader of our field, instead of staying in a perpetual game of follow-the-leader.

"Wait a minute," you may be thinking, "how on earth are we supposed to figure out what Toyota, or anyone else, is going to be doing five years from now?"

By fine-tuning our knowledge of the hard trends. The only reason Tilly Smith was able to anticipate the coming tsunami was that she had learned precisely what signs to look for. That's exactly what we need to do.

>>>Eight Pathways of Technological Advancement

We opened this chapter talking about an onrushing wave of technological transformation. What exactly does that tsunami look like, how big *is* it, and how fast is it approaching?

First, when we say "technological transformation," let's be clear on what the driving force is that we're really talking about. There is nothing in a technology, in and of itself, that drives it to advance; a bicycle doesn't seek to turn itself into an automobile. More accurately, it is the *driving force of human creativity and ingenuity* that generates the hard trend of a continuous increase in human knowledge and technological advancement.

For example, the inventions of written language in antiquity, movable type in the early Renaissance, and digital technology in the past few decades have all contributed to a progressive wave of *increasing literacy* that is a perfect example of the kind of linear, progressive change we talked about in Chapter 1. We are, as a global population, moving from a largely nonliterate population to a thoroughly literate one, and like the progressive democratization of the world, this is not cyclic but is a change that moves inexorably forward in one direction.

Steadily increasing knowledge has not only created steadily increasing technological advancement, it has also created a steadily increasing capacity to communicate and collaborate. Increasing knowledge *combined* with increased communication has created *geometrically* increasing technological advancement—and that self-compounding swell has led to the thousand-foot wave now upon us.

To get a clearer picture of the world ahead, it's helpful to see individual streams within that wave. The hard trend of technological advancement flows through eight specific pathways, each of them a hard trend in itself.

THE EIGHT PATHWAYS OF TECHNOLOGICAL ADVANCEMENT

1. dematerialization
2. virtualization
3. mobility
4. product intelligence
5. networking
6. interactivity
7. globalization
8. convergence

It's not hard to imagine the primitive roots of these eight pathways, going back hundreds and even thousands of years. For example, the move from carving letters into rock to scratching ink onto papyrus and then onto paper is a good example of both pathway 1, *dematerialization,* and pathway 3, *mobility.* Pathway 5, *networking,* was born with the development of the great global shipping lanes, then the railroads, telegraph, and telephone. But even given their early roots, these eight pathways did not become the pervasive driving forces of transformation they are today until the late twentieth century. It took the power of the computer to breathe life into them.

Since first arriving at this list of technology-driven hard trends in the mid-1980s, I have presented it to thousands of audiences, and it has been fascinating to see how people have responded differently over the years. At first, some of these concepts seemed a little arcane or obscure to many. Not anymore. Today they have all become everyday household realities—yet still today we have barely begun to experience their true power and scope.

PATHWAY 1: DEMATERIALIZATION

In the 1987 Oliver Stone film *Wall Street,* there is a scene around the midpoint of the film where Gordon Gekko (Michael Douglas), the überrich Wall Street raider, wakes up his protégé Bud Fox (Charlie Sheen) with a phone call. "Money never sleeps, pal," says the money mentor as he walks the exclusive Hamptons beaches, gazing at the gorgeous dawn and egging Fox on over his incredibly cool, no doubt incredibly expensive cellular phone. The moment was iconic, so much so that the line of dialogue was used in the title of the film's sequel nearly a quarter century later.

Yet to us, watching the scene from our vantage point, the scene seems a little ridiculous: that thing Gekko's holding to his ear looks to us like a cash register. Why? Because we've *dematerialized* our phones; we've literally removed most of their atoms. In the world of *Wall Street 2: Money Never Sleeps*, the phones have become Bluetooth earbuds that are so small we don't even see them.

As technology improves, we are reducing the amount of material it takes to build the tools we use, subtracting atoms from them even as we improve their capacity and performance. The computer—which soars in speed and memory even as it shrinks in size—is itself a microcosm of modern technology. Like our telephones, our computers are getting smaller, lighter, more portable, more economical (in terms of the materials it takes to produce them) and softer in environmental impact. Laptops used to be several inches thick and weigh six or seven pounds; today they use a fraction of the material and accomplish far more than their ancestors—and cost far less.

Whatever you have, you can make it smaller—that is, if you want to. On the other hand, we don't necessarily *want* to make everything smaller, and dematerialization doesn't necessarily mean *miniaturization*. For example, we have the capacity to make our cars much, much smaller, but we may not necessarily want that for all models. However, we *do* want them to be lighter, because then they use less fuel. How do you make something lighter? Dematerialize it.

PATHWAY 2: VIRTUALIZATION

Virtualization means taking things we currently do physically and shifting the medium so that we can now do them purely in a weightless, representational world. The impact of virtualization goes way beyond the world of entertainment. An example of virtualization is *simulation.* As our technological capacity has increased, our ability to model incredibly complex physical realities in software simulations has grown to amazing proportions. Now we can test airplanes, spaceships, and nuclear bombs without actually building them (let alone detonating them, in the case of the bombs).

At the moment, I'm working with a large company on the logistics of their supply chain network. They need to be able to continually improve the way they move things from point A to point B to point C. We found that a good deal of that supply chain network could be virtualized, allowing us to see the invisible and deliver new ways of saving massive amounts of time, energy, and money. All we had to do was convert the physical functions into software models. This would have been impossible ten years ago.

Virtualization has transformed the world of business. In 1990 few people suspected it could be possible to make entire bookstores virtual, yet within a few years, we had Amazon. How do you hold a backyard sale virtually? Through eBay. And it's not only business; the very fabric of society is being transformed by virtualization. Bloggers have virtualized the news industry. With Second Life, the popular online community, millions now live (through their *avatars,* or virtual selves) in virtual worlds, where they play virtual games, go virtual shopping, and interact with their virtual neighbors. (In 2008 more than $1 billion was spent in these environments—and that's a billion *real* dollars.)

Virtualization is transforming our world in ways we're often not even aware of. Today, for example, the time lag from the moment the engineers at Toyota see a car in their minds to the moment it rolls off the assembly line is a mere *twelve months.* How can they possibly take a car from concept to completion in such a short time? Advanced simulation and virtualization. Remember those crash dummies we used to see on television? Today's newer generation of crash dummies are simulated along with the cars: they are so sophisticated they have a pulse, blood pressure, and other vital signs, which is possible because they exist only virtually. We can even perform a virtual autopsy that lets us see what happened to them internally.

Boeing's newest passenger airplane, the incredibly sophisticated 787 Dreamliner, is far lighter, far stronger, far more comfortable (with better air quality and more normal atmospheric pressure and humidity) than its predecessors, and it will have far better fuel efficiency and greater range. The 787 is composed of literally millions of parts. Ten years ago, building a plane like this would have been flat-out impossible. But not today, thanks to advanced simulation and virtualization.

PATHWAY 3: MOBILITY

When I was a kid, I used to visit my grampa and gramma, who lived in Telephone, Texas, a tiny town ninety-seven miles north of Dallas. It was one of those places that was so small you could put the Now Entering and Now Leaving signs on the same post. The town got its name in 1886 from its single telephone, which was located in Pete Hindman's general store. When phones later began showing up in people's homes, they were large wooden affairs that were stuck to the walls like built-in cupboards.

By the time I was visiting Telephone, Texas, most homes had desktop rotary phones: fairly heavy, black things made of Bakelite (the first widely used industrial plastic) that were permanently tethered to the wall by thick black cords. In the 1970s we started seeing different-color phones—and lighter phones. Then modular jacks, so we could unplug our Princess phone and plug it into another room; then wireless handsets, so we could walk around the house; and finally the cell phones that let us walk around practically *anywhere* while we talk.

With the advance of wireless technology (along with progressive dematerialization), we are rapidly being detethered from *everything.* Our mainframe computers became desktops, then laptops, then palmtops, then cell phones.

A few years ago, I-Tech introduced a computer keyboard that is simply a laser-generated image projected onto your desktop. That's a virtual, fully dematerialized keyboard: it's not really there, but there it is! I've seen a prototype of a little device that takes this one step further: it looks like a pen but has a little glass knob on one end that serves as a laser projector. Pop out the two recessed legs and it becomes a tiny tripod. Stand it on your desktop and flip a switch, and it projects a screen onto a wall and a keyboard on the desk. This "pen" is your computer: dematerialization plus virtualization plus mobility. (And by the way, it's also your phone.)

The applications of increasing mobility are endless. In some parts of the world you can buy a can of soda and pay for your parking space with your cell phone. Combining GPS, GIS (geographic information systems), RFID (radio frequency identification), and "presence" (that is, our ability to locate each other automatically through our communication devices), we are beginning to see a transformed version of mobile advertising.

Ten years ago our software and data all resided on our hard drives. Not anymore. We now have *cloud computing* with Web-based applications, like Google Docs, Salesforce.com, Hotmail, and Google Calendar, using software we tap into from distant servers and keeping our data on other servers, allowing our computers to act as "clients"—which means we can hop onto any computer, anywhere, to work on our term paper, check our appointments, and much, much more.

Traditional videoconferencing for the few is shifting to full-fledged visual communications for everyone, as we add live video to every communication device from our flat-panel television sets at home to our cell phones. Videoconferencing has gone mobile.

We're finding ways to unhook ourselves from all the physical anchors in our lives, going mobile with our work, our play, our sports, our shopping, our everything. While some of us will no doubt continue to collect around the water cooler in office buildings, more and more of us are working at home—or wherever we want—on flexible schedules. Like our devices, we ourselves are no longer location-bound.

Information and multimedia communication have been set free. No longer confined to or trapped inside any one network or storage bank, that content now whirls about us like air, all the time, every second of the day. All we need is a wireless device in our hands (or ears) to breathe it in.

You might be thinking that mobile workers have been around for years. True—but the *degree* of mobility has changed, and the degree of practicality and productivity in a mobile context has been transformed. As we continue to raise the bar on what this means by adding high-definition streaming video, accurate speech-to-text, and other powerful new features, we will transform the very definition of mobility.

PATHWAY 4: PRODUCT INTELLIGENCE

You're driving down the road, and a light blinks on your dashboard: one of your tires is about to go flat. Your GPS speaks up: "Service station with an air hose in three miles—take the next exit."

How does your car know this? It's intelligent. It has smart tires, and it's networked (that's the next pathway). It also knows you're low on gas, so it's routing you to the station with the best fuel prices, too.

In the eighties and nineties, as microchip technology became more practical and affordable, we saw an endless parade of consumer goods that suddenly had intelligent features. Self-cleaning ovens, motion-sensing porch lights, and so on. But that was only the warm-up. The degree to which we can now add intelligence to practically any product is about to transform our lives.

The microprocessor offers an almost infinite number of opportunities to imbue a product with intelligence. It's not just your tires that will be intelligent: the road you're driving on is becoming intelligent, too. When I pull into a parking lot, the lot tells me there's one space available on level three, aisle two, four cars up on the right. Soon it will also be able to tell me, "The lot is full, but hang on, some people are unloading a grocery cart on level five—drive on up, their space will be free in a moment."

We already have the capacity to build with smart cement and smart steel, with sensors built into them. Now we have the technology to make roads smart: imagine a road telling you that there's a pothole ahead, or a sinkhole forming. How can we do that? Simple: we use smart asphalt. We already have smart cement that will tell the highway department when the bridge needs to be repaired.

Any tangible thing can be made smart. All you have to do is put a sensor on it and give it the ability to communicate through a *network*.

PATHWAY 5: NETWORKING

In the first years of the new century, the recorded music industry was rocked and nearly capsized by the waves created by a little company named after the eighteen-year-old Boston college student who started it: Shawn "Napster" Fanning. Along with its descendants, Grokster, Kazaa, and others, Napster pioneered a completely new form of music distribution. Rather than storing files in one central location and giving users access, Napster worked through a new technique called *file sharing.*

Recording industry representatives striving to have the growing operation shut down were frustrated in their efforts to nail down the technology's hub: no matter how hard they looked, they couldn't find its central location. That was because no such central location existed. As Gertrude Stein once famously remarked about Oakland, California, "There is no *there* there."

The recording executives had massive money, size, power, and legal clout on their side. Napster and Grokster had networking. It was no contest.

Prior to the invention and proliferation of telephones, we built such networks as the highways of ancient Rome, the shipping routes of Phoenicia and Great Britain, the railways of America. These networks connected us in space but left us still separate in time. Telephones were the first truly modern network, in that they allowed us to start intercommunicating at great distances in real time. We stayed connected by our telephone network for generations. Then came faxes, e-mail, instant messaging, cell phones, and text messaging. Today the average American teenager is capable of carrying on a dozen texting conversations at once, without losing the thread of any one of them. Napoleon was said to have routinely dictated as many as six different letters to six different secretaries at once. With real-time texting via laptop and cell phone, millions of American teenagers are now operating at twice the emperor's capacity.

As networking increases in its scope, speed, and accessibility, we are also enlarging its meaning and application, working not only in the media of text (e-mail, instant messaging) and voice (phone) but also in video and even 3D video. This acceleration is creating fascinating new capacities and unimaginably huge opportunities—as we will see in the pages ahead.

PATHWAY 6: INTERACTIVITY

During the twentieth century, all our mass media were static; then came the Web. The Web was dynamic, with hyperlinks that allowed us to click on content and immediately see more. That ability to interact with our media represented a gigantic leap that we're still just beginning to comprehend. As we continue the process of opening up all our media to become dynamic, we're gaining the ability to interact with *everything.*

Picture this: you're watching a football game on television, and you see a great play, but you can't quite get the angle on that fumble that you wish you could. Wouldn't it be great if you could actually go out onto the field and run around to the other side, so you could see the whole play from a different angle?

But wait—*you can.* We've been hearing about interactive television for years. Internet protocol television (IPTV) is the reason we're finally getting it. With IPTV, you can be an active participant in events where you used to be only a passive observer.

Interactivity is everywhere on the rise. This is why Web sites such as Facebook, YouTube, and Twitter are so popular: they allow us to interact. The more you interact with something, the more engaged you become. You can see this in the way kids play video games. They used to stare at a screen and move a joystick. Now they move through their game environments in three-dimensional virtual space, interacting in real time with other kids from other countries around the world.

We're more interactive today than we were last year; we'll be even more interactive tomorrow. And it isn't just television and video games. From the days of Gutenberg onward, print has consistently been a one-way medium. A "Letters to the Editor" section of a newspaper or magazine could blossom into a moderately lively debate, but only at sedate intervals of time. Radio talk shows, with their entertaining call-in feature, provided a type of interaction. But these were small flourishes that merely decorated what has always been an essentially one-way flow of information and opinion.

No longer. Today social-media applications such as Twitter, YouTube, blogs, and Facebook have rocked the foundation of the news industry. Interactivity is transforming politics and the nature of democracy. It's also transforming marketing and advertising. In the past, mass advertising was a passive experience: all you could do with TV commercials, magazine ads, and billboards was look at them. When you see an ad on the Web, you can click on it—and that makes it a whole new ball game.

PATHWAY 7: GLOBALIZATION

We've had some degree of globalizing for ages, through trade routes, the postal system, and the telegraph. Radio was the beginning of modern globalization, since it didn't need roads or wires but could operate through the air—in other words, it also flowed through the pathways of dematerialization and virtualization. But this pathway became a fully realized, truly transformational force only with the high-speed networks of broadband Internet capacity.

With the explosion of outsourcing and task-sharing software that enables us to easily spread even the simplest procedures around the planet, we have quickly grown familiar with the concept of globalization. But we are only beginning to grasp its true implications.

Globalization doesn't apply exclusively to information. We're seeing the globalization of *everything.* For example, the globalization of economy. As economies become more interlinked with each other, we can no longer afford to blow each other up, because if we take one guy down, we wreck ourselves. This is why free trade is a critical element in the avoidance of war. No country that has a McDonald's within its borders has ever gone to war with the United States, because by the time they have a McDonald's, their economies have become so interlinked with ours, it would be costly and counterproductive to go to war. We might want to think about giving Ray Kroc a posthumous Nobel Peace Prize.

There are degrees and levels of globalization. It's one thing to manufacture and sell products in markets throughout the world; it's an entirely different thing to customize them for differences in the various markets of the world. A Mercedes is a Mercedes, no matter where you buy it—but when you buy a Toyota in Asia, it's different from the Toyota you'd buy in the United States. (For one thing, the steering wheel is on the right—and the car itself is smaller.)

Likewise, it's one thing if the members of your company's board have passports with stamps from all over the world, and quite another when your board is composed of people who actually hail from those different parts of the world. In 2005 Sir Howard Stringer became CEO of Sony, giving the company a top executive who was *not* Japanese for the first time in its history. As our companies' board and staff composition globalizes, we'll reach a point where it won't matter where the company originated. The focus will be more on new job creation than the country of origin of the hiring company. In fact, companies won't be "from" anywhere; or to put it another way, they'll be "from" everywhere.

This is not a political shift, nor will it be the result of some governmental or bureaucratic initiative: it is *technological.* We aren't globalizing because someone thinks we should; we're globalizing simply because *we can.* Technology makes the impossible possible—and when something becomes possible, we do it.

PATHWAY 8: CONVERGENCE

All of these pathways tend to overlap and interact, which only increases their acceleration. In fact, convergence has itself become a pathway of technological advancement.

For example, entire industries are converging. Filling stations and convenience stores converged in the eighties; in the nineties, so did coffee shops and bookstores. Those were mere twentieth-century convergences, though; today it's really heating up. The entire industries of telecommunications, consumer electronics, and information technology are all converging and becoming, in essence, one thing.

There's also product convergence. Look at your cell phone: how many products have converged into that little thing sitting on your palm? The modern smartphone is an e-mail device, a camera, and a video camera. You can do three-way calling on it. And because it has contact management and a calendar, it's also a complete organizer: a Swiss Army knife for the busy executive. The even smarter iPhone took convergence to another level, bringing a genuine Web-browsing experience (with Google Maps, phone directories, and more) together with all the normal phone functionalities, so you could hunt for a restaurant, find it on the map, and dial it for a reservation, all on the same device. Along with all that, plus e-mail, camera, and video camera, plus YouTube player, it was a full-feature iPod, complete with WiFi music store. And of course, there are all those apps!

When I was a kid, the 1966 film *Our Man Flint* spoofed the James Bond craze by creating the ultimate ridiculous secret agent, Derek Flint (James Coburn), whose main tool was a Zippo lighter that sported eighty-two different functions—"Eighty-three, if you want to light a cigar." These days, our cell phones have taken that secret agent fantasy and made it real.

The hybrids and convergences we're seeing are quite amazing; few would have thought we would combine cars and televisions. One automobile manufacturer has even put a miniature microwave in the glove compartment, so you can heat up your sandwich when you're stuck in traffic. (Which would be impossible without the pathway of dematerialization.) Another is talking about placing your iPhone or iPod into its dock on your dashboard and using it as the hub of your car's GPS multimedia system, allowing you to play your streaming-video movies and YouTube files on the video screen in back.

Now we're starting to see the convergence of convergences. The Internet was born of the convergence of the phone and the computer. Google Maps and MapQuest converged the Internet with maps, and now GPS has given us the convergence of MapQuest and our cars—that's dematerialization, virtualization, mobility, product intelligence, interactivity, and networks. Take a close look at where the parts of your car were manufactured, and chances are you've got globalization there, too—which means you have *all eight pathways* converging in a single technology that you use every day.

That is exactly what's beginning to happen everywhere: all eight pathways are interacting with one another, the transforming whole becoming far bigger than the sum of its parts.

>>>Case Study: The Miracle-Earbud

Some years ago, while giving a speech to the leadership of a certain company, I pointed out some hard trends, starting with baby boom demographics.

Technology is enabling a longevity revolution: through genomics, anti-aging therapies, organ clones using advanced stem cell technology, more sophisticated pharmaceuticals, cosmeceuticals, and nutriceuticals, we're in the process of redefining the meaning of "old." There are hundreds of drugs right now reaching the end of their years of testing, all for postponing or resisting the aging process.

Because many didn't save enough for a lengthy retirement, the majority of baby boomers will work well past age sixty-five, albeit not necessarily at their current jobs. For many, *retirement* is shifting to *reengagement*. And how big will that population segment be, the ones who are reengaging in the workforce, many of them trying their hand at entrepreneurial ventures and small businesses, and with the overwhelming majority of the world's money in their pockets? That group will be *huge*.

"And," I told this group of executives, "they will all want to hear what's going on around them. Do you have a market? I think so!"

The company this group represented was Miracle-Ear, one of the world's leading manufacturers of hearing aids. Talk about the perfect business for catching a hard trend! There are 78 million baby boomers in the United States alone who all listened to Jimi Hendrix and Led Zeppelin—boy, are *they* going to need hearing aids. You'd think the Miracle-Ear people would be thrilled—but they were not. Why not? Because baby boomers would not be caught dead wearing a hearing aid. Wearing a hearing aid means you're old, and let's face it, most of us boomers are going to stay in denial about being old right to the bitter end.

This market needs their product—but doesn't want their product.

"What we need," I said, "is a flash foresight."

I told them about the oil executives' problem, and concluded with this thought: "If we can put oil rigs below water instead of on top, maybe we can turn this problem upside down, too—because we're not going to find the solution on the surface. We need to look not at where the technology is today, but where it will be tomorrow. We need to look into the visible future to see what's possible."

We started by looking at technological advancement pathway 1, *dematerialization*, and pathway 4, *product intelligence*. As our cell phones have gotten smaller and smarter, we've seen them embrace more and more functions, Derek Flint–style. Actually, our cell phones are evolving in *both* those directions: some are getting smarter and smarter, turning into multifunction multimedia computers, while others are getting smaller and smaller and focusing on the core function that made phones popular in the first place: talking and listening.

Advances in voice recognition are already making it easier to skip the dial pad function altogether, if you want that option.

Along with all the screen-focused devices, before long you'll also be seeing a cell phone that sports no screen at all and is small enough to fit into your ear. Not a Bluetooth earpiece: the *entire phone* will fit in your ear.

How can we possibly get a phone to be that small? Most of the software and much of the hardware will reside on a server, and the device in your ear will simply access that data. Right now, all the storage and intelligence that's built into our phones takes space and battery power—but once you move those functions onto the server, you don't need all those chips and power sources in the phone itself.

This now raises an interesting problem for cell phone manufacturers: how will they get such a tiny phone to fit comfortably in all those distinctly unique human ear canals? The ear canal is like a fingerprint: they vary enormously, and there's not the remotest chance of having a "one size fits all" model.

"Where will they find the expertise and experience to fit each instrument to each customer's individual ear canal?" I asked the group—and they knew the answer.

Miracle-Ear has more than 1,000 outlets across the United States, many of them in Sears stores, all staffed with professionals who know how to fit a hearing aid to your ear canal so it feels like there's nothing in there, and tune it to just the right frequencies to make sure it maximizes your hearing.

I suggested to the group that they consider collaborating with one of the major cell phone companies to produce a revolution in hearing enhancement: the Miracle-Earphone, or Miracle-Earbud.

Let's bring networking (pathway 5) and convergence (pathway 8) into the picture: add an embedded GPS microchip. Now, as you're walking through a city you've never visited before you can say, "Where's the nearest Starbucks?" and your Miracle-Earbud will whisper into your ear, "Next block on the right." As you walk toward your latte you can ask, "Hey, what's the latest price of Miracle-Ear stock?" and because your Miracle-Earbud is Web-enabled, it can go out onto the Net, come back, and tell you. Or, if you want music, you can ask for whatever song you wanted to hear—you say, "Purple Haze," and a few seconds later you've got Jimi Hendrix in your ear. (As a matter of future fact, you'll want two Miracle-Earbuds. Why? Stereo!)

While we're at it, let's add even more product intelligence. With the Miracle-Earbud we can enhance your hearing so it's better than human. With your human hearing, can you get Dolby surround sound? We can give it to you. How about intelligent noise cancellation? We can do that, too. You wind up on a plane with a crying baby right behind you? No problem: just turn down the frequency of the crying baby—and you're still hearing "Purple Haze."

Do you see what just happened here? We haven't just modified a product—we've shifted our company into an entirely different industry. A moment ago we were in the hearing aid business, a business that boomers don't seem to want any part of. Now, through flash foresight, we're in the leading-edge lifestyle-enhancing gadgets industry. This is no longer a hearing aid, it's a *hearing enhancement device*. Now we can sell it to baby boomers: instead of making it "for people who are getting old and hard of hearing," make it "The Miracle-Earbud: hearing enhancement for people who want to hear *whatever they want, whenever they want, wherever they want—with better than normal hearing.*"

Going from the struggling Miracle-Ear hearing aid to the thriving Miracle-Earbud hearing enhancement device is an example of what you can do when you make the invisible visible and the impossible possible. It's an example of using the certainty of hard trends to transform a business. It's flash foresight.

You're probably wondering whether Miracle-Ear jumped on this idea. The answer is . . . not yet. And I can understand why not: the picture I just sketched out seems so futuristic, so far-fetched; it's a cool idea, perhaps—but is it realistic?

It is *absolutely* realistic—in fact, it's inevitable. If all these features aren't technically possible today, they will be tomorrow. If they don't do it, someone else will. And that's not a guess: it's a certainty, because the advance of technology through all eight pathways is just beginning to enter a period of astronomically accelerating speed.

>>>The Three Digital Accelerators

Throughout this chapter we've referred to the accelerating pace of technological transformation—but we have taken it as a given without really examining what it is, why it is happening, or how we can expect to know where it is headed in the future. The hard trend of technological advancement is one of the prime movers of flash foresight in the twenty-first century. It's time we went to the heart of the matter to see exactly what that approaching tsunami looks like.

A close look at this super-trend reveals that it is actually a braid of three powerful, interlocking hard trends. Each on its own is capable of driving a huge amount of change throughout society, but the impact of the three acting together is enormous. If you think of the forward advance of technology as a car, we are stepping hard on the accelerator—or more accurately, on *three* accelerators at once.

As part of my work in developing what I call a *taxonomy of high technology*, I started charting the progress of these three accelerators in 1982. I was looking for key scientific indicators that could be used as tools for accurately predicting the future of technological transformation. The first indicator began with a simple observation made a few decades earlier about transistors.

In an article in the April 19, 1965, edition of *Electronics*, the cofounder of a little electronics company made an observation: the number of transistors on an integrated circuit for minimum component cost seemed to be doubling about every twenty-four months. The man's name was Gordon Moore, his little company was called Intel, and his observation has come to be known as Moore's Law.

ACCELERATOR 1: PROCESSING POWER

As it is commonly used, Moore's Law refers to the fact that *computer processing power doubles every eighteen months*. In point of fact, this is not an absolutely strict constant; for example, that doubling rate slowed a bit for a few years during the 1970s. But it soon picked up again and has been fairly consistent ever since. And even though

Moore himself has gone on record as saying it "can't continue forever," that rate of doubling shows no convincing signs of slowing for at least another decade, and probably a good deal longer than that.[1]

For example, those gains in speed have historically been obtained by shrinking processor components, but many of these have already reached microscopic levels, seemingly leaving developers few options for further reductions in size. So does that mean Moore's Law is going to grind slowly to a halt? Not a chance.

Now scientists have found that DNA nanostructures (about one-thousandth the diameter of a human hair) can serve as scaffolds for the assembly of computer chips. The process involves placing a long, single strand of viral DNA in a solution with short, synthetic strands. The large molecule self-assembles into various configurations, folding itself into a square, triangle, or other two-dimensional shape, with the short segments acting as "staples." The structures are positioned precisely on a silicon wafer using electron-beam lithography and oxygen plasma etching. Carbon nanotubes, nanowires, and other microscopic components can then be assembled on the scaffold to create complex circuits that are much smaller than any conventional semiconductors. Dubbed *DNA origami*, this breakthrough is one of many that will maintain Moore's Law well into the future.

And here's another example: researchers are now working on developing a way to produce circuits that use photons rather than electrons—a shift that will catapult computer processing speed well beyond today's conceivable upper limits.

Doubling every eighteen months. Think for a moment just what this means.

For example, take a penny, and double it every day: what would you have by month's end? Tomorrow, you'd have two cents; the next day, four, the next eight, and so on. By the end of the week, you would have a whopping sixty-four cents. By the end of week two, your cache of cash would have grown to $81.92. Not too exciting. But by day twenty-eight, just two weeks later, your pile of pennies would exceed *$1 million*; on day thirty it would be over $5 million. If this happened to be a thirty-one-day month, you would end the month with more than $10 million.

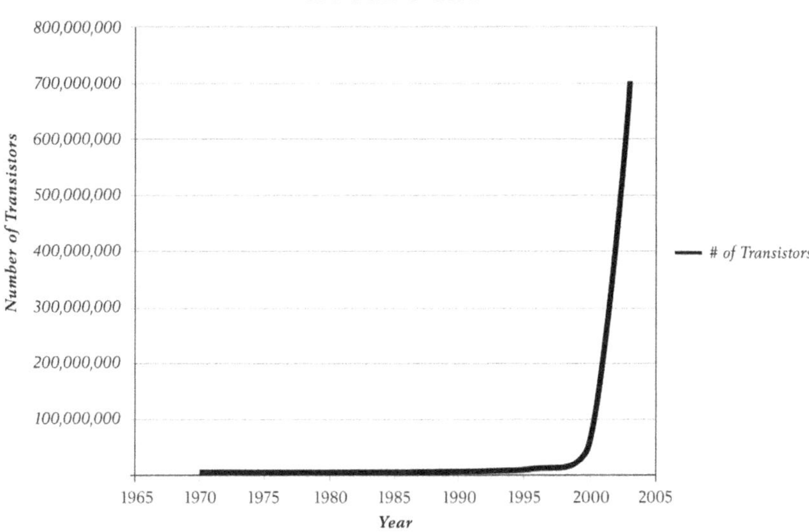

That's exactly what Moore's Law looks like, and why to most people in the 1970s and 1980s, it didn't seem like much to get excited about. Those years were like the early weeks of doubling penny piles, which is to say, not that impressive. It's hard to get excited about sixty-four cents. Going from a five-megahertz chip to a five-*hundred*-megahertz chip took twenty years. But doubling from five hundred megahertz to one gigahertz took just eight *months*—and that was already many years ago. Today, we've hit the "day twenty-eight" point: suddenly that steady doubling of processing power has hit escape velocity, and it's turning our pennies into millions.

This is what is driving the proliferation of all the computerlike functions that now come built into our cell phones, and why our automobiles suddenly have the capacity to diagnose their own impending repair problems.

In 1984 I forecast that we would eventually succeed in sequencing the human genome, but not until about the year 2000. Six years later, in 1990, the Human Genome Project was begun. Years later a rough draft of the complete human genetic code was announced jointly by U.S. president Bill Clinton and British prime minister Tony Blair. When? On June 26, 2000—right on schedule.

How could such an impossibly huge scientific feat have been so accurately predicted, right down to the exact year, sixteen years earlier? It was simply a matter of identifying the relevant hard trend. Given Moore's Law, it was clear back in 1984 that it would take about that long for processing power to reach the level needed to accomplish the task. That's the astonishing power of a hard trend and its capacity to ground us in certainty.

But again, remember what is perhaps the most salient aspect of this trend: it's *so easy to miss* in its early phases.

You can see this in the graph. As you first start doubling, the curve starts out slow. Two become four, which become eight, which become sixteen . . . still looking nearly horizontal, the curve is barely noticeable. But as it picks up arc and momentum, it eventually reaches the point where the graph seems to leap off the page and go *vertical*.

Going vertical: that's where we are right now. And that's only the first digital accelerator. The other two are doubling even faster.

ACCELERATOR 2: BANDWIDTH

The second digital accelerator is the growth of bandwidth, that is, the amount of information that can travel over a given channel.

In the mid-eighties, I emceed the world's first all–fiber optic videoconference in conjunction with Norlight Telecommunications, Inc., in Madison, Wisconsin. In that videoconferenced talk, I described a principle that was then almost invisible but would transform the world in years to come: *Digital bandwidth increases at an even faster rate than the accelerated growth of digital processing power.* Unlike Moore's Law, this principle hasn't been given its own popular name (although some have referred to it as Burrus's Law of Bandwidth); I'll refer to it as *accelerator 2*, or simply *bandwidth*.

As with processing power, the increase in bandwidth started out very slow—excruciatingly slow. If you are old enough to remember the modems we had back in the 1980s, you'll know what I'm talking about, and you're probably groaning as you think about it. To use one of these devices, you would literally stick your telephone handset into a pair of suction cups so the device could pick up the phone's acoustic (analog) signals. Once you'd plugged your phone into your 300-baud modem and gotten online, you could sit at your desk and rewrite an entire book by hand in the time it took your computer (processing power) and modem (bandwidth) to download a single Microsoft Word document. It was *slow.*

Today bandwidth is lightning fast, and not only is it accelerating, but it's accelerating even faster than the doubling of processing power. We think Web sites are sophisticated today because we've got high-quality graphics that load quickly, and even streaming video. But tomorrow it will be common to have 3D Web sites that allow you to walk a virtual tour of your store, new house, or vacation site, in real time. (We'll talk about what Web 3.0 will look like and how it will transform your life and business in Chapter 3.)

How can we know this for certain? Because bandwidth is on a growth curve that's gone nearly vertical—and the number of people using it is accelerating like that, too, which is driving costs down and giving us the ability to do some previously inconceivable things.

The most common analogy used to define bandwidth is a "pipeline." The wider the pipe, the more information flows through it in the form of bits per second. A full page of English text is about 16,000 bits, or 2,000 bytes. One of the early dial-up modems could send 56 kilobytes (57,344 bytes) in one second. Full-motion video takes roughly ten megabytes—twenty times that number—per second.

But don't take the "pipeline" image too literally. What we're really dealing with here is a strand of fiber optic filament. The acceleration in bandwidth that made possible outsourcing to India and ushered in what Thomas L. Friedman dubbed the *flat world* was generated mainly by advances in fiber optic technology, which translated into a huge increase in speed and doubling potential, as compared to glacially slower copper wire. Increasing these fiber optic strands' capacities doesn't require laying down new fibers—it only requires innovation in the switching units at the ends of each cable. In other words, we can easily multiply the capacity of our existing network by orders of magnitude without any substantial new investment in the infrastructure. And as we'll see in a moment, bandwidth will soon transcend even the upper limits of fiber optics, as communications and networking go increasingly wireless.

ACCELERATOR 3: STORAGE

Even as processing power and bandwidth climb at ever-increasing rates, the increase in our tools' capacity to store all the information from that increased processing and bandwidth is going through an even steeper, more dramatically escalating curve. My first computer didn't even have a hard disk drive. Today data storage capacity is so huge it's almost unlimited—and so cheap it's practically free. That's the continuing impact of the third digital accelerator: *The capacity to store digital data is doubling every twelve months—faster than the increase in both bandwidth and processing power.*

The first disk drive was developed by IBM in 1956, way back in digital prehistory. (In 2006 the disk drive turned fifty. That's right: the computer disk is itself a baby boomer.) Called RAMAC, it had a storage capacity of a whopping five megabytes, which took fifty spinning iron-oxide-coated disks, each the size of a twenty-four-inch pizza, along with a separate air compressor to protect the two moving heads that read and wrote the data. RAMAC's total size: about that of two modern refrigerators; total weight: one ton. And should you want to lease one, it would have run you $250,000 in today's dollars. Yet with all that size, weight, and cost, it would hold only the equivalent of about one MP3 song!

The big deal was that this information was fully accessible. "Random access" meant that you could go instantly to any point on the disk and retrieve any bit of data. Before that, if you wanted to find something, you had to rewind the tape to that point, just as with the audiocassettes we used to listen to before we had CDs.

In the early 1980s, when we first started tracking the three digital accelerators, PCs were shipping with floppy drives and hard drives whose storage was measured in kilobytes and then megabytes. By the late nineties we were talking about gigabytes; today it's terabytes—but not for long. Soon it will be petabytes (1,000 terabytes), then exabytes (1,000 petabytes), and so on.

Since shipping its first hard drive in 1979, Seagate Technology reports that by 2008 they had shipped one billion hard drives, a total capacity of 79 million terabytes, enough to store 158 billion hours of digital video or 1.2 trillion hours of your favorite music. And while it took them twenty-nine years to ship their first billion, they project they will ship their second billion hard drives in the next five years.

That vintage 1979 hard drive could store five megabytes, the same as the gigantic 1956 RAMAC device; it weighed five pounds and cost $1,500, or $300 per megabyte. As of April 2008, a typical Seagate drive offered one terabyte of data, enough to hold one solid month of continuous high-definition video around the clock, at the cost of about one-fiftieth of a penny per megabyte.

Here again, there seem to be limits to how far this trend can go—that is, when you look only at what we've *been* doing and neglect to look at what we're *going* to do.

While current laser technologies are continually increasing the amount of data stored by using shorter and shorter wavelengths of light, they are limited by the nature of their two-dimensional design. But scientists at GE are looking at new ways of increasing storage capacity using holographic principles. They have developed specialized polycarbonate materials that "write" data to a disk by chemically altering the composition of the material when exposed to specific types of laser light. This method allows them to use the entire volume of the recording medium instead of just the visible surface, permitting 200 times more data to be recorded on the same size disk. Because surface area is no longer a factor, the size and shape of the media can be more flexible. And data retrieval is considerably faster with the use of parallel reading schemes.

You could someday store your entire movie collection on one DVD. But you probably won't—because even DVDs will soon be obsolete. After all, who buys CDs anymore? We download our music directly from iTunes. My current laptop doesn't even *have* a hard drive; it uses solid-state memory chips, with no moving parts.

My data are sitting on a server I'm linked to on the "cloud." And that's today. What about tomorrow?

>>>Going Vertical

If doubling a penny and suddenly reaching $10 million seems dramatic, imagine this: what if the next month, you started with that $10 million *and kept doubling*? In technological terms, that is exactly what is waiting for us in the next handful of years. As dramatic as the technological changes produced by these three accelerators have been up until now, they are only a hint of what lies ahead. With bandwidth accelerating even faster than processing power, and storage capacity accelerating faster still, all three digital accelerators are coming together like a "perfect storm" to create an enormous force of transformation that is shooting up and off the charts of conventional expectations. We are about to put the pedal to the metal.

The next big technological shift affecting all three accelerators is the *photonics revolution*: using lasers and crystal holography to store information. (Think Superman's Fortress of Solitude.)

We've already been rummaging around in the foothills of this particular mountain of change. Magnetic drives give way to optical drives, and copper cable is joined by fiber optics, the transmission of data in the form of light, rather than magnetic charge. Just as laying down steel tracks for the railroads transformed the economic and social landscape in the late nineteenth century, our crisscrossing the oceans and continents with fiber optics in the late 1990s transformed the modern landscape—only to a far greater degree and in a fraction of the time.

These three accelerators describe a curve that starts out almost imperceptibly slowly. In the eighties, it started curving upward to the point where we could almost start to feel the change. By the end of the nineties it was impossible *not* to feel it. Yet today, oddly, people often seem to feel the technology revolution is over, that the biggest changes are behind us. This is a grave mistake.

As radical a change as we've seen with fiber optics, we've barely scratched the surface of the photonics revolution. Crystal holography is yet another technology that will give us inconceivably vast amounts of data, all stored in three-dimensional and instantly retrievable form. Information about virtually everything, at your fingertips: just add light and stir.

And that's just storage. Moore's Law is also continuing to feed this coming sea change, as our microchips get faster and faster. We've already stepped into the next frontier in processing, too: nanotechnology and *quantum computing.* Researchers have charted the workings of soon-to-be-constructed nanocomputers that store infinitesimal bits of information (called *qubits,* for *quantum bits*) on single atoms.

And what about bandwidth? That may be the greatest shift of all. We have already stepped off our copper wires and onto fiber optic cables, and now we're stepping off those translucent filaments onto . . . thin air. We have become the high-wire artist without the net—and without the wire, flying literally through the air with the greatest of ease. Fiber optics will continue to provide the backbone of communications—but with advances in wireless transmission, our capacity to increase bandwidth, both wired and wireless, has virtually no upward limit.

Photonics, crystal holography, nanotechnology, quantum computing, infinitely extensible wireless transmission—the rate of change ahead will make the days of 1999's "Internet boom" seem like a quiet autumn afternoon sitting on the front porch in a rocking chair watching the leaves turn.

A tectonic shift miles out at sea triggers an earthquake, creating a quiet series of tidal waves that nobody sees or senses. Because of the ocean's great depth, its waves are very small, yet the energy from the earthquake can cause these unnoticed waves to build to speeds of as much as 500 miles per hour—around the cruising speed of a 747. It is only when they approach the shoreline that their true magnitude becomes plain for all to see.

That is what is happening right now with digital technology.

The tectonic shifts in the ocean floor have already happened, and the ripples are flying toward us at astronomically accelerating speeds. Can we even comprehend what this will look like as that relentless doubling of processing power, storage, and bandwidth forms vertical lines that go straight off the charts, and that thousand-foot wave breaks over our shores?

What's critical to remember here is that none of this is a *maybe.* This accelerating rate of change is as certain as the sun rising in the east tomorrow morning, and it's going to sweep across our landscape like the technological tsunami it is. This is going to happen whether we want it to or not. From education to health care, agriculture to energy to manufacturing, it will burst through every industry and every institution, metamorphosing everything and leaving nothing untouched in its wake. It will disrupt catastrophically every aspect of every industry and every aspect of human activity—*except for those who see it coming.*

>>>CHAPTER 2 **ACTION STEPS**

*Being **preactive** means anticipating the future before it happens. Being anticipatory, instead of reactive, allows us to change from the inside out, instead of being forced to change from the outside in.*

- *Make the decision to be **anticipatory,** to become **an opportunity manager.***
- *If you work within a company or other organization, decide that you are going to become an **anticipatory organization,** capitalizing on the opportunities certainty brings.*
- *Ask yourself, "**What are the problems I am about to have?** What problems will my company be facing in the next few weeks, months, years? What problems will our customers be facing? What problems will my spouse, my children, and my friends be facing?" Then look for creative ways to **solve those problems before they happen.***
- *Another good question to ask is: "**What is my ideal future** ten, fifteen, and even twenty years from now? What are some of the steps I could take to shape that future now?"*

>>> *CHAPTER THREE*

Transform

By 1996 it was clear to all that the innovative little company, despite its past successes, was doomed to fail. The *New York Times* had already written its epitaph: "Whether they stand alone or are acquired, [the company] as we know it is cooked. It's so classic. It's so sad." *Time* magazine echoed the *Times*'s pronouncement: "[The company is] a chaotic mess without a strategic vision and certainly no future." So did *Fortune* magazine: "By the time you read this story, the quirky cult company . . . will end its wild ride as an independent enterprise." Incredibly, a year and a half later that quirky cult company was still breathing, but surely its days were numbered; after all, according to the *Financial Times,* "The idea that they're going to . . . hit a big home run . . . is delusional."[1]

But one man's delusion is another man's dream, and that "big home run" was not long in coming. The doomed company all these experts were eulogizing was Apple Computer. The experts were all dead wrong, of course, and just *how* wrong can be spelled out in four letters: i-P-o-d. In 2001 the "cooked," "delusional" company with "certainly no future" came out of nowhere to dominate a market that hardly anyone even realized existed. In 2001, the year the iPod launched, MP3 players represented a $50 million market worldwide; five years later that market was in excess of $2 billion. By the end of 2009 Apple had sold nearly a *quarter of a billion* iPods. And less than six months later it shot past Microsoft to become the world's single most highly valued technology company.[2]

How on earth did Jobs & Co. accomplish this miracle? Answer: a transformation happened, and they saw it coming.

Apple's success with the iPod was the result of many factors, including a corporate culture that holds innovation as one of its highest values, but the core of that success came down to a single flash foresight: The people at Apple saw that technology was *going vertical*. In other words, they saw where the three digital accelerators of *processing power, bandwidth,* and *storage* were going, and because they saw that, they also saw the opportunity to profit from them.

Apple didn't just capture a little slice of recorded music; it transformed the entire industry and threw its status quo into a tailspin. For decades, starting with Elvis, the Beatles, and Dylan, the industry had had a spectacular run as it followed the growing baby boom generation. Like the Big Three automakers, the Big Four record labels—Sony, Universal, EMI, and Warner—built massive organizations with huge profit margins, and they commanded a good three-quarters of the recorded music market. The good times didn't last forever, though. By 2005 they had lost 25 percent of that market share, and the bleeding hasn't stopped.

In view of the growth of P2P file sharing and free MP3 downloads, the idea of charging for downloaded music seemed impossible to most—but not to Apple. Upon its launch in April 2003 Apple's online music store, iTunes, quickly became a major force in music distribution. By the middle of 2005 it had racked up five hundred million downloads. And on February 23, 2006, recorded music hit a milestone that signaled a cataclysmic shift in the industry: the British pop group Coldplay's song "The Speed of Sound" became the *one billionth* iTunes download. By 2007 Apple's virtual music store had become the nation's third largest music retailer. By early 2008 it had surpassed Wal-Mart and become the single largest seller of music in the United States.[3]

What happened here? The tsunami happened. Bandwidth, processing, and storage accelerated so ferociously that suddenly it was possible to buy, store, retrieve, and enjoy a high-quality home stereo experience virtually—and the Big Four record labels did not see it coming. In a business based on marketing a physical product—vinyl disk, cassette tape, CD—of which at least 90 percent is pure profit, what happens when that product suddenly migrates to a medium from which *all* the atoms have been removed? That business collapses. Recorded music was hit by the first of our eight pathways of technological advancement: *dematerialization*.

When Steve Jobs decided to invest in iTunes and iPod technology, he put Apple out in front, ahead of the technological curve. In 2007 Apple became the third largest PC maker in the United States; by early 2008, while much of the market was entering a slump, the company was growing three and a half times faster than the rest of the PC industry. (It's also interesting to note that Apple also clearly saw where the hard trends of *dematerialization, mobility, networking*, and *convergence* were going, which allowed them to see the future of where their customers and their company were heading: they dropped "Computer" from their name, becoming simply "Apple, Inc." A short time later, they launched their next history-making revolution with the iPhone.)

The iPod rode the predictably increasing wave of *storage*: digital accelerator 3.

The iTunes store rode the predictably increasing wave of *bandwidth*: digital accelerator 2.

Predictably, the Big Four television networks began experiencing exactly the same crisis as the Big Four record labels. By 2008 Americans were watching more minutes per day of video on YouTube than on the top ten television shows. Like the iPod, YouTube came out of nowhere to dominate a field that hardly anyone realized was there, becoming a billion-dollar company in the process. Like the recording giants, the television giants were all caught by surprise. It's not that they didn't expect things to change; they knew things would change.

But things didn't change. They *transformed*.

>>>Blur—Streak—*Gone*

According to the *New Oxford American Dictionary, change* means "to make something different," while *transform* means "to make a thorough or dramatic change." It is a difference of degree, but that degree is so extreme that it becomes a *qualitative* difference.

Changing means continuing to do essentially the same thing, only introducing some variation in degree. Build it a little bigger, smaller, faster, higher, longer. Increase the marketing budget. Add a few staff to the department. Build a snazzier-looking SUV. Come up with a new slogan. But GM cannot be fixed by *changing,* nor can the recorded music industry or television networks survive simply by *changing.* Embracing change is no longer enough: we need to *transform.*

Transformation means doing something utterly and radically different. It means nanofusion; it means putting oil rigs at the bottom of the ocean and reimagining GM on a Dell model. In the early 1990s Barnes & Noble superstores *changed* how we shop for books. By the mid-1990s, Amazon was *transforming* how we shop for books, which then transformed how we shop for everything.

As a teenager, I had a collection of my favorite music on long-playing vinyl disks. When eight-track tapes and then cassette tapes came out, that was a great change: now we could hear the music in the car. When the industry moved from LPs and cassettes to CDs, that was an even better change: now we could hear our favorite music without the hisses and scratches. But with an iPod, now you can carry your entire music library around in your shirt pocket. And with the introduction of the Nano, there were no longer any moving parts; nothing to spin. Nothing moves but electrons, and they can be transferred at the speed of light to anywhere. The eight-track, audiocassette, Sony Walkman, and CDs all *changed* how we listen to music; MP3 and the iPod *transformed* it.

One of my favorite images of this distinction comes from the 1977 film *Star Wars,* in the moment when the *Millennium Falcon* (Han Solo's tin-can smuggling ship) shifts into "hyperspace." Up to that point, you can see the stars hanging motionless outside the portholes; then, all at once, the stars shift and blur, change from white dots to white streaks—and they're *gone*. In 1977 that was science fiction, but that's what the pace of transformation in today's reality feels like: blur, streak, *gone*.

In the nineties we were always telling ourselves to "think outside the box." It's a neat image, evoking creativity and unconventional thinking as a way to arrive at ingenious new paths and solutions. But like being proactive, it's a slogan whose time has come—and gone. Here's the problem with thinking outside the box: we all know that no matter how creative we get during the weekend seminar, come Monday morning we're going to have to crawl back *into* the box again and deal with our current reality. The problem isn't that we need new ways to simply step outside the box—we need to completely transform the box itself.

In fact, whatever your box is—your job, company, career, situation—it is going to transform whether we like it or not. There is no field or profession, no business or organization, no country or society that is not going to transform dramatically and fundamentally over the years ahead.

Just ask the Big Four. In October 2007 the popular band Radiohead stunned the industry by releasing its new album, *In Rainbows*, exclusively online, as a downloadable MP3. No CD, just a series of ones and zeroes floating somewhere in the electron streams of virtual space. Before long the Eagles, Joni Mitchell, Madonna, and Paul McCartney had all severed their ties with the major recording labels. What happened to the industry's lucrative CD deals? Blur, streak, *gone*.

>>>There's No Recovery Coming

When I was thirty I visited Glacier National Park in Montana. It's a stunning location, and I returned with a ton of photos of the mountains there. Years later, two kids from my neighborhood took a camping trip there with their dad. When they returned home I asked them how they liked the park.

They shrugged. "Not so great," said the older boy. "Yeah," his little brother chimed in. "Wasn't that impressive. Just a bunch of pine trees. Not goin' back *there* again." They showed me a snapshot of the two of them standing with some friends against a backdrop of sullen haze. No wonder they weren't impressed. A thick blanket of smoke from recent fires, combined with some especially cloudy weather, had completely obscured the mountains.

"Hang on a sec," I said, and went to bring out my photo album from my earlier trip. I showed them a few breathtaking shots of the mountains climbing regally into the sky. "What do you think?"

"Cool!" the younger brother said. "Where's that?" "Yeah," said the other boy, "we should go *there* next time!"

But they *had* gone there. They just hadn't seen the mountains, because the mountains were shrouded from view.

That's where we are right now. We're standing at the foot of an enormous mountain of change—only most people can't see it, because of the fog and smoke raised by events like the recent global economic downturn.

After the world slipped into the recession of 2008 and 2009, people were asking when we were going to really experience a recovery—but the answer was already implicit in the question. What they were really asking was: "When are things going to go back to normal? When are we going back to our old jobs, to our old economic stability? When is life going back to the way it was?" But that's not going to happen. There is not going to be a "recovery."

Economic flux is cyclic change; all recessions are temporary. Oh, things will get better; they are already improving as I write this. But in reality, there will be no *recovery,* no going *back*—only a surge forward into a very different world.

From our vantage point, it's easy to assume that the biggest changes have already happened: the Internet has already turned our world upside-down and changed everything. But that's hindsight, not foresight. The proliferation of the Internet throughout the last decade has been the prologue, not the unfolding story itself. It was not the transformation—it was only the foundation that laid the groundwork for the transformations to follow, the overwhelming majority of which are still ahead of us.

We are at the dawn of an era of technology-driven transformation that will make the changes we have experienced over the past twenty-five years seem tame, mild, and slow. We have crossed the threshold into a time of transformation. And that is the context of the third flash foresight trigger: *Expect radical transformation.*

In the past, it was important to change. Now it's no longer enough to change. In fact, as I tell my clients, *to change is to fail.* We need to transform.

>>>Our Intelligent Future

Among the biggest challenges facing us in the new century is that of energy. The quest for sources of energy has historically been one of the biggest driving forces of colonization, global discord, and war (as well as many great fortunes). Our consumption of fossil fuels now stands as arguably our greatest ecological threat, and it is a prime factor in many of our biggest economic and geopolitical crises. In fact, this is one reason we opened this book by looking at nanofusion and oil drilling. If we can use flash foresight to solve our energy challenges, we will transform our world for the better in myriad ways—creatively, from the inside out, rather than catastrophically, from the outside in.

In Chapter 5 we will look at what flash foresight has to say about the future of oil and other fuels and their implications. But regardless of whether we're using oil or wind, coal or biofuels, nuclear power or nanofusion, our biggest energy problem is that we're asking the wrong question: the central question is not what we should be using for fuel but *how we should be using it.*

The answer to that question is, *with intelligence.* The flash foresight solution to rising energy costs is to transform our use of fuel by adding intelligence to the process itself.

Of the eight pathways of technological transformation we looked at briefly in the last chapter, exploring any one of them in more detail would give us a fascinating look into the visible future, but product intelligence, pathway 4, is perhaps the most vivid example of seeing how dramatically technology is going to transform *everything* in the years to come.

The cost of intelligence is falling even faster than the cost of energy is rising. What's more, it will continue falling for years to come. Can we really say this with certainty? Yes, because it's a hard trend: it is a direct result of the increase in processing power, storage, and bandwidth, our three digital accelerators. As we design new ways to integrate product intelligence into every tool, system, or vehicle that uses petroleum fuel, for example, we counter the rising cost of that fuel with the falling cost of intelligence, allowing us to do more and more with less and less fuel.

In fact, we've already seen how this works. In the seventies we were wringing our hands because we were running out of oil. What happened? For one thing, fuel injection: we married the computer to the internal combustion engine and brought intelligence to the process. Fuel injection had an enormous impact on mileage efficiency and overall fuel consumption. At the same time, developments in technology allowed us to get more oil out of old wells we thought were dry. Thanks to vastly improved data mining and virtualization/simulation modeling, along with new drilling technologies (for example, allowing us to drill sideways instead of only straight down), we developed ways of detecting, reaching, and extracting oil from entirely new places.

And that was only a glimpse of what's possible, as the three digital accelerators head into a vertical curve. The more we add intelligence to the systems that burn petroleum fuels, the more we'll economize and balance that rising cost.

At the same time, while the cost of intelligence continues to fall, the *intelligence* of intelligence (that is, the increasing sophistication and capabilities of embedded product intelligence) continues to rise in an arc that is itself approaching vertical. What we think of today as "smart concrete" will be at the dumb end of the scale ten years from now—and the smart end of the scale will be staggering compared to what's possible today. For example, in the previous chapter we talked about smart parking lots, but the gains there pale in comparison to the savings we'll gain, both economic and ecological, as we create smarter streets and stoplights and allow them to communicate real-time data to everything else. We presently burn up more gasoline stuck in urban and suburban gridlock than we do actually driving out on the freeway. By embedding sensors and microchips in concrete, we create smarter intersections that know what traffic is flowing at all times and communicate that knowledge to the stoplights and to our cars' navigation systems. If our auto tires were inflated to the optimum pressure, we could save millions of barrels of oil. Smart tires that can tell us how much it is costing us *not* to put sufficient air in them will help. And smarter tires that fill themselves while in motion will be even better. Communication means *networking* and *interactivity*—pathways 5 and 6. In fact, these innovations of intelligence will use all eight pathways, and not just the one we called *product intelligence*. It means harnessing the intelligence power of the three digital accelerators to transform our infrastructure.

The impact of smart infrastructure goes beyond fuel savings, too; it also means saving *lives*. If we can build intelligence into our bridges, so they can tell us how stressed they are before they collapse, then we can also build smart levees that let us know before they burst. We can do all these things. The technological capacity already exists; these are not pipe dreams, they are in the pipeline, coming toward us.

In the future we'll bring intelligence to everything that uses any kind of energy. Smart houses that know your habits and schedules as well as the changing cost of electricity in real time, minute by minute. Your house will know exactly how to adjust your climate, lighting, and other power-consuming features in the most economical and optimal-performance ways. Smart cars that know when to use which fuel, according to the terrain, locale, and type of driving you're doing. Intelligence will drive our multifuel future, so that our tools will know when to use different fuels and how to use them for optimum efficiency and productivity.

Right now, 65 percent of all industrial energy consumption in the United States is used to run our electric motors, the great majority of which operate at single speeds. In terms of efficiency, this is like driving your car using only the brake pedal to vary the speed. If these motors were outfitted with intelligent drive units that could control their speed to match the output required, it would reduce their energy consumption by about 30 percent—an absolutely enormous reduction in the electricity needed and greenhouse gases produced.

Dale Morgen tells me that in his latest patent for nanofusion, he's designing a way to make the fuel itself intelligent.

And if we have smart homes and offices and smart power plants, we'll also need to have smart transmission systems—smart grids—or everything will stay dumbed down. Which means smart grids, too, are an imperative.

We can apply the same flash foresight in other sectors of industry, too; for example, our food supply. To a great extent, the history of civilization has been the story of our changing relationship to the earth. Just because we style ourselves as "post-agricultural" doesn't mean that primal link isn't every bit as important today as it has always been; consider the international food riots of early 2008. The need for agriculture will never be obsolete. We will always live on growing things from the earth, just as we will always breathe, laugh, and love. It's part of our human nature.

However, in the face of the transformation that is upon us, we need to reinvent agriculture just as we do our use of fuels. We need to add intelligence to agriculture. Writing about the future of agriculture in 1990 in my book *Advances in Agriculture,* I predicted the use of GPS to plow straight rows by the nineties, and that by the second decade of the new century, farmers would be using fully intelligent tractors and putting biodegradable sensors with wireless transmitters and nanoantennae in their fields, allowing them to tell by computer readout what parts of the field are being attacked by insects, which areas are low on moisture, which sections need a little more phosphorus. Instead of treating all 100,000 acres the same way, they would now treat only the spots that needed it.[4]

Today GPS is commonplace, tractors can drive themselves, and that wireless sensor technology is quickly becoming a reality. With this more intelligent agriculture, we'll know exactly when and where there's an insect infestation, so instead of blasting an entire crop with an insecticide, we can make our field applications with laser precision. And for those applications, we'll use insecticides derived from plants and insects, making them more organic and less toxic to the environment—and to us. Imagine the savings, in energy, time, and dollars, as well as how much we'll reduce the negative impact of overtreatment.

With sensors in the soil, crops will become intelligent, telling us exactly when our crops are thirsty, and which crops, and how thirsty. Instead of pouring entire rivers onto our fields at huge economic and ecologic costs, we'll meter out water only to those areas of the field that need it, when they need it, and in the amounts they need it. How will we know? They'll tell us. And because the cost of water is going up just like the cost of fuel, while the cost of intelligence is going down, smart irrigation alone will effect an economic revolution in agriculture.

>>>Intelligent Health Care

I've known Dr. Ben Durkee since he was a kid; I used to hire him to rake the leaves on my lawn, and as he got older, he learned to use flash foresight to shape his future. When he decided to go to medical school, he pursued both a Ph.D. and an M.D. concurrently. As a twenty-six-year-old third-year graduate student at the University of Wisconsin, Ben won first place in Chicago's Innovation Whiteboard Challenge for a fascinating innovation. Working with his research partner, Matthew Christensen, Ben developed a most unusual pill—actually a combination of two pills—to help in the area of colon cancer. Not to treat it; to prevent it.

The first pill contains a biomarker and a fluorescent molecule. As it travels through your system, the biomarker will seek out, detect, and locate any cancer cells in your intestinal tract. The second pill is a microelectronic tablet that uses light signals to track the fluorescent molecule and communicate its location to an external pager for readout.

Essentially, Ben and Matthew have created a virtual colonoscopy that would allow the easier detection of intestinal polyps *before* they become cancerous. Using flash foresight, it's easy to see that before long, Ben or someone like him will follow with a virtual biopsy.

Consider the implications. Colorectal cancer is the second leading cause of cancer-related deaths in the United States; every nine minutes, someone in the United States dies from the disease. It's generally estimated that as many as 90 percent of these forty-eight thousand annual deaths might be prevented by early detection. But there's a problem: the idea of a colonoscopy is unpleasant enough to be a significant deterrent. Imagine the impact this one intelligent technology could have, in both lives and dollars.

Like energy and agriculture, health care is an area that has been plagued with skyrocketing costs—and one critical key to containing those costs is to take advantage of the sweeping transformation created by the gone-vertical curve of the three digital accelerators and the falling cost of intelligence.

Ben and Matthew's cancer-detecting capsule is a perfect example of what happens when you add intelligence and dematerialization to medical treatment: it becomes far less invasive and far more effective, saves a lot of lives and a great deal of money. We used to have to crack open your chest to do bypass surgery; now we can do it endoscopically with just a few slender probes. The robotic da Vinci Surgical System lets us do minimally invasive prostatic surgery.

Remember when we practiced being inventors with our baby boomer–based new-business brainstorming exercise in Chapter 1? Let's do that one more time. One of the major health problems among the elderly is broken hips. One-quarter of seniors in the United States have a chronic problem with balance, leading to 300,000 broken hips each year—nearly 40 percent of which are followed within the next year by death. In fact, falling is the leading cause of accidental death in adults over eighty-five years of age. And knowing where demographics is leading us, we know we are going to have a *lot* more people in that age bracket in the years ahead. What do we do?

Well, what if we built intelligence into shoes and developed footwear that would monitor and correct balance? Such a technology already exists, originally developed to help astronauts walk on the moon. Could we apply that technology to a shoe for seniors?

In fact, someone already has. It's called the iShoe: the device analyzes pressure distribution throughout the insole and provides a computer readout so that doctors can diagnose balance problems. If an imbalance is detected while the wearer is mobile, the insoles generate tactile stimulation to correct it. And in the event that the person does fall, the shoe can be set to automatically notify emergency services and/or caregivers.[5]

Adding intelligence does some remarkable things to health care. With microprocessing fabric, we can create a smart bed that will take your temperature and read your heart rate. Again, someone has already done it, or something very similar. The LifeShirt is a smart garment, as light as an undershirt, that gathers data from the wearer including movement, respiration, posture, and activity level for twenty-four hours; the system can also gather information on blood oxygen levels, brain wave activity, exhaled carbon dioxide, and more. (It is estimated that the system could save U.S. hospitals as much as $200 billion over the next twenty-five years.) And the Japanese have developed a smart toilet: when you use it, it knows who you are and takes a urinalysis or stool sample. If your sugar levels start looking unusual, it will alert your doctor.

In the early eighties, I applied flash foresight to medicine and began sharing with doctors the kinds of transformational changes they would start seeing when X-rays went digital. When digital technology removed the physical film from the process (dematerialization), the process would not simply improve, it would transform. With digital X-rays, suddenly we would be able to adjust contrast and manipulate the information in ways that would allow us to see things we couldn't see before. And since digital files could be readily transmitted, the information in X-rays would be set free from earthbound constraints, and it would become possible to have instantaneous consultations with experts thousands of miles distant or even around the globe.

This is exactly what has happened over the past decade. In *The World Is Flat,* Thomas Friedman talks about the outsourcing of X-ray analysis: physicians in India read our X-rays during their office hours (our nighttime in the United States), and when our doctors come into the office in the morning, the results are already there for them.

And it isn't just our X-rays; the onward rush of our three digital accelerators is freeing practically every aspect of health care from its past limitations. Imagine this scene.

In the darkest early morning, something pulls you upright in bed. Your breath is strained and shallow; the night air feels clammy on your skin. You glance at the clock: 3:10 A.M. What was it that woke you? Aaah! There it is again—a gripping, cramping pain in your chest. Along with the pain, you are seized by a choking fear: Am I having a heart attack?

You tell yourself to calm down. You could get dressed, get in the car, and make your way to the emergency room thirty minutes away, go through admitting, wait your turn, and then convince the triage nurse you may be having a heart attack and need to get in to see a doctor ASAP—but what if it's only heartburn? Should you sit tight and see how things feel in a half hour? What if it really is your heart, and while you're "sitting tight" you drop dead? What should you do?

Using voice control, you switch on your HD media center and go to the virtual hospital channel. You scan the regional listing, find the hospital you like, and pull it up on the screen: "Elmbrook Hospital—Virtual Emergency Room."

A nurse appears on the screen and says, "Elmbrook VER—can we have your biometric?" You could instead head over to Virtual Admitting, where you'd fill out a series of virtual forms, but given the circumstances, you say, "Sure." (Filling out virtual forms can be just as much fun as filling out paper forms.)

Your HD media center's embedded camera uses facial recognition and a quick eye scan to identify you, and an instant later the people at Elmbrook Hospital have your medical re-

cords: they know your complete medical history, any medications you're on, any allergies you have, and all the rest. In five seconds the nurse is back onscreen asking you what's going on.

You tell her: "I'm having heart palpitations, shortness of breath. I'm concerned I might be having a heart attack."

"Okay," she says, "take out your medical sensor pack and clip the red biosensor to your index finger. Now, take out the yellow sensor and hold it to your chest. We're going to get your EKG, pulse, temperature, blood pressure, and oxygen levels."

Ten seconds later your vital signs have all been recorded, read and interpreted. Virtual triage. She looks up, smiles, and asks, "What did you have for dinner?" You tell her. "Good thing you didn't come in," she says. "It's not cardiac arrest. Chances are, it's indigestion."

What have you saved? Time, stress, worry—and a small ton of medical staff time. Multiply your own experience by the more than 100 million ER visits in the United States every year, and the impact is staggering.

The ER visit has been the great economic sinkhole of the American hospital system. Prime-time television dramas notwithstanding, most people who visit the ER don't need to be there. Even though they are one of the most costly ways to obtain routine treatment, well more than half the nation's ER visits are judged unnecessary. One report estimated that the total annual cost of unnecessary ER and doctors' office visits in the United States is just under $31 billion.[6] That's a lot of money we're flushing down our hospital toilets—most of which we could save with the product-intelligence applications of remote and virtual diagnostics.

Here is just a partial list of the advances in health-care tools and techniques we can see in the visible future:

- remote diagnostics
- remote monitoring
- virtual hospitals

- wireless telemedicine
- regrowing body parts
- in-depth genetic screening
- evidence-based (intelligence- and communication-driven) medicine
- results-based (that is, not treatment-based) funding
- e-enabled patient choice
- e-enabled assisted living
- e-enabled disease management
- e-enabled health records

>>>Anticipatory Health Care

However, the real challenge in health care cuts deeper than the nature of our medical tools and healing procedures or the structure of our health-care insurance system; it has to do with our *thinking.* At its root, the crisis in health care is the same as that in the energy industry, auto industry, or recording industry: we're barreling into the future with our eyes glued to the rearview mirror. The crisis in health care is not really a problem of cost; the system's cost is only a symptom of the disease, not the disease itself. In the ongoing national conversation about health care, just as with the national conversation around energy, we continue to ask the wrong question. And if you start by asking the wrong question, the most you can hope for is really good wrong answers.

The debate on health care typically centers around the question, "Who's going to pay for it?" The question we need to be asking is not "Who's going to pay?" but "Pay for *what?*" The answer, in a word, is *anticipation*; we need an anticipatory approach to health care that prevents as many health problems as possible *before* they happen.

Our present approach to health care is a break-fix model: you come into a hospital broken and we fix you. But consider this: 95 percent of the money spent on a person's health care is spent in his or her last five years of life. As 78 million baby boomers enter their seventies and eighties, that model will collapse—unless we shift it first.

For example, five years ago an uncle of mine who was in his seventies had a medical emergency. There was no room for him in the area hospitals, so they placed him in a hospice for a while. As it turned out, he badly needed surgery, but it took them days to realize it, because he wasn't under observation in a hospital. And that's my uncle's generation. What's it going to be like when the boomers hit that age bracket?

The conventional, allopathic, break-fix model is health care's petroleum: we watch its costs rising through the roof and try to figure out how we can pay for it—but the answer is that we *can't* pay for it. Nobody can. We have to change the *it*.

The beauty of Ben Durkee's cancer-detecting capsule is that it solves a major problem through early detection—that is, prevention. We need to treat as many of our health problems as possible before we have them, not afterward. You can only prevent something when you see it coming. In other words, what we need to be paying for is *medical foresight*. We need to apply flash foresight to our health care.

Of course, many have been talking about prevention for years, and there has already been a fundamental shift in public consciousness toward the concept of *wellness*. However, up to this point wellness has developed as an alternative to the mainstream health-care model. That's going to have to change. Today wellness is something people opt for. Tomorrow it will no longer be a luxury—it will become a core strategy.

In the past we simply couldn't do this, because we didn't have enough accurate information about what health problems lay on the road ahead for each of us. Now that we have mapped the human genome and are making constant and significant refinements to that knowledge, this is no longer the case. The hard trends tell us we are about to have a vastly greater capacity to project and predict health and disease tendencies—and that this capacity will continue to grow at ever-increasing rates.

This will transform not only the health-care system but also the life insurance industry. Right now, we're using actuarial tables that are based on generalizations extracted from history. In other words, your insurance rates are set by a rearview-mirror approach. Life insurance is an educated gamble.

For example, your rates are affected by whether you smoke. But some people smoke throughout their lives and never get cancer, while others smoke and die of lung cancer in their forties. What's the difference? Genetics. There are people who can take a drink and not become addicted, and others who take a drink and become alcoholics. The difference? Genetics.

What if there were a simple blood test that could tell me which disease susceptibilities I've inherited, and which I haven't? There is. Right now there are at least two companies that will provide exactly that service to you—for a thousand dollars. They'll even throw in a lineage search and find out where your ancestors came from. And that's just entering the foothills of the mountain of medical knowledge we will soon be scaling. In January 2008 a retired biotech entrepreneur named Dan Stoicescu slapped down $350,000 and became the first paying customer of a Cambridge-based company called Knome. Knome's service: to deliver the fully parsed sequence of the roughly six billion chemical units of Stoicescu's entire genetic code. Stoicescu was not the first person to buy his complete genetic printout: that distinction belongs to James Watson, codiscoverer of DNA, whose genome was sequenced the year before by a company that donated the $1.5 million in costs to demonstrate its technology.[7]

Note that sequence of costs: from $1.5 million to $350,000 in less than a year. It's easy to predict that the price will go from hundreds of thousands to a few thousand to a few hundred, and eventually, to nothing. The cost of petroleum may be on the rise, but the cost of information is plummeting ever downward toward zero.

Now, instead of betting on my death, my life insurance agent will have the tools to serve as a lifestyle counselor. He'll become a life *ensurance* agent, helping to ensure my long, healthy life. (When I'm alive, I pay; when I die, they pay. They *want* me to stay alive.)

Accenture has already developed a technology that puts a face on this issue: yours. Stepping up to a kiosk outfitted with a video screen and a keyboard for input, you answer a short series of lifestyle questions—questions about diet, exercise, whether you smoke, and so forth—and the video display responds by showing you exactly what you're going to look like twenty years from now. Change the answers to any one question, and you can see the positive or negative impact on the twenty-year-from-now you.

If you answer yes to "Do you smoke?" then you'll see a lot more wrinkles and possibly a grayish pallor staring back at you. Change your answer to no, and you will be stunned at the difference it makes in your complexion and overall facial vitality. It is a vivid display of the visible future, and it packs a powerful emotional wallop.

The biggest barrier to adopting healthier lifestyle habits is that the future is out of sight, out of mind. Sure, we know on some abstract, intellectual level that smoking and eating junk are going to take their toll: but on the abstract level is where it stays—until you take a look at yourself in the Accenture kiosk. Of course, people can step on a scale and see that they are obese and already at risk. But that doesn't show them the visible future, it only shows them the visible present. We need to see the future consequences of today's choices.

>>>Self Health

The shift from emergency remediation to technologically assisted prevention will have enormous consequences on the shape of health care, because it shifts the emphasis from practitioner to patient.

One of the biggest challenges in health care, as in every other industry, is that we're losing practitioners. Our doctors and nurses are retiring in droves. With 78 million baby boomers heading toward their seventies, we're losing our hospital staff.

But note: there's a hard trend at work here, and also a soft trend. Aging boomers will have increasing medical needs: that's a hard trend. But losing a large number of our doctors and nurses is a soft trend. It's *possible,* and given current conditions, even *likely*—but not *inevitable.* With flash foresight, that's a future we can change. If we have drastically fewer practitioners, who are we getting drastically more of? Retirees. One solution: shift from retirement to reengagement.

In the past you'd retire, live five more years, and die. Now the chances are good you'll be around for a good ten, twenty, thirty years after you "retire," and be needing some supplemental income, too. You just don't necessarily want to do the same thing or work as hard. We have hundreds of thousands of people, for example, who've worked their whole lives in advertising, marketing, or corporate sales, and who want to continue to use their skills but don't want to reenter their old professions. Let's attract some of them to become part of the transforming health-care system.

Part-time? No problem. Work from home? Consider it done. You can be a retired or newly trained nurse and answer questions from your home on a computer on your own schedule, just as a JetBlue reservation agent does today.

You can see where this shift is heading: more and more of the actual application of health care is going to be put in the hands of the patients. Or to put it another way: every citizen will become a part of the health-care delivery system. Diabetics already know how to self-diagnose and self-administer. Depending on the medication, why not apply that model to everyone?

In fact, we've already been heading in this direction for decades. In the 1950s and 1960s patients wanted their wise, kindly old family doctors to tell them what to do; today people look up their own conditions on the Internet and often know more about the latest treatments than their doctors do. The three digital accelerators and eight transformation pathways will accelerate that trend beyond anyone's imagination.

The problem is that cutting-edge technology finds its way into the health-care world rapidly when it comes to the actual treatment of disease, but very slowly in relation to the management of our hospitals and health-care systems. There is a huge gap between the technological state of our health-care *diagnostic and treatment techniques* and our health-care *management systems,* including the supply chain, delivery systems, and every aspect of the experience right up through billing and insurance.

In this, the modern hospital is in a situation very similar to that of the Big Four recording labels and Big Three automakers. Doctors are working on the cutting edge when they enter the operating room—but they're working within an environment organized and administered by systems that feel as if they were created in the dark ages. In the same way, there are extremely advanced engineering and prototyping systems inside GM—but that couldn't save them from collapse, because the organizational process and overall thinking there was still reactive and past-focused.

When you go to place an order on Amazon, they already have your credit card number and know all your shipping addresses from past orders. Imagine if we had the same experience at hospitals. And when you ship a package via FedEx anywhere in the world, you can go online and see exactly where your package is at any given moment. If we can do this for a package, couldn't we do it with a patient?

American health care still has a Byzantine approach to patient information. When you go to see your doctor, what's the first thing that happens? You fill in a form, and then you wait . . . and then you wait some more. It doesn't matter when your appointment time is: you never actually see your doctor then.

Why not? Why can't you submit all that information online, the evening before? Why can't your doctor's office know who you are, what your history is, and why you're there to see them, the moment you walk in the door?

When I call my airline frequent flyer hotline, they answer the phone by saying, "Hello, Mr. Burrus." Before I even open my mouth, they know who I am, because they have a smart data system networked with their smartphone system, and it tells them. Why can't they do that at my doctor's office? They could—they just haven't.

Still, as behind the curve as they are, even our entrenched health-care institutions cannot withstand the onrush of technological metamorphosis bearing down upon us. To the extent that our existing institutions fail to budge, we will see independent initiatives leapfrog over the calcified, geriatric systems presently in place to bring innovation to the marketplace.

In Canada, the health-care system is working furiously to integrate all patient records into one central database. As of 2010 only 20 percent of the U.S. patient population have computerized records—a number that will escalate rapidly. Imagine this scenario.

> *Walking down the street, you come upon the scene of an accident; a man is lying on the street unconscious. You flip open your cell phone, place his finger on it (or do a retinal scan, or one of any number of other biometrics) and within seconds, your phone identifies him. Before you get any information, you place your finger on the phone, too, and the medical information bank recognizes you; because you are not a doctor or nurse, you don't get access to the man's full medical records. However, the system notices that you took a course in CPR, so if that's indicated, it tells you. Or it sees that you didn't, so it walks you through the process with streaming video, right on the phone.*

What's preventing this scene from happening today? Only one thing: how we manage our health information. Our digital accelerators are creating an astonishing opportunity to transform how we do this. Increasing storage means we can *maintain* all our records; increasing processing power means we can *interface and collate* them, along with all known medical data, seamlessly and instantly, and *mine* them for actionable knowledge; and increasing bandwidth means we can *take these processes virtual* with wireless access anywhere, anytime, along with full high-def videoconferencing for professional interpretation when necessary.

Health information is a gigantic business, and those companies that grasp the scope of the transformation ahead will be the ones that will effect this shift. Early pioneers such as iMedix, WebMD, and Revolution Health have already taken this lead, and those who do the best job seizing the high ground will do enormously well for themselves in the process, just as Apple did with the iPod.

>>>Welcome to Web 3.0

We've been exploring the future of energy, agriculture, and health care as examples of how every aspect of our world will be transformed as the curve of digital technology's advancement goes vertical. We could choose any one of a thousand other areas, since this metamorphotic wave will leave nothing untouched. But no discussion of the coming transformation would be complete without a tour of the environment in which we have come to spend more and more of our time: the Internet.

To date, the World Wide Web has gone through two basic iterations. The first generation, lasting through the end of the nineties, presented the Web as a flat, one-dimensional way of displaying information that could be accessed by keyword searches. Basically, it was humans interacting with computers, which would soon change. Google's current project to digitize all the world's books and make their contents available via search is an advanced form of Web 1.0.

The Web's second iteration, Web 2.0, has been characterized by the user-to-user dimension of content sharing. Peer-to-peer networking was the application used by Napster to offer music file sharing to the masses. Since then we have seen enthusiastic amateurs from around the world work together to classify and post massive amounts of new content on the collective encyclopedia project Wikipedia. Idea-sharing tools (blogs and Twitter), personality-sharing sites (MySpace and Facebook), photo-sharing sites (Flickr), and video-sharing sites (YouTube) are all examples of the content-sharing nature of Web 2.0, which has given rise to the concept of *social networking.*

Thanks to the underlying technology of XML, which allows machines to talk to other machines over the Web, *applications* as well as individuals can also share data with each other; for example, the connecting of corporate or personal location-based data to Google Maps.

Web 2.0 created an entirely new experience from Web 1.0—but that's all behind us now. Web 2.0 is already old news; the future is Web 3.0.

The hallmark of Web 3.0 is that it is an *immersive* environment. In this new Internet construct, you won't *use* the Web, you will *enter* the Web. Where the essence of the early Internet experience was information search and retrieval, and Web 2.0 was all about interaction and communication, the prime thrust of Web 3.0 will be immersion and multidimensional experience. Today we talk about going *onto* the Web to look for information. In the future that language will change: instead, we will speak about going *into* the Web to learn and interact.

Generations of the Web: 1.0–3.0

GENERATION	KEY ACTION	EXPERIENCE
Web 1.0	search	access to information
Web 2.0	content sharing	social networking
Web 3.0	immersion	3D experience

Since 2000 I have been giving small demonstrations of an early prototype 3D Web browser in my keynote talks, showing audiences what it would be like to step into an inner-spatial, immersive environment to shop and get customer service.

As you click on this site, you have the sensation of stepping into a room where you are surrounded by content of different types on all sides. Turn to the right, and there on the wall is your live newsroom—CNN, *USA Today*, the *New York Times*, the *Wall Street Journal*, NPR, BBC, whatever your favorite news sites and sources are, there they are, all open simultaneously. Now look to your left, and there are the most current projects you're working on. Look behind you: itineraries for your next trip, your banking and investment information, whatever information you like to have nearby.

In the version I use, it feels like you are moving through a virtual environment. We can enter a building, hop into an elevator, go up a floor, and see a whole different room—in this case, a shopping mall that looks and acts just like a brick-and-mortar mall. We walk down the hall and on the left, there's a Porsche dealer. "Wait!" you say, "car dealers don't have display rooms in malls!" Maybe not in physical malls, but in virtual malls, why not? Walk up to a great model and you can open the door and explore the interior in high-definition, open the glove compartment, check out the backseat to see how roomy it is. You can open the trunk and throw in some golf clubs and see how they fit. In fact, you can start it, see how it sounds—perhaps even take it for a virtual spin.

The applications of such an experience will be transformational—not only in and of themselves, but also as combined with their real-world counterparts.

Right now, let's say you and I attend a big trade show on the latest technologies for your industry, whatever it may be. All the biggest suppliers from around the world are there, showing off their latest, greatest new stuff. Even though we're there for several days, dawn to dusk, there's no way we can get to all those booths and see all those displays. I've been to trade shows that feature entire city blocks' worth of the latest technologies. How do you take it all in? It's impossible. So let's make it possible.

When the conference is over, everyone packs up and goes home. What if instead, we just cloned the entire event to 3D virtual? The CAD (computer-aided design) drawings of the building already on file can instantly re-create the entire conference center in 3D form, needing only graphic artists to get the colors right, let the vendors add their virtual products, and presto! you have your fully immersive trade show. Now, when we go home, everything is still there—it's never over! You can click on any and every booth and connect to a real salesperson via videoconferencing anytime you like. And by the way, the vendors are still paying a fee, albeit a fraction of the in-person cost. Now, instead of having a three-day conference, you have a twelve-month conference.

In most of these 3D environments we use, it will seem that you are actually there, looking out into the room. In others, you will watch yourself walking through the room—although of course, it won't actually be *you* who walks through these 3D environments but your avatar, that is, an online representative of you in the virtual environment. An early version of this experience can be found in Linden Lab's Second Life, where several million registered players select an avatar of themselves through which they can interact with others, purchase land, build homes, and conduct business. Another is the enormously popular avatar-based video games, such as World of Warcraft.

Because of runaway multiplication of the three digital accelerators, over the next several years we will see this kind of dimensional experience come to the Web for the general user.

>>>Welcome to Web 4.0: Ultraintelligent Electronic Agents

If Web 3.0 is the future, then what's beyond that? Web 4.0, a further iteration of the online experience that will transform how we do everything. The essence of Web 4.0 is this: instead of our having to go searching for what we want, *it will come to us*.

Generations of the Web: 1.0–4.0

GENERATION	KEY ACTION	EXPERIENCE
Web 1.0	search	access to information
Web 2.0	content sharing	social networking
Web 3.0	immersion	3D experience
Web 4.0	intelligence	personal assistance

Advances in artificial intelligence have created a type of intelligent search that tailors itself to the individual user, learning our parameters and preferences to make our searches automatically more relevant and useful to each of us individually. Soon we will be using a powerful new tool to do a good deal of our Web-based work for us, thanks to an emerging technology called *ultraintelligent electronic agents*.

Because they reside on the Internet, you can access your e-agents from anywhere, regardless of where you are or what device you are using. We will probably use them at first through our laptops and PCs, but they will leap to our phones in no time.

Only you will have access to your personal e-agent. You will use two forms of biometric identification, like your voice and face, or your voice and fingerprint, to identify yourself.

You will be able to select various types of plug-in agent functionality. For example, your financial planner may offer an agent plug-in module to help you manage your money. Your travel agent, if you still have one, might offer a plug-in giving you highly customized and unique travel advice. Your trainer from the gym might offer a virtual trainer plug-in to be with you on the road. The list of possible plug-ins is endless.

Professional psychologists will provide plug-in modules for patients to help guide them through tough situations. Career counselors will provide plug-in modules to help you think through career changes, giving you guidance as you make career path decisions and linking you to the best resources.

You will most likely have one main e-agent you interface with most often, but you will have others that help you both at home and at work. Organizational e-agents will execute tasks on behalf of a business process. Personal e-agents will carry out tasks on behalf of one user. In time, businesses and individuals will delegate basic responsibilities to a customized collection of highly intelligent e-agents.

GETTING TO KNOW YOU

Your e-agent will use neural network technology to learn more about you every time you use it. This is the function, for example, that allows Amazon to build a profile of your preferences by keeping track of your searches and purchases, and how it is able to make personally relevant recommendations. The more time you spend on Amazon, the better it gets to know you and the better its recommendations become. Apple's iTunes has a similar function, called Genius, that will recommend music, movies, and TV shows based on your preferences, and even create playlists and mixes for you with a single click.

Your ultraintelligent e-agents will take this functionality to a whole new level. Imagine sitting down in front of your television, turning it on and, since it is connected to the Web, your e-agent pops up and asks what you are in the mood to watch. Let's say you want an adventure movie that you have never seen before. The e-agent will suggest a particular movie (set in the future because your past adventure movie selections were also set in the future). If possible, it will suggest a movie that has your favorite actors and director, and a plot that has twists and turns the way you like it best. Or, if you want something fresh and different, a complete change from your usual choices, then your e-agent can fill that bill just as easily.

Before showing you the movie, your e-agent might say, "I know you have been wanting to buy a sailboat. I have found several that fit your specifications. Would you like to look at the boats and have me review the materials now or later?"

Your e-agent will monitor your complete health and wellness, reminding you to take your medicine, warning you of potential allergic reactions from new prescriptions, helping you with your diet, and guiding you through your optimum exercises.

Who would be in the best position to supply this health e-agent plug-in module? The person you trust with your life, your doctor. As the world continues to get more complex and as we have access to increasing amounts of information, we will turn to our most trusted professionals for their guidance and help. Trust will be even more important in the future than it was in the past. And those professionals will increasingly turn to highly intelligent e-agents to help them in their tasks.

For many, the e-agent will become a friend, listening to and helping to solve minor problems, responding sympathetically, and suggesting helpful resources. They will be great "listeners" and will respond only when a response is needed and with the kind of response you have found most helpful over time.

WHAT WILL YOUR E-AGENT LOOK LIKE?

You will determine what your e-agent will look like, the voice it will have, and you will even be able to give it a personality. Most of us will rent a public personality to be our e-agent. For example, if you want a little humor in your personal e-agent you might pay a few pennies to rent the likeness and personality of whoever the hot new comic actor is. Some might prefer an action star or pop star. This will create an entire new revenue stream for public personalities. That means there will be a wide variety of e-agents from which to choose.

Disney and Pixar could make their most popular cartoon characters available as intelligent e-agents, mentors, and coaches for children. Your child will select his or her cartoon e-agent (and you will be able to set parameters to filter out objectionable content).

As a mentor, the e-agent might say to a child who has been using the computer for too long a time (determined by the parents), "Hold it—you've been looking at this screen way too long. Time to do something else in the real world, like going outside and playing with some friends."

As a coach, the toon e-agent could test the child on spelling, punctuation, grammar, math, history—in a completely entertaining way, of course. It will also perform functions like reminding them of appointments with friends, to practice their music lesson, or to finish their homework.

A PERSONAL CONCIERGE DESK

Think of your e-agent as a personal concierge desk. Wherever you might benefit from a human agent, mentor, or coach, you will begin to find electronic versions that will serve as virtual assistants of those human advisors, helping you stay on track. You'll wake up in the morning and your e-agent will greet you as you access your Net-enabled TV, computer, phone, or whatever device you're using. It might say, "I see from your calendar you are flying to Seattle this afternoon. It will be raining, so don't forget your umbrella. The flight you were taking is having a mechanical delay, so I rebooked you on another flight. Last night the stock you were interested in hit the price point you wanted, and after accessing all of the best analysts' reports I felt confident in purchasing 200 shares, per your request. Don't forget, this is your day to exercise."

Your e-agent will also serve as a personal researcher and organizer. You won't have to go to Google, Wikipedia, or other information sites, if you don't want to: just tell your e-agent what you need, and it will go search it for you—and a lot faster than you'd be able to do it. And the more you use it, the better it will know you, your preferences, and exactly what it is you're looking for.

Since the Web will go with you wirelessly wherever you go, your e-agent will always be there when you want or need help. Your e-agent will let you know the minute you have a new e-mail or voice mail and ask if you want it now or later (and in the case of e-mail, if you would prefer to read it yourself or have it read to you)—and it will do a much better job of filtering out all your junk e-mail than today's spam filters. It will inform you of traffic delays as you drive and offer alternative routes. Thanks to the growth of smart parking lots, as you enter the airport your e-agent will tell you how to get to the closest parking space available.

Imagine you're on a vacation with your family; you've been driving for hours and you're all getting hungry. Since your car knows your exact location, direction, and destination (thanks to your intelligent GPS navigation system), and since the car will be Web-enabled, all you have to do is speak your e-agent's name and tell it that you are hungry. The e-agent will ask each passenger what they would like to eat and when. Based on the answers, it will access all the electronic menus of each restaurant within a ten-mile forward radius of the car's position. Many restaurants already post their menus and daily specials on the Web because it brings in more business. The e-agent will recommend where to go based on your food preferences and budget limitations, and then provide driving directions to the restaurant.

Sometimes when I talk about such developments, people say, "That sounds terrible—a world where everyone interacts with machines and artificial intelligence, and nobody talks to each other anymore?"

But in fact, it's quite the opposite. The more high-tech we become, the more high-touch we'll need. A whole generation of adults worried that the rise of more and more realistic video games would mean their kids would become asocial, reclusive automatons, incapable of meaningful relationships or social sensibilities. But from all evidence, the kids of Gen Y are just the opposite: they are *more* socially conscious, *more* concerned about the environment and other large-scale social issues, *more* creative and entrepreneurial than any previous generation.

In fact, as we transform into a vastly more high-tech society, we will see our world become more human, not less. There is a simple reason for this, and it goes to a crucial flash foresight principle that governs how all this digital transformation will actually play out in the real world: the *both/and* principle.

>>>When It Comes to Technology-Driven Change, Think *Both/And*

In the late eighties, many futurists began predicting that by the late nineties, our offices would be paperless. We're still waiting. When the late nineties arrived, experts started predicting that within years, we would have no more shopping malls. The malls are still with us.

The same experts predicted that the phenomenal success of Amazon.com presaged the end of those brick-and-mortar dinosaurs, the Barnes & Noble superstores. After all, how can a physical store survive with its mere hundred thousand titles, when shoppers can go online and have instant access to a million titles and more? And yet those stores survived and thrived. Why? Because you can't walk into Amazon.com, sit on a couch, and have a latte while you browse a few magazines and visit with other book lovers.

Executives, managers, and the business and popular press all tend to make the same false assumption about the future of technological change. Every time a new product category is introduced, they assume that the older category will soon vanish.

But that's not the way it works. The hottest new breakthrough technologies do not necessarily replace older ones. Instead they often coexist with them, side by side. Why? Because the old technology has its own unique profile of functional strengths, which the new technology never fully replaces. In the case of paper, it's inexpensive, portable, foldable, you can erase on it—and best of all, it doesn't disappear if the computer goes down. Digital obviously has its powerful strengths as well. Both are here to stay.

We tend to greet innovation with an either/or assumption, but this is not an *either/or* world but a *both/and* world—a world of paper *and* paperless, online *and* in-person, digital *and* analog, old media *and* new media.

A few years ago there was a big debate in the business press: will the computer become a thin client, a device that stores all its data on and accesses all its software from a server, or will it continue to be a self-sufficient device that holds its own software? Which will it be? The answer is both/and. The question is not which will survive, but which are the best devices for which application and situation? For schools, a thin client is perfect: all the kids need is their lightweight device, and they can access all their assignments, homework-in-progress, and reference tools on servers, whether they're at school or at home. And if they lose it or break it, the replacement cost is much lower. When it comes to business users, on the other hand, many of us might prefer having our actual stored data right on our laptops (or phones), so we are not dependent on our wireless connection.

Either/or thinking assumes a zero-sum game, in which the pie is of fixed size and emerging technologies—or emerging markets—must necessarily threaten the existence of the old. But that's not the reality.

For example, book publishers have been in a panic because of the suddenly booming popularity of e-books. But the growth of digital books doesn't mean paper-based books will vanish.

In 2000 marketing guru Seth Godin wrote a book titled *Unleashing the Ideavirus,* and decided to do something very unconventional with it: he gave it away for free on the Internet—not just a teaser or free chapter, but the entire book. In just the first three months, the e-book version was downloaded more than a million times, making it then the most popular e-book of all time.

Publishers thought he was crazy, convinced this would cannibalize sales of the physical book—after all, the hardcover edition cost $40. Who would shell out forty bucks when they could get the entire thing online for free? But Godin understood that it's a both/and world. When the hardcover came out, it flew off the shelves and became a best-seller itself. People who had the digital version in their PCs wanted to have a paper copy they could highlight, write on, hold in their hands, and put on their bookshelves.

This is not to say that volume and market share for the older technology will always remain unchanged. Obviously there will be additional slices taken out of the pie—some smaller, some larger. But the *both/and* integration of new-tech and old-tech combinations has an amazing way of enlarging the pie itself.

And that is the crucial point here: integration. This is why all those paperless-office predictions were off the mark: as we create new technologies, we also keep integrating old ones. Go into a Barnes & Noble retail store and you can find an electronic kiosk for ordering any book online that isn't stocked on the store shelves. People go online to look at Apple products or Lexus automobiles, and some will even buy them there—but many then go in person to an Apple store or Lexus dealer to touch the product, feel it, see how it works, and establish an in-person service relationship before they buy. Today the nation's newspapers, like book publishers, are in a panic, convinced that Web-based media have made them obsolete. The radio and television networks are in the same state. (We'll take a closer look at this situation in Chapter 6.) But the old doesn't necessarily disappear. The secret to survival and new growth for these old-tech organizations is to embrace the new tech and find creative ways to integrate the two. If a newspaper's print version is different from its online version, then having both is a viable option.

Grasping the secret of both/and integration can unleash dramatic new levels of resources, capacities, wealth, and capabilities.

Returning to our discussion of Web 4.0 and the world of ultra-intelligent e-agents, the both/and principle tells us that no matter how sophisticated and useful e-agents become, they will never replace live interaction with another person. Those businesses that most skillfully integrate electronic agents with real-time live help will be the ones that ultimately thrive and dominate their markets.

Actually, you have probably already seen this play out on a simpler platform: the infamous touch-tone "help" menu: "To review your account, press 1; to change or update your account, press 2 . . ." We have all at some point had the infuriating experience of trying to get something fairly simple done over the phone, only to find ourselves in a seemingly endless loop of menu choices, none of which quite get us where we want to go. The companies that learned to adapt this new technology and integrate it seamlessly with exceptionally good live-operator customer service, and make that choice easily and transparently available at any time during the experience, are the ones that excel, survive, and thrive.

The future is not automated help; it is automated help *and* live help. The future is not digital, fiber optic, automated, self-serve, and youth-focused—it's digital *and* analog, fiber optic *and* copper, automated *and* manual, self-serve *and* full-serve, youth *and* elders. The faster things change, the more we will live in a *both/and* world, and one flash foresight key to surviving, succeeding, and thriving in that world is to continually seek ways to integrate the freshly old with the emerging new.

>>>The New Golden Rule of Business

The old Golden Rule in business was to find out what your customers wanted, and give it to them. "Do unto others as they want to be done to." Today, if you ask your customers what they want and you give it to them, you're missing a huge opportunity, because their answers will never give you more than a fraction of your potential.

Our capabilities are changing far too rapidly for this old rule to be useful. Customers today don't *know* what they want, because the things they most want are things they don't yet know are possible. Customers did not know they wanted an iPod until Apple gave it to them. The elderly were not asking for an iShoe that would help prevent them from falling—they had no idea such a thing was possible.

The new Golden Rule in business is this:

Give your customers the ability to do what they can't currently do but would want to if they only knew it was possible.

To survive and thrive, look into your customers' visible future, look at their hard trends, at what you're certain about regarding their future. See what problems they are going to have and solve them before they happen, so that by the time they're just starting to experience the problem, you already have the solution.

And if you don't? Then it's over—the wave will take you out to sea. Because this technology-driven transformation will not wait, pause, or stand aside while you think about it. Blur—streak—*gone.* There are two critical truths about business in this new era that you cannot afford to ignore; we might call them corollaries to the Golden Rule.

1. If it can be done, it *will* be done.
2. If you don't do it, *someone else* will.

If the Big Three automakers don't make the cars of the future, Toyota will—and if Toyota doesn't do it, someone else will. If the Big Four record labels weren't moving fast enough to embrace MP3 technology and the dematerialization of recorded music, Apple was only too happy to step in. If the major television networks don't embrace interactive, personalizable, high-bandwidth IPTV, then someone else will—and a few years from now, perhaps the major television networks will not be ABC, NBC, CBS, and Fox, but YouTube, Microsoft, Google, and Yahoo.

This is going to happen in every field. Blockbuster didn't move fast enough to make the home video rental business virtual—so Netflix did. In the 2008 presidential election the Hillary Clinton and John McCain campaigns didn't grasp the potential of online fund-raising and Web-based voter interaction: Barack Obama's people did. In 1999 Yahoo was the king of search, but if you worked for Yahoo in its search division back then, you were in the basement—because the company itself didn't see the value in search. Google did.

>>>In a New Fish Tank

Back when I was teaching science, I did an experiment once with some students. We set up a tropical fish tank with a pane of glass inserted down the center, dividing the tank into two compartments. In one side, we placed a predator fish, and in the other, a number of the type of fish the first fish would normally hunt and eat. For a few hours, predator went after prey: he tried like crazy, every way he could, to get to those tasty morsels. He rammed against that glass, over and over. Eventually, he stopped trying.

I removed the glass. All the students pressed in around the tank, peering in to watch the predator fish swim on over and gobble up his neighbors.

The large predator fish stayed on his side of the tank.

We grow up trying things that don't work, bumping our noses up against those failures, and eventually we learn to stop trying. But here is what's happening in the world today: technology is removing all those pieces of glass.

Wouldn't it be nice to have bridges that told us when they were about to break? To have crops that knew when to water themselves? To know in advance exactly what illnesses we're heading toward, and how to prevent them? We've learned not to expect these things, because they were always impossible. In this new world of transformation and opportunity, they are impossible no longer.

Unfortunately we tend to be like the predator fish: we don't know the glass is gone, so we don't even try. However, whether we know it or not, down the partitions have come, and as that flood of digital metamorphosis sweeps across the world it is completely transforming every feature of the landscape. We might as well have been released from a fish tank into an ocean. Are you ready to swim free?

No matter what your business or occupation, this challenge is facing you one way or another. The landscape is going to transform so radically that no career path will go untouched. How can you ensure that you will be the one who finds the high ground, who survives and thrives—one who experiences this wave not as disruption, but as opportunity?

Start with certainty; anticipate; transform.

>>>CHAPTER 3 ACTION STEPS

*Change means doing the same thing, only with a difference. Transformation means doing something **completely different**. It's no longer enough to change: no matter what field we're in, we need to transform. There is no profession, career, business, or organization that is not going to transform dramatically and fundamentally over the years ahead—whether or not we want it to. Expect radical transformation.*

- *Go through the **eight pathways of technological advancement** (from Chapter 2) and ask yourself, "How will each of these transformations affect my business? My life? How could I apply each one of these transformations to innovate my life and business?"*
- *Ask yourself, "What impact will the **three digital accelerators** have on my life, my business, and my customers?"*
- *Looking at the example of energy, agriculture, health care, and the Web (with its coming 3D environment and "ultraintelligent agents") as examples, ask yourself: **"How can I expect my own field or business to transform in the next few years?"***
- *"Knowing the **both/and** principle, how can I find new and creative ways to **integrate new and old technologies** in my field to yield better results?"*
- *"How can I **give my current and future customers the ability to do what they can't do but would want to—if they knew it was possible**?"*
- *Start crafting **strategies to transform how you sell, market, communicate, collaborate, and innovate.***
- *Looking at all the possibilities these inquiries have uncovered, remember this: **If you don't do it, someone else will.***

>>> CHAPTER FOUR

Take Your Biggest Problem—and Skip It

The year was 1865, and the British empire faced a problem that possibly threatened its very existence. Spurred by the development of the steam engine, an epic shift had been taking place for decades, an accelerating boost of productivity and standard of living that people were starting to call an *industrial revolution*. It was the fuel that drove this revolution that was at the heart of the problem, or more accurately, the looming shortage of this fuel, as the great British economist William Stanley Jevons had just spelled out with crystalline clarity in his latest book. In *The Coal Question*, Jevons surveyed the matter with thorough precision and predicted that Britain's coal capacity would soon reach its peak, thereafter causing the decay and collapse of the empire.

"The conclusion is inevitable," wrote Jevons soberly, "that our present happy progressive condition is a thing of limited duration."

History would prove Jevons right—and wrong. British coal production did peak within decades, just as he predicted, but it hardly mattered, because by then the Industrial Revolution had learned how to run itself on a new fuel, one that Jevons himself had dismissed as impractical. On August 27, 1859, a retired train conductor named Edwin Drake sank the first successful oil well in Titusville, Pennsylvania. Six years before the publication of *The Coal Question*, the petroleum age, which would carry the Industrial Revolution to heights that Jevons and his contemporaries could scarcely have imagined, had already begun.

It's interesting to note that Jevons's forecast was *not* an example of the Elvis fallacy. The economist did not confuse a soft trend with a hard trend: the depletion of England's coal was indeed a hard trend, and his forecast of Britain's "peak coal" was fairly accurate. So what was his mistake?

Jevons looked at coal in terms of its availability and cost. But even if coal supplies had been cheap and inexhaustible, the nature of the fuel itself would have brought industrial advancement to a grinding halt sooner or later. Can you imagine driving down the freeways of America in a vehicle powered by a coal-fired steam engine? How about flying from New York to L.A. in an airborne steam locomotive?

It wasn't a matter of reading a trend wrong, but of reading the wrong trend. Running out of coal was not the real problem. The problem was running on coal in the first place. Coal was not a problem we needed to *solve*—it was a problem we needed to skip over altogether.

>>>Your Problem's Not Your Problem

Here is an exercise I often do with my clients.

"Close your eyes for a moment and ask yourself: *In my work, what is the biggest problem I'm facing right now?* Keep your eyes closed until you've come up with an answer."

Their eyes invariably pop open again in just seconds; our biggest problems have a way of sitting right on our shoulders, ready to jump in and make their presence known at a moment's notice.

Try this yourself; to get maximum benefit from the exercise, you may want to jot down your answer. Now, with that biggest problem firmly in mind, here's what we're going to do: we're going to take that problem . . . *and skip it.*

The typical approach is to grab that problem and attempt to *solve* it. The problem with trying to solve your problem is that in order to solve it, you engage it, and by engaging it you embrace it—which often leads to getting your wheels mired in the mud of the problem, stuck in crisis mode and unable to move forward.

Flash foresight takes a different path. Rather than engaging with your biggest roadblocks by confronting them, often you'll find you can simply leap over them. This is not a philosophy of denial, avoidance, or procrastination. It is a powerful kind of conceptual jujitsu that teases previously invisible crises out into the open, where we can take decisive action to address them.

The key to unraveling our most intractable problems often lies in recognizing that the problem confronting us is not our real problem; the real problem lies hidden behind the distraction of what we *think* our problem is. *Skipping your biggest problem* means stepping outside the flat plane of the existing situation and gaining a clearer perspective, and this often triggers flash foresights that lead to new opportunities far bigger and more productive than you could have imagined based on the original (incorrect) problem you were trying to solve.

Take Eli Lilly, for example. A Fortune 500 company and member of the S&P 500 index, Lilly was one of the largest pharmaceutical companies in the world, yet they knew they were not invulnerable. In 1992, more than a hundred years after its founding by Civil War veteran Eli Lilly, the company that brought us insulin, penicillin, and erythromycin, had suffered the first quarterly loss in its history. By 2001 Lilly faced a ticking clock. That August a key patent would expire, ending the company's exclusive on Prozac, the drug that had been responsible for a third of its annual sales of $3 billion just the year before.

Lilly was in a panic. In 1999, knowing that the Prozac patent deadline was approaching, the company had ramped up its R&D budget by 30 percent in a quest to find the next pharmaceutical blockbuster. But its profits were tumbling anyway, and so was its stock value. A pharmaceutical company's stock price is tied to whatever exciting new drugs it has in its pipeline, and not simply to how well its existing flagship products are selling. To get new drugs into the pipeline, you've got to solve molecular problems, which is why Lilly had nearly 7,000 researchers on its payroll. As large a staff as that sounds, it wasn't enough. In August 2000, when news of the patent's impending expiration hit, Lilly's stock dropped nearly one-third in value in a single day, deleting more than $36 billion in equity. Now the August 2001 deadline loomed. They had some big molecular puzzles to solve, and solving them would mean hiring at least another one thousand PhD employees—a thousand new employees they frankly did not have the money to hire.

Lilly's problem was, to put it bluntly, *no money*. Or was it?

Actually, the key to solving Lilly's problem was to skip it—because that wasn't its real problem. The real issue was not *hiring more PhDs,* it was *solving molecular problems.*

So what did they do? They created an online scientific forum called InnoCentive, Inc., where they posted difficult chemical and molecular problems and offered to pay anyone who could solve them. By making the site open to any scientist with an Internet connection and posting the problems in over a dozen languages, the company created a global, virtual R&D talent pool that soon found solutions to problems that had stumped its own researchers.

One of the beauties of this strategy is that the company paid only for those solutions that worked. The amount paid depended on the difficulty of the problem. Some of the awards have been as high as $100,000, although most are in the $2,000 to $3,000 bracket. To date, engineers and scientists from Beijing to Moscow have worked at solving the company's molecular problems—without being on the company's payroll. In the following years, other companies followed Eli Lilly's lead, including Procter & Gamble, Dow Chemical, and others.

They created new drugs, and their stock rebounded. Lilly survived—and thrived. (In 2006, *Fortune* magazine named Lilly to its list of top 100 companies to work for, and *Barron's* included it in its top 500 best-managed U.S. companies.)

How did Eli Lilly solve its money problem? They didn't: instead, they skipped it. In fact, their money problem was not the problem, it was only what they *thought* the problem was.

So, what about that biggest problem of yours? Like Eli Lilly, if you hold the problem up and look at it from different angles, you may well find that it is not your true problem—and that rather than trying to solve it, you may fare far better by skipping it entirely.

Here is a suggestion: as you read through the rest of this chapter, keep that problem you defined in the back of your mind. By the time we reach the end of the chapter, perhaps you will have had your own flash foresight.

>>>Solving the Wrong Problem Can Spell Bankruptcy

At the same time Eli Lilly was watching its stock drop precipitously, a one-year-old company was basking in the afterglow of its recent IPO.

Founded in 1999 at the height of the dot-com boom, Webvan.com set out to create the ultimate customer service experience: home delivery of groceries, guaranteed within a specific thirty-minute window of the customer's choosing. This evidently seemed a can't-lose proposition to some, including Yahoo, Goldman Sachs, and other Webvan investors. After all, everyone needs groceries, right? So Webvan did what any ambitious, aggressive, optimistic, and unfortunately myopic entrepreneur would do: it capitalized like crazy. Contracting with the construction giant Bechtel to build it a billion-dollar network of warehouses, the fledgling enterprise bought a fleet of delivery trucks and outfitted itself with enough high-end computer hardware to run the military of a small country. The creators of Webvan had found the perfect problem to solve, and they were going to solve it with good old-fashioned Yankee ingenuity powered by a whopping dose of twenty-first-century technology and boatloads of dot-com cash from venture capitalists.

They were bankrupt in less than two years.

Where did the creators of Webvan go wrong? They set out to solve the wrong problem. As a consumer, where do you spend the bulk of your grocery-buying time? Chances are good that you spend it trudging through the store, trying to find everything you need. Most of us don't really mind driving to the store; it's once we're *in* the store that our time gets drained away.

Here's an inexpensive (and therefore commercially feasible) way to solve that problem: have customers order everything they need online, then assemble their groceries for them so that all they have to do is drive up to the front door and pick them up. Now, instead of maintaining expensive fleets of trucks and drivers criss-crossing town, wasting time ringing doorbells to discover that the customer forgot about the appointment and isn't home, and all the other logistical problems that plagued operations like Webvan (yes, there were others as well), we have a staff of in-store shoppers, networked to our order system by a communication network.

Would this model work? Sure it would. Has anyone tried it? As a matter of fact, they have; companies like New Seasons, in Portland, Oregon, have implemented a system just like that, and it works just fine.

Webvan was not alone; many of the companies that crashed and burned in the early 2000s after the dot-com bubble burst were working at solving the wrong problem. Many companies today are doing that still.

One key to finding the best solution is to make sure you're working on the best problem. It is only when you find the real problem that you find the real opportunity.

>>>Visible Problems = Invisible Opportunities

As Eli Lilly struggled to resuscitate its stock and Webvan watched its collapse, an American politician was sorting out what to do with his future.

Al Gore had a problem. The son of a career politician and a man dedicated to serving the public good, Gore had been in public office for nearly a quarter century. After fifteen years in Congress and another eight years in the White House as vice president, he had finally stood within a whisper of winning the Oval Office. In fact, he *had* won it, as far as he could tell. Unfortunately, the Supreme Court didn't see it that way, and now the ultimate fulfillment of a career of public service, the one goal that, once achieved, would finally allow Gore to make the kind of difference on the planet that he so earnestly wanted to make, would forever elude him.

Or would it?

In fact, Gore's losing the 2000 presidential race may have been among the greatest blessings of his life, because as things turned out, he has arguably had considerably greater influence outside the presidency than he would have had inside it.

As a politician, it is actually extremely difficult to create significant change. Politicians generally are not the ones who create change. Change happens, whether anyone wants it to or not. Advances in technology create changing possibilities, which change what the public thinks, expects, and demands, and it is the politicians' job to adapt to these new realities. It is not politicians' role to *create* change so much as to help articulate and manage the change that is already occurring. Politicians don't anticipate, they react. In skipping public office altogether, Gore took himself out of that more reactive role and put himself into a far more powerful role of influencing public opinion, a position where he could have a more direct positive impact on climate change through the transformation of energy and agriculture.

Freed from the constraints of office, including the need to do battle with Congress, wrestle with the constant scrutiny of the press, and juggle thousands of promises made to constituents and various interest groups, he was suddenly at liberty to pursue his environmentalist vision wholeheartedly. And now he was representing the world, rather than just the United States. Within a few short years, he had won an Emmy, a Grammy, an Academy Award, and a Nobel Peace Prize.

Failing to obtain the levers that controlled the system, Gore stepped outside the system—where he discovered a far greater opportunity than the one he had lost. He didn't solve his problem: he skipped it. In fact, getting elected wasn't really the problem in the first place. The problem was finding a way to have global influence without being bogged down by political baggage.

>>>Peeling the Onion

In the exercise we did above, there is a specific reason I asked you to close your eyes in order to think of your biggest problem: it illustrates a crucial point. Closing one's eyes helps to concentrate one's thinking—but it also shuts out what may be one's greatest opportunities. Focusing on what we have identified as our biggest problem creates a kind of blindness. We start seeing the world through the tinted glasses of that particular problem, and become colorblind to ideas lying elsewhere on the spectrum of possibility.

In the exercise, identifying your biggest problem is an important first step. The far more important step is, having identified the problem, to *open your eyes again and start looking*—because whatever your initial answer to the question is, that's probably not the answer you're looking for. The problem you identified will probably not be the real problem; however, it is often an excellent starting point from which to begin the search for the real problem, a search process you might think of as *peeling the onion.*

A few years ago I visited one of the largest international accounting and professional service firms in the world, and met with the CEO, whom I will call Ed. Ed's company was responsible for auditing many of the world's largest public and private companies, a workload that involved well more than a hundred thousand employees worldwide.

"As CEO," I asked him, "what would you say is your biggest problem?" As you've already guessed, his answer provided valuable insight into what was on the surface of this particular onion.

"Our biggest problem," Ed told me, "is getting enough people on staff to service all our clients globally. There's so much opportunity there, but we just don't have the manpower to service it all." He had put a great deal of effort into trying to locate, review, and hire qualified people, but still they were not able to keep up as well as they hoped.

As we talked, I began asking him for more information and detail about their situation. The specific questions I asked were not really that important, because there wasn't something specific that I was looking for—the point was to *look*. As is so often the case in a situation like this, what was important was the process of questioning and exploring. We were peeling the onion.

Ed had his laptop with him, with wireless access to everything—yet to my surprise, he was unable to find some of the information we were looking for. Why was this? Well, explained Ed, his company was actually composed of member firms in nearly 150 countries, with a dizzying array of different legal and logistic structures. He started telling me about a raft of incompatibilities, how different regions had developed different solutions with different systems and protocols, and how it wasn't at all easy for the various pieces of the whole to communicate clearly and efficiently with each other.

Bingo. We had found our way to the heart of the onion.

It soon became clear to Ed that if he and all his current employees were able to communicate and collaborate more effectively, they would not only *not* have to hire a lot of new people to service all their clients, but they might actually be able to trim and consolidate their staff a bit.

His problem, as it turned out, was not his problem. That is, there was another problem: while Ed's firm was excellent at performing the services they provided to their clients, they were strikingly inefficient in how they managed their own internal information and communication. They had plenty of data, but inadequate systems to exploit them and turn them into action.

Since then, they have mounted a company-wide campaign to consolidate and integrate their global computer networks. Considering the size and complexity of their operation, this has turned out to be a huge undertaking—and one that is well worth the effort. Although they are still only partway through the project, they report that they are already seeing huge gains in productivity and efficiency.

>>>Focus on One Issue

The power of peeling the onion is that it enables you to find that one place where, if you focus your effort, you can be genuinely effective. When the ancient Greek engineering genius Archimedes discovered the principle of leverage, he is said to have declared, "Give me a place to stand on, and I can move the world." Approaching your biggest problem by onion-peeling it, instead of simply trying to solve it, reveals that powerful focal point to stand on.

After receiving my undergraduate degree, I entered graduate school with the goal of teaching teachers how to teach science. The classic first-year grad student's problem was getting through the semester with great grades—but I decided to peel the onion. When I did, it seemed to me that the real problem was not graduating, but becoming the best possible teacher of teachers. What would be the ideal background for a teacher of teachers? Clearly, it would be having some kind of powerful teaching *experience*. Earning a PhD doesn't necessarily mean you have experience. I decided to teach at a variety of levels in a variety of situations while working on my degree. Having heard that junior high was one of the most difficult ages to teach, I took a position at a junior high school that turned out to be one of the first in the nation to have students from the inner city bused in. These kids would be my first teaching experience.

When I reported to my first day there, the other faculty were already complaining about the worst kids from the previous year, and saying how they dreaded having them back again. If you had asked any one of them to close his eyes and say, "What is the biggest problem we're facing right now?" they would all have immediately given the same answer: this particular small group they referred to as "the killer kids." So I said, "Well, why don't you give them all to me?" Which is how I found myself teaching science to a crowd of junior high students known throughout the school as the worst of the worst, the ones who always got into trouble and consistently got nothing but D's and F's in every subject. As one of my new colleagues put it, "They just cannot learn. It's as simple as that."

How do you solve your problem when your problem is *everything?* You don't solve it: you skip it—and start peeling the onion.

My first step was to forgo making any effort to try anything that any of the other teachers had already tried. Not that they were bad teachers; quite the contrary, some of them were quite good, and they certainly had the best of intentions. One or two had even made minor inroads in this subject or that. But it didn't matter: nothing had made any significant or lasting difference. I had an advantage, though: I knew one thing these other teachers didn't know, which was that *their problem wasn't really their problem.* Which meant posing this question: what if they *weren't* terrible students?

I gave them their first test individually and orally: no writing, no paper, no pencils, no hunching over desks; just me and one kid at a time, face-to-face. It turned out that they really knew their stuff. Not only did they remember everything we'd gone over in class, they would even explain their answers using the same hand gestures I'd used when teaching that topic in the first place.

The reason these kids had a history of such terrible grades was not that they weren't smart; they were *really* smart. The problem was that they didn't know how to read or write, at least not well enough to perform at any decent academic level. If they had to write the answers, they would freeze—but they could *talk* the answers.

I got each student a cassette recorder and had them speak what they wanted to write into the microphone, then play it back and write down what they'd said. This helped them learn to connect what they were thinking with writing on the page. It worked. By the end of the school year, not one of those kids was failing.

>>>Skipping Death

As the junior high story points out, the *skip your biggest problem strategy* is not only for the boardrooms of multinational corporations. In fact, it can be a lifesaver in even the most personal and individual of situations.

Once, after a speech in which I'd covered a number of flash foresight triggers, a small crowd of people from the audience waited to talk with me, most of them wanting to discuss their particular biggest problem and see if we could find ways to skip it. One woman caught my eye; there was a contained urgency in her manner. Nevertheless, she waited until every other person had gone through the line and there was no one left but the two of us.

"I have a problem I can't skip," she said.

She had recently been handed a diagnosis of terminal cancer, she explained. The tumor was growing fast; she had about six months to live.

"My life has become a living hell," the woman said. "I don't want to die, but I know I'm going to, and I can't stop thinking about it. How do I skip *that*?"

Like William Jevons, she was staring at a hard trend, only it was not coal that was running out, but the very days and hours of her own life.

"I'm so sorry to hear about your prognosis," I began. "Of course we all know we're going to die some day. But it's different when you know when." She nodded, and we were silent for a moment.

"May I offer a possibility?" I asked. She nodded. "Why don't you save thinking about dying for the day you die—and start thinking about *living* so you can enjoy the time you've got?" Her face changed; she smiled, and I could see, she got it.

About a month later, I heard from her; she said that simple shift had transformed her life. She had indeed begun focusing on enjoying life and the pleasures, beauties, and joys of life, she told me, where before she had been focusing almost exclusively on her feelings of dread, fear, and panic. She knew she was dying; this was a problem she could not solve—but she could skip it.

In another instance, someone used flash foresight to skip over the reality and finality of death itself.

As a young girl, Natalie Cole had appeared on stage once with her father, Nat King Cole, and had never forgotten the experience. However, it was not until her midtwenties that she launched her own successful singing career. Her ascent to stardom was soon followed by a plague of personal challenges, including a gnawing drug problem and a struggle to find her own identity as distinct from her famous dad's.

Finally, a decade and a half after becoming a recording star, Natalie was ready to mend the fences and embrace her family legacy. It was time to fulfill a dream that had first sprung to life when she was just eleven years old, and record an album with her father. There was just one problem: he had died a quarter century earlier, when Natalie was only fifteen—a full decade before she cut her first successful album.

Natalie's dream was clearly an impossible one; but technology can let us turn the impossible into the possible. She had heard about some techniques of digital engineering that were just starting to emerge, and she asked a childlike question: would it be possible to digitize her dad's old recordings and extract just his voice from the full sound—so she could then mix it with her own? She began exploring this idea, and eventually she succeeded in singing what was in essence a live duet across the seemingly impenetrable barrier of time. Joining her father in a rendition of his signature song, "Unforgettable," she created a CD that went straight to number one on the charts and held that position for weeks. *Unforgettable . . . with Love* won seven Grammy awards and sold more than 11 million copies, becoming one of the best-selling albums of the decade.

Her father being dead was a problem that would have stopped most people. Natalie skipped over it.

Natalie Cole's achievement, by the way, highlights one of the core tactics of the *skip it* strategy: *look to technology*. Skipping over the apparent problem and peeling the onion to find the single most powerful issue to focus on has always been a powerful strategy, but the faster the rate of technological change, the more abundant are its possibilities. Natalie Cole was not a technologist; she didn't know the details of how this brand-new technology worked. She didn't need to. And neither do you.

When he predicted the demise of industrialization, William Jevons knew about the fledgling petroleum industry but dismissed it as of limited use and short life span. There were probably people in Natalie Cole's life who were skeptical that her digital-mix idea would yield a result high-quality enough to release to market, just as there were naysayers at Eli Lilly who couldn't imagine the Internet being a reliable replacement for on-staff PhDs. No doubt there were Cro-Magnon individuals who didn't believe this whole using-fire idea would ever really catch on (What good is it—it burns everything!) or that the wheel had much practical application (It's so hard to get it to stand still!). We've been doubting the future of technology as long as we have had the capacity to imagine and invent. But today, in a world of digital vertical transformation, it's more crucial than ever. Because today, if it can be done, it *will* be done.

>>>Suspend Judgment

The secret to Natalie Cole's achievement was not that she had special knowledge that others didn't; it was that she was willing to ask that childlike question. In other words, she was not daunted by what appeared to be impossible. To put it in different terms, she was willing to *suspend judgment*.

Suspending judgment is not an easy thing to do, because it often runs counter to our habits or instincts—but it is an act that has great rewards.

Judgment blinds us from seeing new opportunities as well as hidden problems. When we hear about a new technology, read about a radical idea, or start looking outside the box in any way, often our first instinct is to judge—that is, to assess the value of this new information based on past experience. But the past does not equal the future. Becoming aware of the instinct to judge lets us take a breath, resist that knee-jerk assessment, and remove the blinders that keep us from seeing the invisible and doing the impossible.

For example, suppose someone told you they were going to start a bank in Michigan in 2009. You would judge this to be a bad idea—but I have a friend who did just that, and it has been very successful. He was able to resist the tendency to judge the idea based on the crises in Detroit and Wall Street, and has done quite well as a result.

Another friend has a large interest-only jumbo ARM that was about to reset in March 2010. He had never missed a payment and had a job, so he was told by others it would be impossible to get a loan modification—but he did. His new loan, secured in January 2010, was at 3 percent for the first two years, 4 percent for the next two years, and 5 percent for the remaining twenty-six years, with no payments for the first two months. Everyone prejudged this as an impossibility. But that didn't stop my friend from making it happen.

The *skip it* flash foresight trigger is one I've seen many people use to access enormous new opportunities. The key to using this trigger effectively is to start by making yourself willing to suspend judgment.

>>>Skip Ahead to the Finish Line

In the fall of 2006 I took a few weeks off to go on an East African photo safari through Uganda, Kenya, and Tanzania. In many of the villages we passed through, there were hardly any of the trappings of modern life: no banks, no television, no radio, no electricity. In many places, there was no running water. Climbing a mountain in Uganda's Bwindi Impenetrable Forest to spend time with the great mountain gorillas there was like going back to the era of hunters and gatherers living in tribes. With the sound of distant drums beating and natives singing, our guide hacking through the rainforest with a machete as we climbed to elevations of 8,000 feet and more, it felt like we had been dropped into an old Johnny Weissmuller *Tarzan* film from the 1930s.

My companions and I took a tiny chartered plane into Kenya's Amboseli Park, a wildlife preserve spread out over about 150 square miles of swamps and semiarid vegetation, and were dropped off in the middle of nowhere. As we looked around, we saw no visible signs of civilization. It was impossible by any visual clue to fix our location in time. We knew we were in Amboseli Park, but we could as easily have been in Jurassic Park.

The illusion was soon amplified: as we began our trek into elephant and lion country, we suddenly encountered a small knot of Maasai warriors. The three men were dressed from head to toe in their traditional garb, the way their people had dressed for centuries. It was as if they had stepped out of a time machine sent from many centuries in the past. Except for one little detail: two of the three Maasai were chatting on cell phones, courtesy of the Mobile Telephone Networks (MTN).

Chances are, you've never heard of MTN, but in the years to come, you will. Founded in 1994, this Johannesburg-based company is now the number one telecom in fifteen out of the twenty-two countries where it has a presence. In two-thirds of those markets, it has more name recognition than Coke. MTN specializes in providing services to emerging markets, particularly in countries in Africa and the Middle East. Here is a partial list of the languages that are today being spoken over MTN phone lines:

> *Afrikaans, Arabic, Dari, English, French, Fula, Greek, Hausa, Igbo, Kinyarwanda, Ndebele, Pashto, Portuguese, Sotho, Swahili, Swati, Tsonga, Tswana, Turkish, Venda, Xhosa, Yoruba, and Zulu.*

Many of the regions MTN serves have little or no infrastructure. How on earth do you bring cell phone service into an area where there is no electricity, let alone cell towers? If you're MTN, you skip the problem: you bring the electricity in with you.

When they enter a new market, one of the first things MTN does is set up a branch of the MTN Foundation, which provides a huge array of community support services that can range from health and educational initiatives to building small power plants. In the less developed areas, where there is no reliable electricity (or none at all), the MTN Foundation puts in small generating stations and an electrical network. (More about those generating stations in a bit, because they are no ordinary electrical plants.)

In the process, MTN's customers acquire far more than a communications system. Because if you live in one of these emerging economies, you don't just need a way to talk to others. You need radio and television, banks and credit cards, personal computers with Internet connectivity—and as it turns out, the humble MTN cell phone can fulfill every one of these functions. With miniaturization, mobility, networking, and convergence, your cell phone becomes your radio, your high-def television, your computer, and much more. As your region's economy advances, your cell phone also becomes your bank, so you don't need to build those big stone buildings (or charge those big fees, either, as ING Direct has shown); it becomes your house key and car key, your heart rate monitor and baby monitor. It serves as a multimedia training and educational tool for everyone in your community, from the youngest schoolchildren to seniors. The cell phone provides all the services you didn't have last week—and it does all this without destroying your ecology or burdening your country's economy with the weight of a colossal copper, steel, and concrete infrastructure.

If you're living in New York or San Diego, London or Sydney, Tokyo or Mumbai, it's hard to fully appreciate the significance of an MTN cell phone. In San Diego, all those features are nice, but we already have our banks and credit cards, our television and Internet access. All this cell phone convergence stuff is interesting, but not vital. Not so in emerging nations. There they are not just intriguing new features for our toys and gadgets, they are the doorway into the twenty-first century—which they acquire by skipping clean over the twentieth.

I noticed a similar example of a skipped-over infrastructure problem many years ago on a visit to Ecuador, where they had installed broadband wireless access virtually everywhere in the country. After arriving back home to the United States, I was struck by the fact that we couldn't get the same service here that everyone had in Ecuador! They had skipped the wired stage altogether. This is also one of the secrets to the Indian economic miracle: to a significant degree, India skipped over the more tedious copper wire and fiber optic stages of data transmission and went right to satellite and wireless communications.

>>>The Curse of What Works

Seeing MTN's impact in Africa made me think of a recent visit to Oregon to tour the magnificent Bonneville Dam, and of how much more advanced the inhabitants of Kenya are, in a curious way, than those of the American West Coast.

Over the four years from 1934 to 1937, as part of America's massive New Deal commitment to the nation's infrastructure, the Army Corps of Engineers built a new lock and powerhouse over the Columbia River on Oregon's northern border with Washington state. When the new lock system was opened in 1938, water from the Columbia River poured through, creating Bonneville Reservoir. It was the largest single-lift lock in the world, and its construction provided cheap power to the region. By damming up the water, the Bonneville had let loose a flood of new jobs. Woody Guthrie immortalized the impact of this engineering miracle in his song "Roll On, Columbia":

At Bonneville now there are ships in the locks,
The waters have risen and cleared all the rocks,
Shiploads of plenty will steam past the docks,
So roll on, Columbia, roll on.

The dam was declared a national historical landmark in 1987. As such landmarks often are, however, it is a marvel tinged with historical irony. In the early twenty-first century, the New Deal is very old news, and the great infrastructure that elevated our grandfathers in its construction now smothers us with its enduring presence.

The Bonneville Dam's seventy-five years of history passed through my mind on that visit; I feel a special connection to the dam, because my dad helped build it. Dad was part of the design team, and later became part of the sales team that generated business for the generators there.

My dad worked for Allis-Chalmers when it was a mighty company. A major force in the nation's World War II manufacturing effort, Allis-Chalmers had two big divisions, tractor and electrical. Speaking about the massive electric generators his company built, my dad once said, "The good news is, we made them so they'll last a hundred years. That's also the bad news."

While Africa's problem is that it has no infrastructure—a problem MTN and other flash foresight–minded entrepreneurial businesses are engaged in skipping—America's problem is the opposite: it has tons of infrastructure. Generators like the Allis-Chalmers behemoths and the Bonneville Dam facility are gigantic, inefficient, costly to run, costly to maintain, and gradually breaking down. The problem is, they still work. So what do we do, dismantle them all? It's the same with our highways and bridges, our municipal water and sewage systems, our power grid.

It is the curse of the legacy system: it works too well to throw it away, but not well enough to move us forward, and it's growing more dilapidated and more of a handicap with every passing day. It is an anchor, holding us back as we strive to drag our way into the twenty-first century. We have a decision to make: are we going to sink by the weight of our old stuff?

In a way, emerging nations like Kenya, Ecuador, and India have the advantage of necessity. They had no choice in the matter; it simply wasn't possible to retrace the whole historic progression from copper-wire telegraph to telephone and dial-up modems, to higher-speed modems, DSL, and cable, and eventually to fiber optic broadband and wireless. They were forced to skip the problem of the twentieth-century legacy telecom system.

For those of us in the already-emerged nations, here is the salient question: having the luxury of choice, can we exercise the judgment to make the leap anyway? Can we muster the courage, born of flash foresight, to let go of our legacy systems and skip into the visible future?

China seems to be in the midst of making that epic choice.

In its headlong embrace of twentieth-century-style industrialization, China began driving down the same road the industrialized nations of the West had traversed over the past few centuries. Only a few years ago, China was heading pell-mell into a full-blown American-style industrial age nightmare of urban sprawl and smog. This would be a worrisome development indeed; the earth may be able to support one superpower fueling its massive growth on hydrocarbon fuels—but not two or three.

Now, however, it is starting to appear that China may have decided to skip the problem. While the United States continues to waffle, dither, and equivocate over how to embrace greener, more twenty-first-century approaches to industrialization, China is endeavoring to leap to the head of the pack.

"China has emerged in the past two years as the world's leading builder of more efficient, less polluting coal power plants, mastering the technology and driving down the cost," observes the *New York Times*'s chief Hong Kong correspondent, Keith Bradsher. "While the United States is still debating whether to build a more efficient kind of coal-fired power plant that uses extremely hot steam, China has begun building such plants at a rate of one a month. China has also doubled its total wind energy capacity in each of the past four years, and is poised to pass the United States literally any month now as the world's largest market for wind power equipment."[1]

China's embrace of the *skip it* principle is also showing up in its approach to cars, as Bradsher reports:

"It is behind the United States, Japan and other countries when it comes to making gas-powered vehicles, but *by skipping the current technology* [emphasis added], China hopes to get a jump on the next."[2]

Chinese leaders have already adopted a plan for China's automobile industry to make that country the world's leading producer of hybrid and all-electric vehicles.

The crippling problem of legacy systems is not a dilemma of nations only; it is also the routine scourge of companies, organizations, and bureaucracies of all sizes, who easily become so handicapped by their expensive, outdated computer hardware and software systems that they lose all hope of retaining any competitive edge. It seems easier and less expensive to keep using the old systems—but it only seems that way if you're looking in the rearview mirror. Look out the windshield into the future and you get a very different picture. With your eyes on the visible future, based on the certainty of hard trends, it suddenly becomes apparent that making the change from the inside out will be less costly by far than having to make it from the outside in. Staying with the old, the legacy system, is a lot more painful than transforming with the new.

The challenge of legacy systems goes beyond hardware and software; it also applies to our *processes*. Scratch the surface of practically any company or organization and you find ways of doing things that have been developed and implemented because, to some extent, *they work*. Supply and inventory processes, accounting and customer service processes, research and decision-making processes, organizational and communication processes, all of them so bloated and cumbersome yet so entrenched they can seem almost impossible to abandon—yet staying with them can be suicidal. Selling CDs in retail stores was the legacy system for distributing music, a process that the Big Four record labels have clung to like driftwood in a shipwreck. Apple didn't bother trying to get a piece of that market, instead skipping it altogether. Analog processing was the legacy system for photography until the early nineties, as was analog signal for cellular phones until the mid-nineties. Polaroid and Motorola both held fast to their analog positions long enough to completely lose their former market dominance, never to regain it. Why? Sheer stubbornness, habit, arrogance? No, more because it simply seemed like the safer course of action at the time.

And that is the real problem, bigger by far than our aging highways and dinosaur generators: not just legacy systems but legacy *thinking*.

For most of history, weighing the value of holding on to or letting go of outmoded technologies was an issue we could safely ignore or postpone most of the time. Not anymore. In the new technological environment, our tools and systems become antiquated with astonishing rapidity. Because of the pace of change, dealing with legacy systems is something we have to learn to do constantly, because what is cutting edge today will be out of date before the steam cools on tomorrow morning's coffee.

In the old world, the rule was: "If it ain't broke, don't fix it."

In today's world, the rule is: "If it works, it's already obsolete."

An especially poignant example of this new rule is the One Laptop per Child project. Established and spearheaded by professor Nicholas Negroponte, founder of MIT's celebrated Media Lab and one of the creators of *Wired* magazine,[3] the OLPC educational computing group was founded with the dream of leveling the global playing field and bringing the underprivileged children of the world into the twenty-first century by supplying them with inexpensive laptop computers. The group spent years developing this simple, bare-bones laptop as a tool of transformation for emerging markets. At its launch, the nonprofit program announced a goal of shipping more than seven million of its "$100 laptops" to children in developing nations and emerging markets throughout the world.

The OLPC idea was and is a bold and ambitious plan, but the OLPC group is looking at the future through the eyes of the present, not the future. A powerful idea for investing in the future of the world, the concept was crippled by its own legacy thinking. By the time the $100 laptop concept had been conceived and designed, it was already obsolete. It was a good idea—but not a great idea. A great idea would be this: forget the computer altogether, and build the plan around smart cell phones instead.

The cell phone is the only infrastructure inexpensive enough, accessible enough, and practical enough to serve this vision. These people need to be able to communicate and collaborate, not just work in isolation, and the OLPC computer can't give them telecommunications. What's more, literacy rates tend to be low in emerging populations. I'm not sure how well a Maasai warrior is going to take to typing on a keyboard—but he can talk on a phone as readily as anyone.

The computer cannot function as the hub of all those activities individuals and businesses need to engage in to move significantly forward in Africa. The cell phone can.

The economics of it tells the story. At the time of its announcement in January 2005, the OLPC computer was supposed to cost less than $100 to produce, yet that figure began inching upward immediately; by 2009 it had doubled. India declined to commit to the project, stating its intention to build a laptop instead for $10. In Africa, as of this writing, the cost of manufacturing a cell phone is about $1. MTN executives tell me that soon that cost will be down to ten cents. And here's the irony: for all practical purposes, the cell phone is no longer just a cell phone—it is itself a computer.

Picture this: there is a tiny chip built into your cell phone that projects a beautiful digital screen onto a wall, and a second chip that beams a virtual keyboard in the other direction onto your tabletop. Wherever you go, if you can find a blank wall, push a button on your phone, and there's your television/computer screen and keyboard. This technology is just now becoming commercially available as I write these words.

Who could have possibly foreseen it? Actually, you could—because you already know about the eight pathways of technological transformation, and just half of these eight would have foretold the whole story:

- **DEMATERIALIZATION:** We can now pack a functional computer into a little handset that only a few years ago would have needed to be designed as a laptop.
- **MOBILITY:** What used to require a wired or cabled television or computer can now be done on a wireless mobile device.
- **NETWORKING:** The more individuals we connect to the same network of ever-expanding bandwidth, the more diverse kinds of activities and services we can provide over that network, which increases its value even as it brings down its cost.
- **CONVERGENCE:** Banking, broadcast, video, and Internet access have all converged with telecom in a single device.

Put these all together and you have a good description of exactly what MTN is doing; and it is helping to transform the African continent in the process. Focusing on this kind of technology might have put the OLPC project a good deal further ahead in the realization of its goals—but it was hampered by a legacy image of what a "computer" looks like.

>>>Skipping Scarcity

One of the most pervasive aspects of legacy thinking has to do with our fundamental economic worldview. As a consequence of advancing technology and our three digital accelerators taking the world into a vertical curve, we are now in the midst of a transformation not simply in our tools and our environment, but in our very relationship to the concept of wealth and scarcity.

As the world goes vertical, something alchemical is happening: we are shifting from an *economy of scarcity* to an *economy of abundance*. This is more than some philosophical construct or dreamy image of real-world-as-utopia. This is a very real, fundamental shift occurring in our world as a result of our basic unit of economic exchange.

Our economic model of operation has always been predicated on the idea of scarcity because, in a context of material goods, *every transaction depletes*. If I give you an acre of land, a truckload of lumber, or a barrel of oil, then my own stores are obviously now depleted by that same amount. Economics is called the "dismal science" because it is the study of the ongoing process of depletion. But unlike physical resources (interestingly, though, much like love), *knowledge increases when you share it*. This is because of a curious property inherent in all networks.

> *As the nodes in a network increase arithmetically, the network's value increases exponentially.*

The fax machine is a good example. The first generation of facsimile transmitter/receivers were incredibly expensive, yet of very little value. If you were one of the handful of people who had one, you could use it to communicate only with a handful of other people. But once a few tens of thousands of businesses had fax machines, suddenly everyone needed one: their value went way up and their cost went way down.

Of course, dematerialization and networking quickly made fax machines obsolete as e-mail took over the function. Now the Internet has taken this progression to a hypermagnified degree, astronomically raising the value of knowledge while lowering the transaction cost to virtually zero. The Internet has been the central manifestation of the digital technology that has ushered in this new economy.

This has not happened all at once. First we went through a preliminary, transitional phase where we used the Internet primarily as a one-way avenue, to *inform*. During this transitional time, we tended to view knowledge (and the majority still do so) in the same way that we used to view gold, land, steel, and all the basic elements of industrial economy: in terms of transaction and depletion, in other words, in terms of scarcity. You got richer if you hoarded it or were able to make access to it more expensive. But that math doesn't work with our Internet-enabled knowledge economy. You can't get richer hoarding knowledge: you get richer by *sharing* it.

It has been only in the last few years that we have begun learning how to unleash the Internet's genuine potential as an interactive pathway for unlimited knowledge sharing and communication. As we make the leap from using the Internet primarily as a tool for information to adding the higher-level functions of knowledge sharing and communication, we tip over the threshold into a new type of economy.

The industrial age was based on leveraging a scarcity of resources, for example, mining the earth of its limited metals and turning those raw materials into high-margin products. Wealth existed largely in the form of scarce, tangible, physical material resources, such as land, oil fields, mineral rights, factories filled with machines, and so on. But in the current era, with the sharing of information and knowledge having become the basis of wealth, the old math no longer applies.

In a scarcity-based economy, you increased value by acquiring material assets and then limiting people's access by the ticket prices you charged at the door. In the new abundance-based economy, you increase value by developing *immaterial* assets and *enlarging* people's access, creating as broad a free user base as possible and then charging for services that leverage that magnified user base, such as Google's AdWords. If Amazon gave away the Kindle e-book reader for free, instead of trying to make it an income base, then everyone would be buying books from Amazon, and they would make far more money. Zappos routinely upgrades customers' shipments from standard shipping to overnight, for no extra cost, just to "wow" them. Familiar examples of companies that have adapted to this new economic model to some degree are Apple, Google, and YouTube; another is MTN.

A knowledge (immaterial) economy follows the dynamics of *magnification* and *abundance*. As our technology dematerializes, there is a polar shift from the first set of principles to the second. That's what is taking place right now, and it ushers in an entirely new set of dynamics in the business world.

In a scarcity economy, for example, breaking news of current events is a commodity hoarded by the few: the *New York Times*, Associated Press, the major TV and cable news networks. In an abundance economy, blogging and podcasts put the power of the media in *everyone's* hands. Here is a vivid demonstration of this shift: *Time* magazine's Person of the Year in 1991 was Ted Turner, founder of CNN, in honor of his network's coverage of the first Gulf War. Fifteen years later, *Time*'s Person of the Year was "You." As *Time*'s cover story put it:

> *2006 [is] a story about community and collaboration on a scale never seen before. It's about the cosmic compendium of knowledge Wikipedia and the million-channel people's network YouTube and the online metropolis MySpace. It's about the many wresting power from the few and helping one another for nothing*

and how that will not only change the world, but also change the way the world changes.[4]

This epic shift was a long time coming. For thousands of years, we have imagined what life in an abundant economy would look like, and introduced ideas and mechanisms into our social contract to try to realize such a world, at least inasmuch as possible. From the ancient Greek idea of *democracy* and revolutionary concept of *citizen rights* in Rome to the Magna Carta, the American Constitution, the abolition of slavery, and women's suffrage—each innovation that advanced the cause of individual freedom served as a foretaste of an economy of abundance. But throughout these past ages we still operated within a world of physical scarcity, and therefore a prevailing mind-set of scarcity. However, since the mid-twentieth century, for the first time in history, our advancing technology has allowed us to create a world increasingly circumscribed by abundance rather than scarcity.

The baby boom is the first generation that has grown up in a world where the expectation is that our physical needs will be more than taken care of. Their parents, the World War II generation, grew up with the mind-set that by working hard, it was possible to get ahead and provide for your family. The boomer mind-set was that it was possible for *everyone* to have plenty, not just those special few who worked extra hard, a mind-set that sees abundance as normal for all, not a hard-won prize for the few. This worldview was at the root of the idealism of the 1960s.

Yet even for the boomers, this sense was mixed, and that lingering sense of scarcity passed down from parents who recalled the Great Depression and World War II was still strong. Not for today's formative generation. Generation Y, sometimes called the Millennials (or the Echo Boom, since as the children of the boomers they represent another huge bump in population), have taken the expectation of abundance even further. In the sixties, blacks and women in America fought for equal rights. To this new generation, racial and ethnic diversity is *normal*. To the Millennials, digital abundance is a commonplace experience: there's little that can't be had with the click of a mouse. Some say they're spoiled and unrealistic. Of course, parents have said this for generations, including the baby boomers' parents. The dark side of the boomers, Millennials, and other youth in the countries of the traditional industrialized world is that many have a sense of entitlement—and entitlement only feeds scarcity as part of legacy thinking. The good news is that Millennials and younger are reading the future much better than most boomers. The three digital accelerators are creating a world of abundance the likes of which we've never before dreamed, and as increasing numbers shift to an abundance mind-set to match the new realities, they will discover a powerful tool for shaping a better tomorrow.

In the past, scarcity and a mind-set of entitlement were a problem to be *solved*. Today, they have become a problem to be *skipped*.

This is not to ignore the fact that scarcity and privation still exist, still less to minimize their awful and very real impact in people's lives. The numbers of those who have no shelter, whose health is compromised by inadequate nutrition, who go to bed hungry every night, are in the hundreds of millions. In fact, poverty and economic inequity are arguably the single greatest driving force behind the spread of fundamentalist terrorism and other forms of radicalized violence around the globe. But that is exactly the point. Such poverty exists not because we lack the abundance to care adequately for all the world's people, but because we still operate largely out of a scarcity mind-set that has already become obsolete.

To a great extent, we and our institutions continue to operate on the fundamental basis of us-or-them, zero-sum economics: there is only so much to go around, and if *they* get it, then it won't be there for *us*. But that is legacy thinking.

Scarcity says, "I'm going to keep all my ideas to myself and sell more than anyone else." Abundance says, "By mentoring, coaching, and sharing all our best ideas, we're going to create a powerful tide that raises *all* our ships."

There is a catch, though: if we keep trying to run things with the old mind-set, it will blow up in our faces. Just ask the Big Four record labels, or the Big Three auto manufacturers. If you approach the new landscape with a scarcity mind-set, you guarantee your obsolescence and demise.

There's no going back: abundance is the name of the new game. Us-or-them, you-or-me, the fundamental rule of the economic game from prehistory until last year, is suddenly obsolete. We sink or swim together.

Thinking back to Chapter 1, let's apply this new rule to the question of how to transform an automaker to make it "the best automaker on the planet." Now we know how to take that idea a giant step further. Imagine what would happen, what different strategies we would develop and decisions we would make, if we shifted one small word in that mission statement: if we made it our mission to become "the best automaker *for* the planet."

>>>A Tale of Two Telecoms

MTN has an intriguing business model. It is not driven purely by profit, at least not in the conventional sense. Instead, its operation is directed by what it calls a "triple bottom line," a cord woven of three strands of equal importance: social impact, environmental impact, and financial profit.

As we saw earlier, when they bring phone service into an area that has no electric power infrastructure, MTN brings power plants into those areas. But they don't bring in nineteenth- or twentieth-century technologies, they go twenty-first century all the way: their power plants are based on renewable energy, in this case, biodiesel produced from waste cooking grease and plant materials. Not only is this a relatively nonpolluting operation, it also avoids the undesirable side effect of making the region dependent on international petroleum politics. In fact, it helps to *build* the local economy. MTN has stated that part of its mission is to be a carbon-neutral organization. One of its current goals is to reduce fuel consumption at its power stations by 1,000 percent. How? By using wind and solar.

Says John Ludike, a senior manager with MTN, "It's not just

about infrastructure and financial feasibility, it's also about having an impact on the communities in which we operate, putting people in touch with each other.

"Part of our licensing agreement in many of these markets," explains Ludike, "is that there has to be a transfer of capabilities in the countries in which we're operating, as well as of the manner in which we select our talent. We put quite a bit of time and emphasis on working with our international management to put those capabilities back into the communities."

Once you have electricity, you can charge your cell phones—but the process doesn't stop there. Once you have electricity, you have light and you can pump water. And once you can do that, MTN discovered, it's not just lights that illuminate and water that starts to flow. Ideas start flowing, too, and you see an acceleration of economic, intellectual, and cultural development. The entire area begins to grow.

MTN moves into its poorer new markets realistically. To avoid problems with collection, it started in many of these countries with prepaid cell phone service. In some countries, it started out with bare-bones service: local phone minutes, period. As the markets have grown, in some areas it's been able to expand to the point where it customers want more advanced services, such as data, Web browsing, and 3G service, which supports streaming video transmission over phone lines and advanced services such as mobile banking.

In every country MTN has entered, the economy has grown consistently. As an area grows economically, its residents start wanting more cell phone features, and they also become able to afford them. As they use more features, they see more growth, which lets them afford more features. It's good for MTN. It's even better for its customers. MTN is not really a telecom company, it is an *economic empowerment agency* disguised as a telecom company.

The abundance-economy orientation of this approach becomes strikingly clear when you stand it side by side with another telecom giant that also came of age in the mid-1990s.

Like Enron and Arthur Andersen, the name WorldCom has

become an icon of the twenty-first century's mistrust of the Big Corporation, synonymous with the excesses of merger-and-acquisition fever, executive greed, and wholesale fraud. Founded in 1983 as Long Distance Discount Services (LDDS), the company assumed the name WorldCom in 1995 in the midst of an aggressive and ambitious campaign of mergers and acquisitions. Its $37 billion merger with MCI Communications in 1997 was then the largest in history, a record that would have been broken by its merger with Sprint two years later (also knocking AT&T out of the number one spot for the first time), had regulators not prevented that marriage from being consummated.

Five short years and $11 billion worth of fraud later, the company filed for bankruptcy.

Like any business, a telecom company grows by acquiring new customers. Broadly speaking, there are two sources for new customers: you can grab them from existing companies through intense competition and mergers and acquisitions, or even by pushing the limits on business ethics and the law; or you can seek ways to provide abundant opportunities for growth for your customers. The first approach typically reflects a model of economic scarcity, the second one of abundance. WorldCom committed suicide in the 1990s following the first strategy; MTN is thriving with the second.

So just how is MTN doing? It recently doubled its footprint, adding about a dozen more countries in Africa and the Middle East and growing to well more than 40 million customers. It's too soon to see major results in its newer markets, but in the markets where it started out, it has made a measurable difference in the lives of the people it serves.

"In our original thirteen markets," reports Ludike, "we have seen a definite increase in social and economic impact. . . . Mobile [telecom] has had a major impact on these people's lives."

And MTN is not the only one. For example, another company, Zain, is doing something similar in the same region of the world, using the three digital accelerators and the eight pathways to create abundance for its customers as it drives growth for the company. Zain's goal is to quickly become one of the top ten telecom companies worldwide. The strategy is working. In 2008 it had $3 billion in sales, with 55 million subscribers. By 2011 it is on target to *double,* with $6 billion in sales and 110 million subscribers.

There are many other such companies that are using the spread of abundance to drive their growth—and using their growth to further spread abundance.

Right now everyone is talking about the role of India and China in the world economy. Seldom does Africa enter the discussion. And no wonder: Africa's challenges, especially the extreme poverty and notoriously intractable political instability of so many of its nations, are well known. The barriers to significant economic growth seem almost insurmountable. But make no mistake: it is possible to provide economic growth, prosperity, and abundance to any village, town, or country on the planet.

"You would be very surprised to read the economic forecasts," adds Ludike. "You'd be surprised to learn how much China and India are investing in Africa. We've been looking at where the population growth is going to be: the growing economies are going to be in the emerging nations."

Africa, for decades the global poster child for the ravages of scarcity, may well emerge as a new icon of abundance. It's too early to say for sure just how this scenario will unfold. But we can predict a few things about it with confidence: the first is, it *will* unfold. And the second: it will happen largely through finding ingenious ways not of solving those problems, but of *skipping* them altogether.

>>>The Coal Question, Revisited

We opened this chapter talking about William Jevons and how the Industrial Revolution skipped its coal problem by latching on to petroleum. If you're like a lot of people who hear this story, there may be a question that's been nagging at you:

Did we *really* skip that problem . . . or just postpone it?

You're right to ask, because the truth is, we never *entirely* skipped the problem Jevons had identified. The United States today derives more than half its electricity from coal; for China the figure is 80 percent. Coal is, in fact, still the single most prevalent fuel worldwide in the production of electricity.

And if there is something about Jevons's story that sounds familiar, it should. A little over a century later, a group called the Club of Rome wrote a book oddly reminiscent of Jevons's work. The 1971 *Limits to Growth* predicted that we would run out of oil within twenty years and forecast the demise of the modern way of life. That didn't happen, of course: as we saw in Chapter 3, advances in drilling and extraction, along with new technologies like fuel injection, allowed us to push the limits of the possible much further than *Limits to Growth*'s authors foresaw. What's more, astronomical advances in product intelligence will hugely enhance the efficiency with which we use the oil we have.

But still, we know we can't go on relying on petroleum and coal as the world's chief sources of power forever.

In a larger sense, Jevons's *coal question* is with us still, only it would be more accurate to call it the *hydrocarbon fuel question*. Our prevailing model of industrial power is one based on harnessing potential energy by extracting and burning fossil fuels: coal for electric motors, and oil for internal combustion engines. If coal was the nineteenth century's big problem, oil was the twentieth's; but we are now living in the twenty-first.

A butterfly cannot thrive by seeking to solve caterpillar problems. These are not problems we need to solve—they are problems we need to skip. And in order to do that, we need to look at another flash foresight principle, which is what we'll explore in the next chapter.

>>>CHAPTER 4 **ACTION STEPS**

A difficult problem can easily become a roadblock so large that it seems impossible to get around it. The result is often procrastination and paralysis. The key to unraveling our biggest problems is to recognize that they are typically not our real problem. Skipping our biggest problem, instead of trying to solve it, sets our minds free to discover and engage with the real problem.

- ***Refer back to that "biggest problem" you brought to mind*** *in the beginning of this chapter. As you've been reading, have you been getting glimmers of ideas about ways you might skip that problem altogether?*
- ***Don't get stuck; move forward.*** *Often you can't see the real problem because you're blinded by what you perceive is the problem. Forget about what you* ***think*** *the problem is. Often the real problem—and its solutions—will surface once you eliminate the perceived problem.*
- ***Peel the onion.*** *Think of your problem as the top layer of an onion: peel it back by listing the components of the problem. Keep asking yourself, "Why is that a problem?" and when you find an answer, then ask, "And why is* ***that*** *a problem?" Eventually you'll find yourself at the heart of the problem—often sooner than you might expect.*
- ***Focus on one issue at a time.*** *Sometimes a problem seems complex, with many components working against you all at once. Don't try to solve everything at once. Keep peeling the onion until you find one problem you can address.*
- ***Look to technology for help.*** *Today's technology offers a wealth of options for solving numerous problems. Can't find a good typist for your company? How about using dictation software? Need a way to get more ideas for products or services? Use online surveys to ask your customers what they want. Look at what you need done and find a technology solution to automate it for you.*
- ***Suspend judgment.*** *Snap judgments and knee-jerk assessments, no matter how sound they may seem to be, often obscure valuable insight.*
- ***Skip to the finish line.*** *Every problem has a solution—some better than others. There are many paths to the same destination, and some don't have roadblocks. By asking yourself if you can skip the problem completely, you free your mind to look beyond the roadblock. That is usually where the best solution lies.*
- ***What are the legacy systems in your field?*** *Ask yourself, "Would it be wiser to let go of the old stuff right now and skip into the future?"*
- *Look at every current strategy you are using and ask yourself: "Is this strategy based on the principle of scarcity, or based on the principle of abundance?"*

>>> CHAPTER FIVE

Go Opposite

The Detroit-area school districts were in trouble. It was the early 2000s, and while the American automobile industry had not quite entered the steepest part of its slide toward catastrophe, the region's economy was already suffering. The federal No Child Left Behind program had created onerous new school costs in testing and administration, even as the district faced draconian budget cuts. It had pushed school administrators into an escalating series of Sophie's choices: which program cuts would cause the kids to suffer least?

My graduate school days teaching science to junior high school kids ranks as one of the greatest experiences of my life. It was so gratifying, in fact, that my consulting business has an education division dedicated to helping our nation's schools. As part of this work, we created a program we call Designing Thriving Schools, which is a variation of a workshop I do with corporations and other organizations called Competitive Advantage. The program, which revolves around creating flash foresights and actionable strategies relating to whatever challenges are facing the organization, uses two decks of cards, one consisting of Strategy Cards and the other of Technology Cards.

Now, in the early years of the new century, we were in the Detroit metro area taking leaders from a number of school districts through the process. Someone brought up the problem of their crushing budget squeeze, so we set out to explore the issue and see if we could trigger a flash foresight. The participants tried out idea after idea for cutting costs, but nothing was gelling. Someone pulled out a Strategy Card that bore the phrase CREATE INCOME STREAMS and said:

"Hey—what if we looked for ways to generate an income?"

Someone in the room laughed out loud. (Always a good sign, by the way: in a brainstorming context like this, laughter is usually a signal that some sort of breakthrough is about to make an appearance.) A public school in a struggling urban district—acting like an entrepreneur? It was totally outside the box. I loved it.

"Sounds impossible," someone commented.

"Which probably means you're on to something," I added. "All right, let's shuffle through our Technology Cards and see what we have."

We went through half a dozen cards, and then someone drew out the Technology Card called PROCESSOR SHARING and asked, "Is there some way we could use this one?"

Here's what the card says:

> *Distributed computing allows networked computers to share processing power, turning idle computers into a collective supercomputer.*

"Well," I mused, "let's see. Does your school have any idle computers that are networked?"

No, they told me, their computers were all pretty much in use throughout the day.

"Throughout the day," I repeated back. "Okay . . ." and I let it hang, the unfinished sentence suggesting a flash foresight principle: *Opposites work better.* Sure enough, within moments an idea flashed within the group.

"That's it!" shouted the woman who had first pulled out the CREATE INCOME STREAMS card. The others turned to look at her, and she explained excitedly: "They're busy during the *day*. But what about at night?"

In fact, this school had several *thousand* computers that were all networked together and were completely idle from the close of each school day until eight A.M. the next morning—nearly sixteen hours a day. Not counting weekends.

"We've got sixteen hours of computer time every day," she went on, "that's eighty hours a week—with weekends, more than a hundred twenty hours! Times, what . . . say, four thousand computers? That's . . . half a million computer hours every week." She turned to me. "But what can we do with all that potential computer power?"

She radiated exuberance. There's nothing so thrilling as that moment when you suddenly see the invisible.

I said, "Why not lease it out?"

And that's just what they did. They went searching for a company whose products no parent could object to, and eventually leased out their "supercomputer" to a pharmaceutical firm who used the raw number-crunching power of their network of PCs, turning them into a giant after-hours parallel processor to help work out chemical formulas to find treatments for cancer and other diseases.

Months later, that school district was earning six figures per year from that one flash foresight. Rather than being forced to cut some of their most cherished programs from the budget, they were able to supply the needed funds from their own coffers. They hadn't had to sacrifice a thing or invest a dime to generate those funds, either; all they'd needed was a flash foresight.

Coming on the heels of the last chapter, you may have had the thought that this school, faced with the problem of budget cutbacks, *skipped the problem* instead of trying to solve it. And you would be absolutely right. But this also illustrates another flash foresight principle: *Go opposite*. Public school systems generally are on the receiving end of funds. This school system decided to see themselves as fund *generators*.

That's not the end of the story. Another school district nearby heard about this and got inspired to seek out their own flash foresight. Let me take you up onto the school's rooftop and show you what they found: they decided to rent the roof out for advertising space.

"Advertising?" you might be wondering, "on the *roof*? Why? Who would ever see it? There's not a single kid, teacher, or parent who ever goes up there."

True—but the Detroit Metro Airport is not far away. Between 30 and 40 million people pass through that airport each year—which translates into an exposure of about one hundred thousand people *per day*.

>>>Opposites Work Better

In the previous chapter, we explored the idea that our biggest challenges are often quite different from what we *think* our biggest challenges are. But in searching for the real problem we want to address, it's not always easy to know where to look. One way to help tease that insight to the surface is to note where everyone else is looking—and then look in the opposite direction.

It is often breathtaking how quickly this strategy makes the invisible visible and reveals surprisingly practical solutions to problems you didn't even realize you were facing.

Remember our inventor friend Dale Morgen? Dale recently told me about a patent he has filed on his new design for a certain component on ocean liners. The science of shipbuilding has worked for decades on the design of its biggest transoceanic vessels, says Dale, tinkering with every imaginable way to change and refine the precise shape of the bow in order to get optimum performance as it cuts through the waves. Incredibly sophisticated work has gone into this pursuit, and it seems to have pretty much exhausted the field. "So what could possibly be left to invent?" Dale asks rhetorically, and then smiles. "The stern."

According to Morgen, a good 30 percent of the drag an ocean liner experiences from contact with the water comes from the rudder, and that figure is vastly higher when the ship starts to change direction. Dale's patent describes an intelligent rudder. The blade itself has movable surfaces that can adjust to very fine tolerances and actually change its shape, thus adapting to create far less drag as it maintains course. Dale estimates that his intelligent rudder should reduce drag by as much as 80 percent, resulting in gigantic savings in fuel.

Designers have focused on the ship's front; Dale went opposite.

In the introduction we briefly explored this counterintuitive idea as the quintessential flash foresight strategy, noting such examples as nanofusion (going small instead of big) and underwater oil rigs (rather than spend more money trying to protect rigs on the water's surface, put them on the ocean floor), and cited a brief list of examples of successes in diverse areas that arose from flash foresights that were triggered by the *go opposite* idea. Let's revisit that list and take a closer look at just how each one found success through taking the path of *going opposite.*

AMAZON.COM

Jeff Bezos looked at how Barnes & Noble had taken the traditional bookstore to a new level of size and substance, creating the modern superstore, and went the other way: he shrank the size to nothing and made it completely *insubstantial.*

It didn't take Barnes & Noble, Borders, and the other major book retailers long to create their own versions of virtual book superstores. But by the time they caught up, Amazon had gone in an opposite direction again: it added consumer electronics, toys, clothing, home and garden accessories . . . in short, *everything.* Next he rented excess technology capacity to any size company, acting as a virtual IT department. Having become the first major virtual bookstore, it now became a virtual *unbookstore.*

CROCS

With the popularity of television's *Sex and the City,* fancy Manolo Blahnik shoes were all the rage when the show ended in 2004—but who could afford them? Lots of shoe manufacturers tried to emulate the svelte, chic little footwear. Not George Beodecker. He went in the other direction—and created an absolute sensation with his undeniably ugly line of plastic clogwear.

DELL

Dell looked at the PC industry's reliance on retailers and did something else: direct marketing. All the other personal computer manufacturers created their own line of models and then offered them to consumers to buy through retail outlets; Dell showed its consumers the full range of options, on the Internet, and then invited them to design the models they wanted themselves.

JETBLUE AND SOUTHWEST AIRLINES

JetBlue looked at the hub-and-spoke system used by legacy carriers, and decided to do the opposite. Launching its low-cost airline based on a point-to-point system, it profited while others suffered and went into bankruptcy.

The founders of JetBlue came from the opposites-work-better culture of Southwest Airlines. Southwest does almost everything the opposite of the legacy carriers, right down to how it puts you on the plane. Instead of assigning you seats on the plane, it assigns you a place to stand in line at the gate while waiting to board. Sounds crazy, but it *works*. By 2007, as measured by number of passengers carried per year, Southwest Airlines had become the largest airline in the world.

KIVA

When Matt Flannery and Jessica Jackley visited rural East Africa in 2004, they were stunned by the economic conditions they witnessed. Not the poverty—the entrepreneurial ingenuity. The people they met were far from helpless victims of poverty. But because the amounts of capital funding they needed to create their tiny enterprises were so minuscule (a grant of even $100 would often be enough to get started), they fell through the cracks of conventional seed-capital operations. After all, what kind of venture capital firm would front a loan of a hundred bucks, when that piddling amount would barely cover the transaction costs and FedExing of contracts for a typical investment?

Matt and Jessica's, that's what kind. In 2005 the two did the opposite of big venture capital firms by founding Kiva, "the world's first peer-to-peer microlending operation." By 2009, well over 600,000 individuals had made microloans through the Kiva Web site at a full repayment rate of more than 98 percent, to more than a quarter of a million individual entrepreneurs (more than 82 percent of them women), and the total value of all those tiny microloans topped $100 million.

NETFLIX

Blockbuster Inc. created a fortune with its model of home video rental stores. Upstart Netflix stole its thunder by doing the opposite. It was not simply that Netflix skipped the physical real estate altogether and made it a virtual operation. Equally critical was its upside-down business model: instead of charging for each video rented, Netflix let its customers take as many videos as they wanted at no extra cost above a monthly subscription rate.

Blockbuster struggled to catch up, adding a rent-by-mail program and a much-touted "no late fees!" policy . . . but in the anticipatory climate of digital verticality, catch-up is always a day late and a dollar short, and soon Blockbuster was forced to shutter hundreds of stores in an effort to stanch the bleeding.

STARBUCKS

Used to be, coffee was an inexpensive and generic accessory to the meals we ordered at restaurants, like the rolls and butter. You went to coffee shops for the sandwich and the conversation; the actual cup of coffee cost a quarter and nobody gave it a thought. Starbucks changed all that. It put coffee at the center of the experience (with sandwiches and pastries as a sometime accessory). Instead of your basic Joe plus decaf options, there were now dozens of exotic variations of brew, and we were happily paying three and four dollars for the experience.

It's hard to fully appreciate this, now that the Starbucks empire is such a commonplace fixture of modern life, but imagine what the idea would have sounded like in 1990 (when Starbucks still had only a handful of outlets)—a global empire based on stores where people come in to buy a $4 cup of coffee? Insanity.

VOLKSWAGEN

During the 1960s, while American cars were getting bigger, sleeker, and cooler, this German company gobbled up a huge chunk of the American market with its squat, ugly little WWII-era "beetle." The core belief that "bigger is better" ran very deep in sixties culture, the decade that championed the muscle car. Through its now-famous ad campaigns, Volkswagen trumpeted the unabashedly counterintuitive slogans "Think Small" and "Small Is Beautiful." It worked. The VW Beetle is arguably the best-selling single car design in history.

All these years later, there is still a powerful strain of flash foresight in Volkswagen's DNA. The company recently opened a new factory in the heart of downtown Dresden for its Phaeton model that is the polar opposite of everything you've ever imagined an automobile factory would be. For one thing, it's transparent: its walls are made of glass. Its floors are made of not concrete but Canadian maple. It is so clean, the workers wear white gloves. A few years ago, when Dresden's opera house was flooded, the VW factory floor was loaned out for a production of *Carmen*.

ZAPPOS

During the dot-com boom, while many companies launched flashy and seemingly innovative bombs that crashed within a few years or months, there were a handful who were more careful about the direction they took. Zappos is a great example: the online shoe retailer not only survived the dot-com crash, it went from its ground-floor start-up in 1999 to over $1 billion in annual sales ten years later.

One way it accomplished this phenomenal feat was by doing things a little differently from most companies. Actually, a *lot* differently. This is evident in the company's ten core values, which it publishes on its Web site:

- Deliver WOW through service.
- Embrace and drive change.
- Create fun and a little weirdness.
- Be adventurous, creative, and open-minded.
- Pursue growth and learning.
- Build open and honest relationships with communication.
- Build a positive team and family spirit.
- Do more with less.
- Be passionate and determined.
- Be humble.

One of its more unusual strategies is a wonderful example of *going opposite*. Zappos takes every new employee through a four-week training program; for two weeks they learn about the company's history, its culture and philosophy of customer service, and more, and for the next two weeks they work the phones. All this is at full salary. However, at the end of the very first week, the company makes the new hire an offer: all the salary they've earned so far plus a $2,000 cash bonus to leave, today, right now, without going any further in the training, and not join the company.

They call it their *quit-now bonus*. The offer stays in effect throughout the remaining three weeks of training.

Why would they do such a thing? Because they want to make sure the people they hire really want to work there. Says CEO Tony Hsieh, "When we started this policy in 2007, about 3 percent of our new hires took the offer. In 2008, we noticed that fewer than 1 percent were taking the offer—so we raised it. Actually, it started out at a hundred dollars, but we keep raising the offer when we see that not enough people are taking it."[1]

Some companies offer incentives to *join*; others offer even more enticing incentives to *stay*. Zappos offers you $2,000 to *go away*—and the atmosphere and morale at Zappos headquarters is among the best of any workplace in the country.

>>>The Opposite of No Money

There is hardly any conversation where the idea "that's impossible" more commonly enters the picture than the conversation about budgets and finance. Only in this context, the phrasing usually goes like this: *We can't afford it.* But flash foresight allows us to see the invisible and do the impossible, so the phrase *we can't afford it* becomes an irrelevancy.

Anytime you hear someone say, "But we can't afford it," or hear yourself saying it, know this: you are probably looking at the wrong *it*. As we saw in the last chapter, our biggest problem is typically not the problem at all. And once we've figured out which problem really needs solving—in other words, once *skip it* has given us the *what*—then *go opposite* is one of the most fruitful ways to approach the question of *how*.

Here are three examples, involving an elementary school, a college, and a Fortune 500 company.

A PINT-SIZED THINK TANK

The Detroit area school system mentioned above was not the first we've seen use flash foresight to come up with some innovative approaches to revenue generation. In the late 1980s my education division worked with a school district in northern Wisconsin that was struggling to raise enough funds to meet its schools' needs. They had been approaching leaders in the business community and asking for money—a strategy that had met with mixed results. As leaders in the community, these prominent businesspeople were constantly being approached by people representing one good cause after another. Clearly, they were very community-minded, but there were only so many dollars they could contribute.

We decided to look for a way to turn the situation on its head.

"We're asking them for money to help us solve our problems," I suggested. "What if instead, we ask them to give us *their* problems?"

Kids are loaded with creativity. The problem is, if that creativity is not focused on something constructive, it can get them into trouble. These schools had hundreds of creative kids whose creativity wasn't focused on anything in particular. What if we took some big real-world problems and gave them to these kids to see if they could come up with some creative solutions? What would motivate them to try? We could tell them, "Hey, we're adults, and we don't have the answers!"

We found a municipality that was struggling with a major waste disposal problem that they were about to turn over to an expensive New York firm. Instead, they gave the problem to all the students in a local school—and sure enough, they came up with an idea that worked and solved the problem. The municipality paid the school a lot less than they would have had to pay the consulting firm, yet to the school, it was a major windfall.

When I shared this story with a school district in Illinois a few years later, they jumped at it and asked for my help in finding some businesses to approach. As I was consulting to Motorola at the time, we put the two parties together. Some people from Motorola's R&D department met with a group of elementary school kids, who triggered flash foresights for the R&D team that led to a new design for a cellular flip phone, which eventually made its way to the market under the name StarTAC—one of the most successful and influential cell phone designs of its era.

The kids deserve credit, and so does Motorola: they could have talked to a group of PhD researchers, but instead, they *went opposite*—and their elementary school–aged think tank helped them create one of the most successful phone designs of the day.

A SHRINKING BUDGET PROBLEM

I met recently with the dean of a school of engineering at a major California university. We had only about twenty minutes to talk, so we got right down to business: he had a problem. The governor of California had recently established a 10 percent budget cut for all education, across the board.

"This is huge," he said. "We've got a good 30 percent more engineering students coming in next semester, yet somehow I have to *cut* our budget by 10 percent. And what can I cut? We can't reduce the fixed costs of campus and facilities. The only thing we can really cut is staff. So we're looking at a 30 percent *increase* in the student body, with a 10 percent *decrease* in our teaching staff. How can this possibly work?"

This was a big problem, indeed—so big that it clearly needed not solving but skipping. It occurred to me that the opposite of cutting staff is *hiring* staff, so I asked him how much the average engineering faculty member made. He told me the average salary figure. Then I asked, "How much does each faculty member bring in to the school, on average, in research moneys and grants?" This latter figure turned out to be about twice the average engineering faculty salary.

"That could be the answer right there," I pointed out. "You need to be hiring—not firing. The only way I can think of for you to handle that 10 percent budget cut is to hire more engineering professors."

Opposites work better.

The dean went to the chancellor with his exciting idea—which, not surprisingly, was immediately shot down. He could see the visible future, but his boss could not. He called me up and told me what had happened. "But you know what?" he added. "I'm going to do it anyway. I'm hiring ten new people. I'm sure I'll get my hand slapped, but because we'll bring in more money than we're spending to hire them, it'll all work out."

CREATING A MILLION-DOLLAR AD

In the world of American sports, there are many contests, many arenas—and then there's the Super Bowl. In American advertising, there are millions of opportunities to promote a product, but there is only one ultimate ad slot: the Super Bowl ad. The single most heavily watched American television broadcast, this is also the most expensive ad slot in the calendar, costing as much as $100,000 per *second* of airtime. The big consumer goods companies typically throw their biggest advertising budgets and top PR talents at these tiny peepholes of superconcentrated public exposure.

For years, Frito-Lay had heavily advertised its Doritos corn chips in the Super Bowl, spending millions upon millions of dollars. In preparation for the 2007 event, they decided to do the opposite. "Instead of hiring the very best pros and paying them millions," they said, "let's hire complete amateurs and pay them nothing!"

Sound crazy? Crazy like a fox—with flash foresight. Because of the explosion in processing power, storage, and bandwidth, the ordinary consumer now has the capacity to make a high-quality, television-ready ad on the desktop—and Frito-Lay knew it. Instead of passive ads, they *went opposite,* getting their target audience engaged—and by making the ad itself newsworthy, they also got valuable free media exposure.

They launched a contest called Crash the Super Bowl for consumers to create their own Doritos commercials. The public would vote on the best ad, and they would run the winner during the Super Bowl. The vote was so close that they ended up running not one but two of the consumer-created ads—and the ads were so good that they ranked fifth in a Nielsen survey of most popular Super Bowl ads that year. One of the ads cost $200 to make.

Much to Frito-Lay's surprise, consumers got so engaged they continued submitting their ads long after the Super Bowl. Two years later Frito-Lay ran the contest again. This time the winning commercial was ranked by *USA Today*'s Super Bowl Ad Meter as the year's best ad. It also won the two unemployed brothers who created it a cash prize of $1 million.

>>>Simple Opposite, Big Impact

Sometimes a simple application of *go opposite* can have enormous consequences. This is what happened when researchers for Procter & Gamble asked what must have seemed like an absurdly simple question: what if, instead of washing clothes in hot water, we washed them in cold, and they came out as clean as if they'd been washed in hot?

In 2003 the consumer giant's Department of Global Sustainability (yes, they have a division so named; Len Sauers is its vice president) conducted an extensive audit of the environmental impact of its various products. One of the more significant findings was that among all its household products, the single category "laundry detergent" consumed far and away the majority of energy in the home. Why? Because of the energy consumed to heat the water that washes clothes. In fact, from 3 to 4 percent of the average total U.S. household energy bill is used to heat water for laundry.

P&G researchers spent years working on a genuinely effective way to create a cold-water version of their laundry soap Tide. The goal was to have a product that worked fully as effectively as the standard hot-water product, with no compromise in effect, and that could be sold for the same price. As it turned out, this proved to be an enormously complex task.

The result, which they released to market in 2005, was a new detergent named Tide Coldwater. Here is how P&G describes the solution:

> *Like regular Tide, Tide Coldwater contains surfactants. Surfactant molecules have two parts: a hydrophilic ("water loving") component and a hydrophobic ("water hating") component. The hydrophilic part breaks the surface tension of water, while the hydrophobic part is attracted to oil and grease in soils, loosening and removing them from fabrics.*
>
> *Tide Coldwater is designed with an increased amount of surfactant chemistry that allows it to penetrate easily into fabrics, and with an increased amount of polymer technology to*

suspend dirt particles, helping to prevent them from redepositing on fabrics.

"Using cold-water wash," Len told me, "we found the average monthly home energy bill was reduced by about the same amount as it costs to buy a month's supply of laundry soap. Which means you're basically getting your clothes washed for free."

But the truly ironic thing about this effort is that none of that money is going into P&G's pocket. The product costs about the same, and the consumer saves money—but what's in it for P&G? It turns out to be a question with big-picture implications.

Look at the numbers involved. Some 3.5 billion people use P&G products every day—three and a half *billion*. The people at the Global Sustainability Department suspected that if they could find a way to move their customer base from hot-water wash to cold-water wash, it might add up to some pretty significant environmental impact. They were right. If every household in the United States were to switch to cold-water wash, we would eliminate four million tons of CO_2 emissions per year—the equivalent of 8 percent of the Kyoto target.

Before tackling the U.S. market, the company mounted a campaign in Holland to educate people about the environmental benefits of cold-water wash. When they began, about 2 percent of the Dutch population were washing their clothes in cold water; after an eighteen-month advertising campaign, that number rose to 50 percent. In the same time frame, with a similar advertising effort in the U.K., the cold-water-washing population there went from 2–3 percent to 20 percent.

>>>Bringing Power to the People

We have an electricity problem. "Knowledge is power," goes the popular slogan. True enough, but here is another truth: increasing knowledge *takes* power.

As of late 2008 the total amount of information uploaded to

Facebook every month was about 70 terabytes, or 70,000 gigabytes. All the videos on YouTube came to about 530 terabytes, nearly eight times that number. Yet even all that byte-chomping streaming video scarcely holds a candle to the prodigious information appetite of Google, whose servers process about 1 *petabyte* of information—that's 1,000 terabytes, or 1 million gigabytes—every 72 minutes.

Will that number continue to increase? You're good enough with flash foresight by now to know the answer to that one. This points to an aspect of our "going vertical" world and digital accelerator 3, *data storage*, that we haven't addressed yet. The good news about storage is that it's getting cheaper and cheaper. The bad news is that it's also gobbling up more and more electricity. All this needs servers, and those servers need to run on electricity, which is why Google and Microsoft have been building server farms. (In fact, Google built one recently along the Columbia River, not far from the Bonneville Dam.) When you store data on a CD or DVD, it does not use any electricity until you want to access it. But servers that store data are never turned off, because all that content has to be available at all times.

As information processing continues going vertical, our need for high-quality electricity is also going vertical. This is a technology-driven hard trend: in other words, not a guess, but a certainty. Where are we going to get the power?

This brings us back to William Jevons and *The Coal Question*. While the internal combustion engines of the industrialized world run largely on oil and its various derivatives, coal continues to be our number one fuel for generating the electricity that powers our motors—including those that drive our computers—and whether or not we are in danger of running out of coal, we cannot long continue burning it at such profligate rates if for no other reasons than environmental ones.

Yet the fuel itself is not the only problem: there are the power plants themselves. Right now, generators and transformers around the world are running at about 90 percent capacity. How long would it take to build new plants? At least three years, longer to design them. The U.S. electric infrastructure—not just power stations that generate electricity, but also the infrastructure required to transport it—is three to four decades old.

Let's be anticipatory: we're going to be using a lot more electricity, and we need to find smart ways to generate it—fast.

During the 2008 presidential election season, T. Boone Pickens, the billionaire oilman turned wind-power evangelist, bought a good deal of television ad time to make a flash foresight point: the United States, Pickens said over and over, is the Saudi Arabia of wind.

But of course, there's a problem. Wind farms can harness the power of nature and generate vast amounts of electricity. But how do we get all that lovely electricity to the buildings where we need it?

This is the Achilles' heel of the wind-power dream: transmission is a nightmare. There is so much loss through long-distance transmission (only exacerbated by the fact that the nation is still wired with a dumb grid) that trying to generate power on a wind farm and then get it to the population centers where it's needed is a financial washout and an engineering disaster.

For all the promise of wind, transmission looms as the intractable thorn in its paw. While hundreds of designers, inventors, and technicians labor over ways to solve this problem, an IT engineer and entrepreneur named Mark Cironi has figured out a way to skip it instead. And he did it by looking at what everyone else was doing, and then going opposite.

The wind industry has, in the main, pursued its goal by building bigger and bigger wind turbines and placing them in remote areas that offer greatest access to wind flow unfettered by interference from such distractions as buildings and other manmade structures. (Trees, of course, can be cut down.)

Through his company, Green Energy Technologies, Cironi took an approach that turns those criteria on their head: instead of bigger, he suggested, let's build them smaller—and instead of placing them in remote, open areas, let's put them in the most congested places we have: in our biggest cities.

"This was a major void in the wind industry," says Mark. "With solar, on-site generation is commonplace—you see those panels going up on buildings and homes everywhere. But that kind of on-site application has been practically nonexistent with wind."

To create his novel approach, Cironi teamed up with Dr. David Spira, one of the country's foremost authorities on wind; Dr. Spira ran NASA's wind tunnel program for years and was the person who put up the first wind turbines in the United States.

Instead of the familiar uncontained windmill, with its slender vanes carving through the open air (and, alas, not infrequently carving through unsuspecting birds as well), Green Energy Technologies' model is based on what is called a shrouded system: similar in design to a jet airplane's turbine engine, the contained set of blades serves to amplify or augment the force of the available wind.

"They've experimented with shrouded systems in Australia and Germany," says Mark, "but nobody had really considered building a commercial application. So we decided to do that."

And then Cironi and his team did something brilliant. They took the existing technology of an electrical generator, only instead of putting power into the generator and having it run a turbine, they took existing components and simply reversed the entire design, making the turbine run the generator.

"Instead of propellers," Cironi points out, "we had to come up with *impellers,* because we wanted to run the whole model in reverse."

To give a sense of just how opposite this is: a conventional windmill unit stands as much as 225 feet high, with blades measuring from 150 to 200 feet in length. Cironi's unit is about 25 feet tall, with individual blades under 10 feet long.

As he puts it, "You can only make these wind turbines so big, and then you've got to start getting smaller, so you can provide them to the people who are going to use the energy."

The results are impressive. "With an average wind of 13 or 14 mph, the user will realize between 120 and 140 kilowatt-hours a year. With a big enough roof, so that you could space them far enough apart so the wind wash from each unit wouldn't interfere with any of the others, you could put up a 100-kWh or 200-kWh system."

Translation: at current rates, a rooftop system like this will generate about $20,000 worth of electricity per year. As of this writing, Cironi's distributor, a major Chicago construction firm, is proposing installations atop some of the city's largest buildings, as well as in New York's Battery Park.

Even more fascinating is the technology that has made this possible.

"We have a built-in anemometer measuring the wind speed and direction every second and feeding that information to the system," says Cironi. "Rather than use a gear box, we use embedded software to manage how the system applies resistance on the motor at certain rpm, adjusting the operation of the motor in real time to every minute fluctuation in the environment."

It's our old friend, technological advancement pathway 4, *product intelligence.*

"There's a lot of intelligence embedded in the system," explains Mark, who worked at IBM for years and was formerly a regional manager for Oracle. "Working with PLCs [programmable logic controllers] is kind of second nature to people who automate shop floors and other manufacturing applications. But integrating PLCs into a turbine system was not commonplace.

"We could not have done this even five years ago," he adds. "A lot of the automation we use just wasn't in place yet."

Right now, according to Cironi, domestic demand for electricity is expected to increase by 20 percent by 2020, while production capacity is projected to increase by only 10 percent, leaving a shortfall of 10 percent. Mark projects that their on-site wind generation approach could fill at least half that gap.

The Green Energy Technologies rooftop shrouded system is a beautiful example of several flash foresight principles working together: it lets the wind power industry *skip its biggest problem* (line transmission); it applies *go opposite* for its essential concept; and it *transforms* the centuries-old idea of a windmill by adding product intelligence.

What if we went a step further? The unit is intelligent, but what if we designed intelligence into the blades themselves, much like Dale Morgen's design for smart ship propellers? Right now, the entire blade can turn and feather, changing its angle of axis to vary the amount of air it cuts into. What if the individual vanes were engineered with the embedded intelligence needed to change not only pitch and angle but also *shape,* in real-time response to the most minute variations in environment?

>>> Buried Treasure

Buried under 54,000 square miles in the northeast corner of Alberta, Canada, the Athabasca Oil Sands comprise the largest reservoir of bitumen, a semisolid form of crude oil, anywhere in the world. The more than 2 trillion barrels of this extra-heavy crude make the Athabasca site a resource roughly equivalent to the world's total known conventional petroleum reserves. There is, in other words, another entire Saudi Arabia's worth of oil right here in North America.

The problem is, how do we get it out? Unlike free-flowing oil deposits deep underground, this relatively shallow bitumen-sand mixture cannot be mined via traditional deep-well drilling. Conventional surface mining methods (including strip mining, open-pit mining, and mountaintop removal mining) dig out the mixture and then separate the bitumen from the sand using caustic and highly polluting agents. They are not only an environmental nightmare, they are also energy-intensive themselves, which rather defeats the purpose of the enterprise.

Dr. Bruce McGee had a different idea: instead of gouging out that bitumen-sand mixture, why not leave it all in the ground and separate it there?

In fact, there is already an established method for doing this sort of in situ processing using *deep steam injection* to heat the bitumen in the ground, liquefying it enough so that it can be pumped to the surface. But there are considerable negatives involved in the process. For example, heating the water to make the steam consumes a massive amount of natural gas (Alberta's tar sands industry now consumes 4 percent of the region's entire natural gas output, and that percentage is climbing). It also consumes a huge amount of water, a precious resource in the area, and generates a fair amount of CO_2.

Again, McGee went in the opposite direction: instead of a high-heat process, he designed a low-heat process.

Back in 1980, while a student at the University of Alberta, McGee was inspired by an idea he heard in a lecture by one of his electrical engineering professors. Through his company, McMillan-McGee Corporation, which he founded in 1995 while working on his PhD, McGee at first used the process to reclaim contaminated sites, heating polluted soils at low temperatures to vaporize the toxic chemicals so they could be collected and extracted from the soil. McMillan-McGee has established itself as a major player in the remediation business and is routinely contracted by the Department of Energy for reclamation jobs. In 2004 Dr. McGee formed a second company, E-T Energy (the E-T stands for Electro-Thermal) in order to apply that same process to the Athabasca treasure trove.

E-T Energy uses the exact same process as McMillan-McGee—only toward opposite ends: instead of using it to suck harmful substances out of the soil, it is using it to pull out a precious substance.

Drilling a series of thin holes, workers insert a series of pipes with electrical power running through them, creating a grid of electrodes. By running current between the electrodes, they heat the soil up to about 200° F, which liquefies the bitumen to a viscosity similar to 10/30 weight motor oil, allowing it to be pumped to the surface.

It is a remarkable process, for several reasons. First, it is fast and very effective: 75 to 80 percent of the oil in the treated area can be recovered within a year. Deep steam injection, by comparison, will take ten years or more, and open-pit mining disrupts the area for two or three *decades*.

It is also highly economical, costing far less than any of the other surface mining methods. And, in distinct contrast to the other methods, it is very environmentally friendly, using only a fraction of the water, needing no additional fuels for power (it draws its modest power needs from the existing power grid), and generating no caustic by-products or pollutants.

According to E-T Energy's estimates, its technology could reach about 400 to 500 billion barrels of Athabasca oil, and process 70 to 75 percent of that total to the surface. Taking the more conservative numbers (70 percent times 400 billion barrels) translates into a potential yield of about 280 billion barrels—some 30 percent more than Saudi Arabia's entire reserves.

>>>The Stone That the Builders Rejected

I promised to revisit the question of the world's oil problem. Part of that problem is the geopolitics of oil. It is politically and economically disastrous for the United States and other developed democracies to have our futures in the hands of petroleocracies such as Saudi Arabia, Iraq, and Venezuela. Approaches like McGee's will allow us to skip that problem altogether.

But what about skipping the oil problem itself?

Our national response to the rising cost of fuel in recent years has been to develop a policy based on ethanol derived from corn. This has proven to be a colossal error in judgment—a classic case of acting out of hindsight instead of foresight.

According to some studies, it takes ten gallons of fuel input to grow enough corn to produce seven gallons of ethanol output. That's operating at a net loss, like spending a dollar to make seventy cents. Worse, because the ethanol industry is based on corn, which is the central crop in the food and feed industries, we have put our fuel supply in direct competition with our food supply, creating economic shock waves felt around the globe. The cost of basic food staples worldwide has risen so drastically in the past few years that riots over grain prices have broken out in several parts of the world. Yes, Brazil has run a brilliant ethanol-fuels program based on sugarcane for decades. But the cane material they use is the waste product left over from the sugarcane animal feed process; food and fuel production are complementary there, not competitive. Building a biofuels industry on corn in the United States has proven to be a problem in itself. It would be like building a fuel program in Asia based on rice: you might feed your machines, but you'll starve your people.

Dan Gautschi, a soil-reclamation expert and CEO of SunEco, had a different idea: instead of using one of our most prized plants for fuel, what if we used one of our most despised?

Gautschi has been in the environmental remediation business for twenty years. When pollution caused by industrial wastewater starts to throw an ecosystem off kilter, Dan is one of the people companies call to come in and deal with it. His principal client base in that business has been water-treatment plants, and he has spent a good deal of those twenty years fighting their number one nemesis: algae.

Dan Gautschi has been battling algae for two decades. Now he has discovered a way to turn his old enemy into a friend. It turns out that algae, quite literally the scum of the earth, may prove to be worth more than gold. Algae exist everywhere, in every nook and cranny and every environmental extreme—deep beneath the ocean, within volcano vents, beneath the polar ice caps, in the fiercest desert. Whatever the environment, algae exist and thrive there. Algae are one of the oldest organisms on the planet (perhaps *the* oldest) and they are extraordinarily versatile. Certain strains of algae can even produce . . . oil. In fact, they can produce a very rich, highly usable grade of oil.

Dan is not the first to pursue the idea of using algae to produce oil for fuel; in fact, the big oil companies are spending hundreds of millions of dollars in research to try to develop just the right genetically modified strain of super oil-producing algae.

There is, however, a catch. Once you've come up with your perfect oil-producing monoculture in closed-pond isolation, you have to allow it out into the open environment to ramp up for large-scale production—and then one of two things happens: either it is killed off by the local species, who have had millions of years to hone their dominance; or you've produced an organism so strong that it kills off everything else. In the first case, your project fails. In the second, you've created a monster that could wreak environmental havoc on a catastrophic scale. Neither prospect is very appealing.

So Dan and his team went in the opposite direction: rather than attempting to breed a single oil-specific species as a monoculture in a closed-loop system, they work with a natural polyculture—a naturally occurring mix of various different algae—and cultivate that in open ponds out under the sun, moon, and stars.

It's a fascinating process. The algae farm operates on a cycle (a "growing season," so to speak) of three to four weeks, depending on ambient conditions. For two-thirds of the cycle, the algae are fat and happy. For the last third, the team subjects the algae crop to stress, steeply reducing its food supply. The algae respond by kicking into survival mode, switching from the photosynthetic phase to a heterotropic phase. Like a bear preparing for hibernation, the algae start to build up fat—and there's your oil production. At the end of the cycle, they harvest the oil-rich algae by separating them into three streams: the oil rises to the top, a beautifully purified water comes out the middle and is recycled, and what settles to the bottom is a nutritious green matter that turns out to make great livestock feed.

That's right: instead of competing with the agricultural stream by consuming corn or other food crops to produce ethanol, Gautschi's process actually *contributes* to the agricultural stream. "It turns out the cows love this stuff," says Keith Meyer, CEO of Sunthenoil, the SunEco sister company that sets up the actual algae farm-site operations. (The company's name describes the overarching premise: through the medium of algae, solar energy is converted directly to oil—*sun then oil*.) "It's high in protein, high in fat content, and has trace amounts of vitamin E."

Oh, and did I mention the land he uses? The algae don't need agricultural-grade land to thrive; in fact, they prefer exactly the sorts of conditions that make conventional agriculture impossible—opposites again. Sunthenoil has a major development project in the Salton Sea region of the California desert. It is one of the more wretched, infertile stretches of land in the nation: with a salinity level higher even than that of actual seawater, the Salton's brackish water is loaded with pollutants and agricultural runoff. In fact, the Salton Sea itself was created in only the last hundred years as a direct result of man-made runoff. Entire species of fish have ceased to live there, and there have been massive die-offs of pelicans and other birds.

And to Gautschi's algae, it's Club Med.

"Our model for this kind of algae-energy farm was developed to be suitable for locating anywhere—the Gobi Desert, the Sahara, it doesn't matter, as long as we have water and supplemental organic matter, which could be green waste, manure, human waste, degraded or digested paper pulp, or practically anything," says Meyer.

At $30 a barrel, the process is quite cost-competitive. It uses about one-quarter the water of an agricultural crop on the same land footprint, and has a yield of about 33,000 gallons of oil per acre-foot of water (given the depth of their algae ponds, that's about one-fifth of an acre of land). In large-scale trials with JB Hunt, the trucking company that handles much of Wal-Mart's business, the product performed beautifully. Running the trucks on one-half petroleum diesel and one-half algae diesel, they found zero loss of power or fuel economy—and an 82 percent reduction in particulate emissions. And because the algal oil has a slighter higher lubricity than petroleum-derived oil, it's easier on the engine.

"The stone which the builders have rejected," says Psalms, "that has become the cornerstone."

There could hardly be a more poetic expression of *go opposite*—and one would be hard-pressed to find a more practical expression of that idea than Gautschi's oil-from-algae process: taking the most marginal, unproductive, inhospitable land, growing a crop of the most primitive, "useless" life form on earth—and producing clean water, fresh cattle feed, and abundant biofuel oil.

>>>The Future Always Wins

The both/and principle tells us that revolutionary processes like Dan Gautschi's oil-producing algae won't replace petroleum fuel; they will exist side by side. Cironi's wind cube, McGee's low-impact bitumen-harvesting process, and Gautschi's algae farms are just three among the hundreds of ideas that will prove fruitful as we move into our multifuel future. What's interesting to contemplate is who will be the ones doing it.

Bruce McGee and his E-T process, as we saw above, could yield an entire Saudi Arabia's worth of oil right here in North America, with far less economic and environmental (let alone geopolitical) cost. Yet here is the ironic thing: McGee and his partners could not find a single executive at any of the major oil companies who would stick his neck out and give it a try. In fact, the only way they were able to demonstrate the efficacy of the technology was to get their own oil leases and fund the process themselves.

"It has been quite a struggle to try to get the major oil companies to properly evaluate the technology," says George Stapleton, a director of McGee's E-T Energy, "because they're making money doing it the way they've done it for forty years."

The way we've always done it is the biggest hurdle we face going forward successfully into the future. The real barriers today are no longer technical or material—they are attitudinal. We have habits that go back centuries, even millennia, habits of protecting our own egos and petty fiefdoms, habits of fighting change and being proprietary about knowledge. In an economy based on scarcity, that attitude was the rule of survival; in an abundant economy, it's suicide.

One of the principles of digital transformation is: "If it can be done, it *will* be done—and if you don't do it, someone else will." Sunthenoil's Keith Meyer makes a telling observation that reflects exactly that principle.

"What's so interesting is that the oil majors will probably miss the biofuels opportunity. They will dabble, and they'll even announce big R&D projects, like Exxon's genetic research funding announcement—but they'll miss the opportunity to drive the industry. This is the way it's always been through history: the coal guys should have become the oil guys, just as the stagecoach guys should have become the railroad guys, who should have become the airline guys. But they didn't. They all missed the paradigm shift. And they're missing it again."

As they always do: there will always be giants of the industry, whatever industry it happens to be, who try to drive into the future with their eyes fixed firmly on the rearview mirror. There will be those farsighted and foresighted entrepreneurs who have the flexibility and creativity to look into the visible future. The two will invariably come into conflict, to some degree—but flash foresight allows us to know where to place our bets. One thing you can know for sure about the future: in any battle with the past, the future always wins.

When Southwest tried to launch its little airline (then called Southern Air), it was nearly buried by lawsuits filed by the majors to keep it from flying; it took three years of court battles before it was able to put its first plane in the air. It might seem a bit irreverent to compare the San Antonio upstart to one of the great scientists of history, but Southwest's story reminds me a bit of Galileo's. In Galileo's time, the sun was thought to revolve around the earth; the astronomer was tried, convicted, and condemned (the sentence fortunately commuted to house arrest) for suggesting that the truth lay in the opposite direction.

There's something about *going opposite* that seems to invite resistance.

This is not really surprising. After all, it is in the very nature of the idea that what we're looking for are those insights that lie in the direction nobody else is looking. The fact that this is where most of the great scientific, technological, and social breakthroughs have come from throughout history doesn't seem to have changed the basic human fact of herd mentality.

Not long after that 2006 conference, where I shared the idea of underwater oil rigs with an audience of insurance underwriters, I had the opportunity to explore the practical ramifications of this thought when I met a man named Curtis Burton, CEO of Buccaneer Energy and the founder and driving force of a project called DeepSTAR.

Curtis was one of the first people involved in floating production rigs back in the late 1970s and early '80s. He moved up to the North Sea in '82 to work there, and then to Norway in '87, and found they were starting to do some very deepwater work there, up to 2,000 feet in depth.

In the early nineties, Curtis managed to get a small budget from Texaco, despite their doubts in the outcome, for a project to bring together all the oil majors, pool their resources and best thinking, and explore the possibilities of going even deeper. He persuaded more than two dozen oil companies and some forty services companies (drillers, suppliers, et al.) to join him in creating the DeepSTAR project in the Gulf of Mexico.

Conventional wisdom was, you couldn't make any money in deep water. At the time DeepSTAR began, 2,000 feet was as deep as operations were going; as one executive at Texaco put it to Curtis, "Going any deeper than 2,000—flat-out impossible." But Curtis was right: it was possible to go deeper than 2,000 feet—way deeper. Of the roughly 3,000 sub-sea oil wells around the world today, many reach down 10,000 feet, and some go as deep as 20,000. Bringing all the players together, many of them arch-competitors, to form DeepSTAR was the force that moved the major oil companies into the frontier of deepwater production. It was the largest successful R&D in the history of oil and gas.

How did they do it? I was curious to know.

Human beings can operate at depths of 600 or 700 feet, Curtis explained; below that, the operation needs to rely on technology. Around 2004 they had a breakthrough: they discovered that they could place an electrohydraulic multiplexer—essentially a sophisticated, robotically controlled valve tree that controls the flow of oil and shunts it to different destinations—right down on the ocean floor.

They had not considered putting the entire operation on the ocean floor, but when I related to Curtis my talk at the convention, projecting to the group that before long we would place entire drilling-and-extraction operations on the ocean floor, Curtis nodded and said, "Oh yeah, I can see that. It'll happen."

He paused, then added this intriguing afterthought.

"Typically, when you tell people forward-thinking things, you get one of two reactions. Maybe two people out of a hundred listen, consider what you said, and say, 'That's interesting.' They see that it's possible. And the other 98 percent? They dismiss you out of hand—because they see you as a threat to the status quo." He sighed and shrugged. "Being a prophet is a lonely existence."

>>>Through the Looking Glass

Doing the opposite has always been a smart strategy for breakthrough. Today, though, it has special implications, because in so many ways our entire world and everything about it is going through an intensely rapid and comprehensive reversal. The acceleration of digital technology is turning conditions on their heads, creating a profound shift in the core nature of what works:

SHIFTS IN THE DIGITAL AGE		
slow	→	*fast*
static	→	*dynamic*
stability	→	*flux*
maintain	→	*transform*
adaptive	→	*anticipatory*
dumb tools	→	*smart tools*
material economy	→	*immaterial economy*
scarcity	→	*abundance*
isolated	→	*integrated*
competitive	→	*collaborative*

As we saw in the last chapter, this shift from an economy based on *substance* (physical resources) to an economy based on *knowledge* (immaterial resource) has triggered a polar shift in the very nature of wealth and the anatomy of success. This is so because of the simple physics of it: when you share a physical resource with someone else, your own store depletes—but when you share knowledge, it *increases*.

Because of this polar shift in the nature of wealth, we have moved into an era when suddenly it makes sense to collaborate rather than to compete. The open-source movement in software is a dramatic example of this. The globally realized nature of the economy has turned the rules of geopolitics upside down, too, although nations are still in the process of catching up to this fact. In a world that now functions as one fully integrated economic organism, the idea of one nation profiting *at the expense of* another makes increasingly less economic sense. But protect and defend is a deeply ingrained impulse, and it will take some doing to unwind this pattern of thinking. Unwind it we must, though, if we are to flourish in a world run by new rules.

A few years ago, I went out to dinner with my goddaughter and her husband, Andrew. Fresh out of business school with a brand-new business degree, he had just taken a job at a software company.

"In the past," said Andrew, "they've always jobbed out their sales, but now they've decided to build an internal sales force. That's where we come in."

The company had hired eight young recruits, all straight-A students, like Andrew, right out of business school. I asked him what approach he planned to take.

"It's going to be really competitive," he said, "because these other guys are really sharp, too. It's going to be intense, but I'm determined to do whatever it takes to outperform them and be the best. If I want to excel, I'll need to really rack up the sales."

"That is definitely one way to go," I said.

"Why?" said Andrew. "Is there some other approach you'd suggest?"

"Well," I ventured, "that approach is okay, but it's a scarcity model. An abundance model would be to meet with those other seven guys right away and say something like this:

> *Look, this is the first time this company has ever had an internal sales force, and we need to make it successful—because if we do, then we'll be successful. So here's what I'm going to do. When I find anything I do with a client that works really well, I'm going to meet with you guys after work and tell you about it. If I try something that doesn't work, that really bombs, I'll tell you about that, too.*
>
> *And here's what I'm thinking: if any one of us is falling behind or really having a challenge, let's meet and talk about that, and find out how we can get that person caught up. If we all pool our knowledge instead of competing, we'll all get smarter and better together faster.*

"Pretty soon," I concluded, "you'll find you're not just the best salesperson—you're the sales *manager.* And then an executive. And soon you'll be going to a bigger company."

He decided to try this direction and see where it would lead.

A few months later, Andrew told me what happened. He had met with his colleagues at the new job and presented his ideas, just as we'd talked about. They liked the plan, too, and enthusiastically agreed to pursue an abundant, collaborative strategy. However, their boss did not care much for the idea. He didn't want them sharing their knowledge; he wanted them working independently and competing with each other.

"It was pretty clear that he had a scarcity mind-set," said Andrew, "and that was effectively going to prevent us from working together. It's a good company, but I could see that my future would be limited if I stayed there."

In fact, Andrew had already moved on and taken a job with Oracle, where his career is now thriving. And the company he left behind? Of the original sales team, all but one have left the firm—and Andrew's former boss has been demoted from manager to rep.

Even the idea of *cooperation* contains within it the assumption that your interests and mine are inherently in conflict, but we will temporarily set aside those cross-purposes to find some cautious tactical common ground. Really, *cooperation* is about protecting your piece of the economic pie and doing everything you can to make it bigger. *Collaboration* is working with everyone else, even your competitors, to make a bigger pie for all—which is exactly what Curtis Burton did when he created DeepSTAR, one of the most successful R&D projects in the history of the petroleum industry.

The move from scarcity thinking to abundance thinking, from zero-sum competition to one-hundred-sum collaboration, is not just a "nice" or "moral" idea. In the twenty-first century, it's plain good sense. Scarcity says, "I'm going to keep all my ideas to myself and sell more than anyone else." Abundance says, "By mentoring, coaching, and sharing all our best ideas, we're going to create a powerful tide that raises *all* our ships—and we'll *all* sell more as a result."

Which brings us back to Southwest Airlines for one more example of its insistently counterintuitive, upside-down oppositeness.

In the early 1990s a South Carolina–based aircraft services provider named Stevens Aircraft threatened to sue Southwest for trademark infringement, claiming that Southwest's new slogan "Just Plane Smart" was a direct knockoff of Stevens's slogan "Plane Smart." Nothing new here: just one more big-bucks corporate lawsuit, right? The litigants get down and dirty, the courts get clogged, and the lawyers get rich.

Only this time, these particular corporations decided to *go opposite.*

Stevens's chairman, Kurt Herwald, proposed (rather publicly) that instead of a lawsuit, the companies send their top warriors to battle it out, like jousting knights of old, in an arm-wrestling tournament before an audience of their employees and the media: the best out of three matches would keep the slogan, and the loser would donate $5,000 to a charity of the winner's choice.

Southwest sent this reply:

> *Our Chairman can bench-press a quart of Wild Turkey and five packs of cigarettes per day. He is also a fiercesome [*sic*] competitor, who resorts to kicking, biting, gouging, scratching and hair-pulling in order to win. When really pressed, he has also been known to beg, plead, whine and sob piteously. Can your pusillanimous little wimp of a Chairman stand up against the martial valor of our giant?*

—and of course went on to stage the match, proudly producing a video of the entire proceedings. (At one point the video shows Southwest chairman Herb Kelleher in training, doing a sit-up—with assistance—so that he can reach up and take hold of a cigarette and down a shot of Scotch.)

After the burly, thirty-seven-year-old Herwald beat the sixty-one-year-old Kelleher (who wore one arm in a sling and smoked a cigarette during the entire match), Herwald declared that he was going to share the slogan anyway—and both competitors ended up giving donations to their favorite charities on the spot. The result? No court costs; two charities (the Muscular Dystrophy Association and Ronald McDonald House) got healthy donations; both companies got to use the slogan; both companies got a healthy dose of public goodwill and great publicity; and hundreds of employees had a blast at a famous Dallas wrestling arena.

For an airline born in a three-year court battle, it was quite a moment: Southwest had *gone opposite.*

>>>CHAPTER 5 ACTION STEPS

One powerful way to trigger a flash foresight is to take note of where everyone else is looking, and then look in the opposite direction. Looking where no one else is looking helps you see what no one else is seeing—and then do what no one else is doing.

- *Make a list of everything your competitors are doing and then look at each item on the list and ask yourself,* ***How can I gain an advantage by doing the opposite?***
- *What is the current way of thinking regarding any subject in your industry? Then* ***think the opposite*** *to see new opportunities.*
- *With any particular project, goal, or objective, break that into its component parts and then look at each part, asking yourself:* ***Is there a way to gain advantage by turning that one step, component, or aspect on its head and doing the opposite?***
- *List the key elements or steps that everyone in your field does and ask of each one in turn,* ***Is there some creative way to do the exact opposite of what everyone else already does?***
- *The future always wins. Know that "the way we've always done it" is almost certain to become obsolete—and soon.* ***The pathway that will be most profitable in the years ahead is the pathway nobody is taking yet.*** *If it can be done, it will be done—and if you don't do it, someone else will.*
- ***Collaboration creates a bigger pie.*** *Look at every action you are taking now in your work and ask yourself:* ***Is there a way I could be more effective in this area by collaborating with others?***

>>> CHAPTER SIX

Redefine and Reinvent

In a town of 16,000 residents, fully one-quarter of the population worked at the company whose address served as a statement of corporate philosophy as well as its physical location. Since the turn of the twentieth century, Newton, Iowa, had been the Washing Machine Capital of the World, and its crown jewel, the Maytag corporation, was headquartered at One Dependability Square.

On October 25, 2007, two years after the company was acquired by Whirlpool following record losses, the Maytag plant ceased production and closed its doors. Here is how author Elizabeth Edwards describes the scene:

> *That last day, some of the Maytagers unlaced their work boots, placed them neatly side by side, and walked to their cars in their socks, their boots symbolizing what they were leaving behind, the part that could not come with them on the next part of their journey. The boots would be now—and for as long as Maytag could stand the image—lined up together by the plant door as the Maytagers once had been. It was, in a sense, like they had left the map of what their life was supposed to be at the*

place where the map no longer comported with the ground. The gesture was sad and angry and beautiful.[1]

It is a poignant picture, the row of empty boots defiantly evoking a way of life decimated by a cruel shift in corporate economics. It was also fully predictable—and preventable. The core of the tragedy at Newton, Iowa, was that the offices at One Dependability Square were doing the same thing as 99 percent of the rest of corporate America: they were depending on the wrong things.

In the twenty-first century, the one and only thing you can depend on is *transformation*. This means you can't go backward, and you can't stand still; you can't rest on your laurels, and you can't keep doing what you've always done, even if you do your best to keep doing it better. The only way to survive, let alone thrive, is to continuously reinvent and redefine.

Reinvent and redefine what? *Everything.*

>>>The *Reinvention* Imperative

In past chapters, we talked about the waves of technological acceleration that are transforming every aspect of our landscape. We also explored the urgent need to anticipate, take the initiative, and change from the inside out, even as all these transformations are coming at us from the outside in. This chapter is about creative strategies to *transform* from the inside out.

Transformation is an accelerated, magnified force of change. Redefining and reinventing is a way of harnessing that wild force and applying it to a product, a service, an industry, a career.

In a sense, transformation is a hard trend, while reinvention is soft. Transformation is going to happen, all around us and also *to* us, whether we want it to or not. Reinvention, on the other hand, will happen only if we make the decision to do it—and if we don't do it, someone else will.

You might think of it this way: we have each been dealt a hand from the same deck of cards. We cannot change what's on these cards; they are the transformational hard trends of our world and our future. And if that were all there was to it, there would be no point, no hope, no options to change or improve the future; it would all be *predefined*. But that's *not* all there is to it, because you also have a wild card in that hand. That wild card is *you*. You have the option to anticipate the coming transformations in your field, your industry, your career, and your life, and approach them preactively. How? By redefining and reinventing. Redefining and reinventing means seizing the opportunity to rewrite your own history—before it happens.

In the coming years, dramatic new developments are going to be flying at you so fast, from so many places and so many competitors, that it will become easier than ever to be overwhelmed. In a transformational time, disruption multiplies. The only solution to this increasing dilemma is to become experts at reinventing ourselves, our careers, and everything we do.

Otherwise, we'll have to leave our boots at the gate.

Your basic nature, personality, and talents don't change much over time. But what you know, what you learn, and what you do can change a good deal. People who have been laid off or fired from their jobs can hope they will find another job just like the one they lost, or they can learn new skills and shift from an industry in decline to working in an industry that is growing, both today and into the visible future.

Larry, a friend of mine (and husband of one of my key employees), spent years managing fast-food chains until he was laid off in 2009 as the economy hit bottom. Instead of waiting for another job in that same industry, which was facing increasing competition, he decided to reinvent himself. Since he was in his mid-forties, with grown kids and a new baby, many would have looked at Larry's position and thought it was too late in life for him to take on an entirely new career. Larry saw it differently.

The growing numbers of obese people and the increase in diabetes are soft trends that can be changed by reinventing the fast-food industry. However, Larry wasn't too interested in trying to reinvent the whole industry—but he *was* interested in reinventing his own career. Looking further at the hard trends, Larry saw the 78 million baby boomers getting older with increasing health needs, and he saw that as information technology, knowledge, and delivery systems improve, nurses would in the future be doing more and more of what doctors are doing today. He decided to go back to school and become a nurse.

When you combine self-reinvention with the certainty of hard trends, you are bound to create a huge win, both in the marketplace and in life.

Lee Iacocca and Hal Sperlich reinvented an entire marketplace back in 1983, when they redefined the family station wagon. At the time, station wagon sales were not growing, even though baby boomers were in their prime childbearing years and the nation was bursting with new families. A puzzle: why, if they needed the product, were they not buying the product? Because purchases are more emotional than logical, and are often statements of identity as much as—or more than—a rational act of fulfilling a practical need. Baby boomers may have needed a set of wheels with substantial family room, but, Dodge realized, they did *not* want to look and act just like their parents, even if that's exactly what most were doing most of the time. Baby boomers did not want to identify themselves as a generation of people who drive station wagons.

But vans? They were kind of cool (at the time)—and more important, their parents never drove vans. Chrysler introduced the Dodge Caravan in November 1983, creating an entire automotive category—the minivan—that it would continue to dominate for the next quarter century. It was a stroke of flash foresight, based on the hard trend of baby boomers and their needs (along with the eternal insight that people don't want to look or act like their parents).

Reinventing oneself has always been a powerful strategy. But in the past, corporate and product reinvention was an *option*; today it is an *imperative*. We live today in a unique context, an environment we've never seen or experienced before. We have never had this kind of processing power and bandwidth, this kind of runaway acceleration in technological capacity, and it has completely transformed our relationship to the concept of *stability*. In the past, stability and change were two contrasting states: when you achieved stability, you did so *despite* change. Today change itself has become an integral part of stability: today you can achieve stability only by *embracing* change as a continuous and permanent state.

One Dependability Square might have fared better if it had changed its address to One Transformation Square.

"We'll never have another Maytag," said Paul Bell, a Newton police officer who also serves in the Iowa legislature. "Maybe we shouldn't have had a company here that the majority of people worked for. We put all of our eggs in one basket."[2]

But the problem was not that they put all their eggs in one basket; it was a question of *which basket*. It wasn't that Maytag did anything so horribly wrong. This was no Enron or WorldCom, and there was no single product calamity or business fiasco that brought the giant down. It simply got disconnected from the accelerating pace of change. In an era of increasing competition, cost-cutting through outsourcing, and increasingly well-informed and more fiercely discerning consumers, the Maytag corporation reacted to every new shift with increasing sluggishness. It was a classic case of a solid company resting on its laurels and expecting to continue profiting from an established identity that was sorely in need of reinvention.

It used to be that the big ate the small; now it's the fast that eat the slow. Fast is the new big.

"You know," observed Newton's mayor, Chaz Allen, "a hundred and fifteen years with one company was a great thing, but it's a different world now."

It sure is, and not just in Iowa. It's a different world everywhere, and it's getting more different by the second. If you hope to stay ahead of the accelerating curve of change, it's no longer sufficient to do a good job and make incremental improvements on that good job you're doing. It's necessary to continually redefine and reinvent what it is you do in the first place.

In the past, great companies and great figures like Iacocca might innovate and then go for another decade before doing anything innovative again. In those days, that worked. It doesn't work anymore. The world has changed, and more important, change itself has changed. Information and new knowledge now travel around the world at the speed of light, and technological innovation proceeds at close to the speed of thought. Today you cannot just reinvent now and then: to survive and thrive in a time of vertical change, you have to be redefining and reinventing yourself *continuously.*

If you are a business, this means you have an urgent question in front of you every day: are your customers changing faster than you are? Are they learning faster than you are? Because they are changing and learning *fast*—and if you are not already designing and providing the solutions to the problem they are going to have next week and next year, you are behind a curve you cannot afford to be behind. And this is true whether you are an individual, a small business, a multinational corporation—or a town in the Midwest. (Or anywhere else in the world, for that matter.)

That's not the end of the Newton, Iowa, story. Two months after the Maytag plant closed, a Scottsdale, Arizona–based company named TPI Composites announced plans to build a new plant there. TPI Composites manufactures the blades used in wind turbines for commercial energy production. A portion of the old Maytag plant itself is now occupied by another new company, Trinity Structural Towers, which manufactures the enormous towers used for those same wind turbines. From washing machines to wind turbines: welcome to the new century.

Like so many towns and cities around the world, Newton seems to be in the process of reinventing itself, yet it is doing so more by reaction than by anticipation. Change is always a lot harder when it happens from the outside in. What if, instead of trying to hold on to the status quo, Maytag had actively sought out the visible future?

Maytag's famous television ads featured a Maytag repairman confessing to the camera that he was lonely because nobody ever called him. It was a cute idea: the machines ran so well, went the obvious subtext, that nobody ever needed the repairman. (They were built, after all, at One Dependability Square.) But what if, instead of sitting around waiting for the phone to ring, that guy had been in the lab dreaming up ways to reinvent the washing machine?

That is exactly what Professor Stephen Burkinshaw did. After thirty years of textile chemistry research, the British scientist created a washing machine that skips the problem Procter & Gamble sought to solve with Tide Coldwater: it uses almost no water at all. Instead, Professor Burkinshaw's Xeros washer uses small nylon pellets that, when slightly damp, generate a small electrical charge (much like rubbing your feet on a nylon carpet) that electrically attracts dirt, pulling it out of your soiled clothes and sucking it into the pellets' interior. The same pellets can be used for about a hundred wash cycles, or about six months' worth for an average family, before being replaced and recycled. The process not only uses less than a tenth of the water of a conventional washer, it also uses only a tiny fraction of the energy, because it has no need of a spin or rinse cycle.

In a July 2009 article previewing the Xeros washer, *Fast Company*'s Cliff Kuang pointed out that if every American home had a Xeros, the savings in carbon emissions would be equivalent to pulling 5 million cars off the road. His review concluded breathlessly, "This thing could be a world-changing invention."[3]

>>>Reinvent *Everything*

Recently I met with a group of people in the heating and air conditioning business. When we came to the flash foresight principle of *redefine and reinvent,* one of the gentlemen in the group raised his hand.

"I can see how that would relate to things like electronic gadgets and auto manufacturing. But air conditioning is basically air conditioning. How would this be relevant to our business?"

"Let's back up a step," I suggested, "and first take a look at what it is you do. You're not really in the heating and cooling business—you're in the *environmental remediation* business. Your job is to provide technology that makes people's environments livable and comfortable.

"Last evening, for example, in my hotel room, every time the AC came on it created a rattling noise that made it nearly impossible to talk on the phone. Sleeping was a problem, too. Do you see where you guys come in?"

The man shrugged. "They needed someone to fix the AC."

"Perhaps," I replied, "but is there a bigger opportunity here?"

There was indeed, and as we looked more closely at that hotel room situation, that opportunity became clear: *noise cancellation.*

All sounds are composed of specific wave forms. The applied science of noise cancellation is based on the fact that when you combine a given sound wave with the opposite wave form (its *anti-sound,* so to speak), the two cancel each other out. At the moment, all the significant patents in this area are for noise-canceling headsets. Why not create noise cancellation for heating and air conditioning systems? All you have to do is identify the offending sounds the system creates (usually a fixed pitch, which is easy to identify and cancel), set up a small speaker system broadcasting the opposite wave forms at the same volume, and you've got completely silent heating and air conditioning for hotels and offices, and ultimately (when you can bring down the cost scale) for homes.

There's probably some patentable design in there, and there's certainly an opportunity for an enterprising HVAC company to reinvent its own industry.

Redefine and reinvent is not only about transforming the products we offer; it's about transforming how we do *everything.*

Because of my travel schedule, I spend a good amount of time in hotels. Typically, room service is pretty good. If I want coffee and breakfast at six A.M. and call for it the night before, the knock on the door might come at six o'clock, or it might come at five to six, or at ten after. At least, that's normal at a Hilton, a Hyatt, an Anatole, a Renaissance—but not at certain Marriotts.

At those Marriotts that have implemented a new system, that knock on the door comes precisely at the time you requested it. Not a minute early, not a minute late, but right on the dot. How do they do that? By using the technology known as *artificial intelligence* (AI). They have a computer in the kitchen equipped with what's called an *expert system*. The expert system knows all the precise parameters that will have an impact on time lapse: how long the service elevator will take to get from any floor to any other floor, exactly how long it will take the waitstaff to walk from the kitchen to the elevator, exactly how long it takes each dish to cook, and so forth. It has a complete map of the hotel and keeps track of every order, so if there are multiple breakfasts to deliver, it knows in which order they should be dropped off. The system tells the kitchen staff exactly when to start cooking your breakfast in order to have the hotel employee knocking on your door, tray in hand, at exactly the minute you asked for it.

You might at first think, what's the big deal? Five minutes give or take, does the customer really care? But here's what happens. The first time your meal shows up on the dot, you might not even notice; after all, anyone can get it right every now and then. The second time, third time, fourth time, you start noticing. Hey, this is getting weird! By the fifth and sixth time, you *expect* it—and now, when you stay at any other hotel and your meal comes minutes early or minutes late, Marriott has trained you to be disappointed. They have used technology to redefine customer service.

Remember the Miracle-Earbud idea from Chapter 2? In that example, we didn't simply modify or improve a product, we reinvented the company by shifting it into an entirely different industry. A few moments beforehand, we were in the *hearing aid business*, an industry that baby boomers don't seem to want any part of. One simple flash foresight later, we're in the *leading-edge lifestyle-enhancing electronic gadgets business*—an industry that has baby boomer written all over it, and every other generation, for that matter.

Amazon redefined not only the bookstore but also the shopping experience itself. Southwest redefined the air travel experience, transforming our expectations of something costly, inconvenient, and irritating to something inexpensive, easy, and enjoyable. Apple redefined the PC and has continued to redefine everything it touches, from phones to how we listen to music to how we purchase entertainment.

Reinventing is not the same thing as adding a feature, a tweak, or a twist. Once something is reinvented, it never goes back to being the way it was before—because reinvention harnesses the power of transformation. Blogs redefined the news industry. Twitter reinvented blogs and communication. Mark Burnett (creator of *Survivor, The Apprentice,* and other reality shows) reinvented television.

As Newton, Iowa, has discovered, it isn't only companies and industries that need to reinvent themselves: so do towns and cities.

Las Vegas knows this. Every few years it seems to re-create itself in an entirely new image. From the gambling and nightlife capital, it became *the* location for family-oriented getaways, then it metamorphosed to the X-rated "What happens in Vegas stays in Vegas" theme. Now they're going highbrow, putting up new medical centers, a symphony hall, and a center for the performing arts. And they're working on putting in what they hope will be the nation's most prestigious furniture wholesale showroom, giving Las Vegas the unlikely title of Wholesale Furniture Capital. One thing you have to give Vegas: they never seem to run out of creative ideas for reinventing their city.

Take New York City, as another example. Looking at classic films from the seventies—*Taxi Driver, Little Murders,* or *Dog Day Afternoon*—you see a dark, gritty atmosphere that was a reasonably realistic reflection of Gotham street life at the time. In the nineties Rudy Giuliani cleaned it up and polished the Big Apple to a sheen.

On the other hand, look at what happened to New Orleans—not just the disaster itself, but also the aftermath. What a tragedy. If we had a national philosophy and leadership that embraced continuous reinvention, we would have said, let's take all the money we're going to spend restoring that area and use it to build the first green city: solar panels, energy efficiency, a smart grid, smart streets—make it the model city for the twenty-first century. Will we rebuild Haiti to be a new version of the old Haiti, or reinvent Haiti to thrive rather than just survive in the years ahead?

Likewise, when the American auto industry collapsed in 2009, instead of giving federal bailouts to bankrupt GM and Chrysler so they could go back to doing business the same old way, why did we not use the catastrophe as an opportunity to completely reinvent the American automobile?

Unfortunately, it's human nature to dig in our heels, to protect and defend our existing turf. How do we get past that reflex and build our businesses and our lives on a foundation of continuous self-reinvention?

>>> Forget the Competition

One way to get past the protect-and-defend impulse is to jettison some of our most cherished core principles of the competitive marketplace—principles that *used* to work. In fact, we need to redefine and reinvent the concept of competition itself.

When it comes to the competitive environment, there are two things you can be sure of: (1) competition is more intense today than it was a year ago, and (2) a year from now it will be even more so. How will you survive in an increasingly competitive world? By *not competing.*

The old rule was to do what the other guy is doing, only do it either cheaper or better. Price and quality: these are the two great classic parameters of competition. But in a world gone vertical, this entire concept is obsolete. As change accelerates and pressure increases, there is a natural tendency to focus on what the competition is doing, but doing so is a recipe for disaster, because it mires you in a futile and never-ending game of catch-up while distracting your focus away from where it needs to be: on the visible future.

Trying to compete is a scarcity-thinking game; the organizations that are winning in the new century don't bother competing. Instead, they leapfrog the competition by redefining anything and everything about their business.

Marlin Steel Wire Products, a Baltimore-based manufacturing company, faced stiff and growing competition from China and its incredibly low labor costs, until president Drew Greenblatt decided to stop trying to play the competition game. Leaving the low-margin end of the market to the Chinese, Greenblatt automated his production line and began specializing in more high-end products like antimicrobial baskets for restaurant kitchens, finding customers for his higher-priced product line in places like Japan and Belgium. Marlin's sales grew from $800,000 in 1998 to $3 million in 2007. "I was losing a hundred thousand dollars a year just a couple years ago," said Greenblatt, "and now I'm shipping wire baskets to New Zealand."[4]

Another company that struggled with lower-priced competition from China was a small firm that made hats for painters. Realizing they would never survive going head-to-head on price, they started focusing on special-branding their hats, silk-screening company logos, favorite customer quotations and sayings, and other highly personalized information on their product—a type of service possible only with the small runs and rapid turnaround that China could never hope to offer. Leaving China to its strengths—size, scale, and low-cost labor—they used their smallness (and their proximity to the end customer) as a strength, and captured their niche.

Earlier I mentioned that Amazon redefined both the bookshop and the shopping experience. Brick-and-mortar bookstores that compete on price have been, for the most part, driven out of business by online bookstores like Amazon and BarnesandNoble.com, which offer an unbeatable combination of price, convenience, and book availability. In the late nineties people were predicting that the huge Barnes & Noble superstores would disappear. But they didn't.

Why not? Remember the *both/and* principle from Chapter 3? Barnes & Noble is a great example of new and old technologies existing side by side. What's more, which is the relevant point here, the brick-and-mortar Barnes & Noble stores survived because they provide an experience that online shopping cannot.

Barnes & Noble decided that a bookstore should be more than a place to shop and buy books. Before Amazon and the Web came along, Barnes & Noble reinvented the book-buying experience, based on a blinding flash of the obvious: most people who go into bookstores love books and reading. So why not provide them a place to do that? They created a unique and total experience, focusing on the joy of reading, lifelong learning, and discovery, a place where you could relax, read, and learn, not just shop.

Amazon used technology to redefine how we shop for books. But Barnes & Noble found and focused on its uniqueness, *doing what its competitor couldn't.*

Note that Barnes & Noble competed based not on price but on *customer experience.* Shopping at Wal-Mart is not a great experience, but you can't beat their prices: they compete on *price.* Ben & Jerry's ice cream tastes good, but they don't compete on just taste, or on price—they compete on *values*: Ben & Jerry's has been a strong advocate (and financial contributor) for various social issues from their earliest days in business. Zappos competes on *customer service.* Apple competes on *design, customer experience,* and *innovation.* Here is a partial list of all the things you can compete on:

- price
- reputation
- image
- service
- quality
- design
- time/speed
- values
- customer experience
- innovation
- knowledge
- loyalty

And there are more. You could compete on just one item from this list, or two—but why not use *reinvent and redefine* to compete on them all? Look at each one and ask, "How can I redefine how we compete on—" and then fill in the blank. If you don't, someone else will.

>>>Decommoditize Continuously

One inevitable by-product of advancing technology is *commoditization.* Someone makes an innovative breakthrough, and by doing so they stand out as unique in their field. However, because of the breakneck speed of technological advance, pretty soon everyone else is offering those same features.

When Steven Spielberg produced *Jurassic Park* in 1993, audiences were astonished at how lifelike the computer-animated effects were. *Look at those dinosaurs—they look so real!* A year later, the same tricks were showing up in television commercials, and a few years after that, we could reproduce them on our home computers. When the Apple iPhone was released in June 2007, one of the most dramatic new features was the way the screen image automatically swiveled when the user turned the phone, flipping from horizontal to vertical and back again. It was magical. In less than a year, all the other smartphones had it, too.

In both cases, what happened? A product feature that was special, unique, even astonishing, rapidly became a standard feature. In other words, it disappeared. This is why the reinvention imperative is about not occasional reinvention but continuous reinvention. This is why Hollywood films and Apple iPhones have to keep pushing the envelope if they want to survive—and why you and I do, too.

Every product or service has the potential to become a bland, vanilla, me-too commodity that competes on price alone. More important, any product or service can be taken in the opposite direction and made unique, and therefore far more valuable. In the nineties the idea of *kaizen,* continuous improvement, was all the rage. No more: the pace of transformation is too fast. What's needed is *continuous decommoditization.*

Decommoditization means going against the natural tide of entropy, the tendency for our products and services to settle into a watered-down version that seems safe and caters to the broadest marketplace (read: lowest common denominator). The truth is that there is nothing safe about commoditizing.

Toshiba learned this lesson the hard way. In the mid-nineties, Toshiba was the best-selling brand of laptop. Laptops as a category were then on the rise and in the following decade would unseat desktops as the most popular category of personal computer; laptop sales overtook desktop sales for the first time in 2008. This future development was thoroughly predictable: dematerialization (pathway 1), mobility (pathway 3), and the three digital accelerators made it abundantly clear. But not everyone in the PC industry was looking into the future. If Toshiba had maintained its market lead in laptops, it would have stepped into a huge increase in revenue and profitability. But it didn't.

What happened?

In 1996 I happened to be consulting to Toshiba. "By the early 2000s," I pointed out, "laptops will become the new desktop—just as smartphones will later become the new laptop—and people will use them largely to get on the Internet." I suggested they outfit every laptop model with a built-in modem. In fact, here was the idea I floated: when the laptop first powers up, the start-up screen says, "Welcome to Toshiba Mobile Customer Concierge . . ." and then offers the users an array of online services to help them get the most use out of their laptop's new features as a mobile worker.

There were some at Toshiba who liked the idea . . . and some who didn't. As so often happens in big companies, there were two forces at work: one looking to the future and one clinging to the past. And as so often happens, the one clinging to the past won out. The Mobile Customer Concierge idea never happened; instead of investing in the laptop experience of the future, Toshiba put its resources into introducing an entire new line of *desktop* computers. *After all, all the other PC manufacturers are doing it,* they thought. *We should, too.*

They could not have made a worse move. Toshiba was known for its capacity to miniaturize. Creating a line of desktops was not only an investment in a disappearing past, it was also a commitment to a product category where they could not even use their particular strength. Their desktops were like all the others. With this move Toshiba effectively crippled its brand: it moved from its place at the head of the pack to being lost in the thick of it, becoming one more me-too product in a declining category.

Toshiba had the opportunity to take advantage of a future opportunity and solve its customers' future problems: by anticipating the increasing mobile worker trend it could have done what Apple later did with iTunes and completely redefined an entire market segment, thereby making itself the automatic market leader. But instead of *de*commoditizing, it turned itself *into* a commodity—and in the process lost its market lead. Thus far, it has never gotten it back.

This is not just about electronic gadgetry. *Anything* can be decommoditized, even things we take for granted. In the nineties Starbucks decommoditized coffee, Victoria's Secret decommoditized underwear, and Herman Miller decommoditized the chair. Today, Glacéau Vitaminwater and a host of others are decommoditizing water (and making huge profits), Gdigital and others are decommoditizing electricity, and 1-800-GOT-JUNK has decommoditized junk removal.

Some years ago I spoke in Singapore for a presentation honoring all the past global winners of the Ernst & Young Entrepreneur of the Year awards. One of the winners was a young woman who had built a business around importing French wine to China.

This was a fascinating study in decommoditization. When she began, not only could the Chinese not make French wine, they couldn't drink it, either. Their traditional wine is quite sweet, completely unlike its European counterpart, in part because of the different nature of the soil and growing conditions there. When this entrepreneur first brought in her line of French wines, her Chinese customers were adding sugar to it to make it palatable. She had to educate their palate, for example, by making wine tastings a popular event. They didn't know what "good" was, in relation to Western wines. In other words, she had to completely redefine the entire product category in order to participate in it. Now she has a huge business there. And the Chinese are never going to impose a trade embargo on her wine. Why not? Because it doesn't compete with what they produce. It is a completely decommoditized product.

In the midst of explosive and continuous transformation, one clear dependable strategy for staying ahead of the curve is to create in yourself and in your company or organization a habit of continuously decommoditizing. Anything and everything can become a commodity; and any product or service can be decommoditized. You can wrap a service around a product and decommoditize it, or you can wrap a service around a service and decommoditize it, or you can wrap a new product around an existing product. The combinations are limited only by your imagination.

One of my favorite stories of decommodization concerns a Wisconsin flooring entrepreneur named Tryggvi Magnusson.

An expert who had helped develop the technology used in flooring laminates, Magnusson had consulted to the biggest and the best: Armstrong, Formica, Shaw, Masco, and the other giants in flooring. In the nineties, he began toying with an idea for creating long-lasting, great-looking floors.

The problem with floor finishes, he reasoned, is that people walk on them. If nobody ever walked on the floor, it would look great for years. But of course, that would defeat the point of having a floor, right? Magnusson had a flash foresight, sparked by a combination of *go opposite* and *skip it*: what if, instead of creating a finish that will better withstand wear, you skip that whole problem—by creating a finish that nobody walks on?

He developed a new coating system that contains an abundance of ceramic particles. Harder than stainless steel or industrial-grade diamonds, ceramic is second in hardness only to natural diamonds. With his ceramic-based coating in place, people walk on the ceramic particles—not on the floor finish. Magnusson patented his WearMax technology and in 1997 formed a company called Trustor Coatings to market it. Sales went from zero to $25 million—in his first year in business.

Not content to rest on his laurels, Magnusson continued to innovate. A few years later, he noticed that his flooring manufacturer clients were looking for something fresh and new—and they were also growing impatient with the sixty- to ninety-day wait for container orders to come from overseas. To solve the second problem, he developed From the Forest, a supply company based purely on U.S. woods and using only raw materials sourced from managed forests so as to preserve and protect our natural resources. To address the first need—for something new and different—he did something extraordinary: he decommoditized wood.

He took maple and began experimenting with heating it to cook the sugars in the wood, and found that he could bring out new colors, not by adding coatings to the wood, but by bringing out different natural hues and shades from within the wood itself. The result is a new color process, which he can customize by using a variety of exotic woods and varying the lengths of time he cooks them.

Tryggvi Magnusson created not one but two successful companies—by decommoditizing *floors.*

>>>Reinvent the Old by Using It in New Ways

In the summer of 1993 I was invited to speak to a group of several thousand critical care nurses at the annual conference of the Society of Critical Care Medicine in Seattle. Before I spoke, my host spent a few minutes giving me a sense of what their daily routine was like and what sorts of challenges they faced. During that briefing, I was surprised to learn that during the typical thirteen-hour shift, these nurses were spending an average of four hours talking with their patients' relatives. That's nearly *one-third* of their entire time on the floor.

That amount of time seemed extraordinary, until I realized, these were not just nurses, they were *critical care* nurses. If you had a parent, sibling, or child in critical care and you couldn't physically be there by their side twenty-four hours a day, what would you do? Chances are good you'd be calling every chance you got, wanting to know if there were any changes in your loved one's condition. And who would you call, the doctor? No, the doctors are not always near their patients. You'd want to call the person who's right there on the floor, within earshot of your loved one's room. In other words, you're going to call the nurse. Which is exactly what everyone was doing—and more than 30 percent of the nurses' actual productivity and caregiving was being siphoned away from their patients because of it.

These nurses were just like you and me and everyone else: they were *busy*. Between all the technology they had to manage, with computer systems and phone systems and monitoring systems constantly changing and upgrading, managing prescriptions and medications, filling out charts and handling paperwork and ordering tests and following up on tests and doing a myriad of minor and not-so-minor procedures, they still managed to spend some time actually interacting with their patients. It's a mind-boggling load of tasks they juggle in an underpaid, understaffed, and highly pressured profession—and they had to spend nearly one-third of that time letting worried relatives know if there were any changes in condition.

Addressing the group, I made them a promise: "I'm going to give each of you more than three hours a day of completely free time," I said, "time you can use to do whatever you want. Put in more time with your patients, catch up on your paperwork, grab a few minutes of downtime to put up your feet and keep your sanity . . . whatever you need to do to make you more effective at your job and improve your life, you'll have an extra three hours plus to do exactly that. And best of all, we're going to do this without spending a dime."

You can probably imagine the word forming in thought bubbles over their tired and skeptical heads: *Impossible*! Nevertheless, they listened as I outlined a plan. They decided to try it. But before we look at the strategy we used there, let's take a brief detour, stepping back in time to a similar event nearly a decade earlier.

In the spring of 1985, while speaking at a meeting of the International Food Service Executives, I was presenting some thoughts on how, because of the geometric growth in processing, bandwidth, and storage, the pace of technological change was rapidly accelerating and would soon accelerate beyond anyone's imagination. Speaking about how this would affect our perception of value, I said, "In the years ahead, time will become more and more valuable. In fact, time will become the currency of the nineties and beyond. If you can find creative ways to save people time, you'll thrive—but if you waste people's time, you won't survive.

"What happens at your restaurants? The better you are, the more you are in demand, which means the busier you are, which means people standing in line, waiting for a table. The better you are, in other words, the more you are going to annoy your customers and drive them away—unless you can find a way to give them back that stolen time.

"Here's a thought: instead of making them stand around huddled by your entryway waiting, why don't you let your customers roam the nearby stores while they wait? I know what you're thinking: then how will they know when their tables are ready? So here's another thought: why don't we give them pagers?"

This was in 1985, remember. Back then, pagers were a fairly new technology. A pager on your hip meant you were someone *really* important. The only people who used pagers in those days were surgeons, highly placed businessmen, and big-time drug dealers.

In that audience there were some 300 owners of leading restaurants, and some of them had a major flash foresight.

About a year later, the first restaurants started giving their customers pagers. It caught on, and today there is an entire industry built around producing those cute plastic disks with the buzz and the little flashing lights that restaurants hand out to their patrons. In fact, since cell phones have now made pagers all but obsolete, chances are good that these days, going out to dinner on a busy evening is the only time you ever come into contact with a pager.

Flash forward to 1993. By the time of my critical care nurses' convention, we had arrived on the other side of the pager boom. While they were still a new and rare technology in 1985, by 1993 they were everywhere; moms were putting pagers on their teenage kids' hips so they could buzz them for dinner. In fact, by this time pagers were not only common, they were already beginning their decline—because mobile phones were now in the ascendancy. Within a few years, everyone would be carrying cell phones, and pagers would go back to being a niche technology.

This presented a perfect opportunity for our critical care

nurses—and I'll bet you have figured out what the strategy was. As my host explained the nurses' situation and how incredibly stressed their schedule was, a *go opposite* thought flashed through my mind.

Who uses pagers? Doctors. What's the opposite of doctors? Patients.

The strategy I proposed was simple: go out into the community and ask companies to donate all their old pagers to the hospitals—and then give those pagers, not to the nurses or doctors, but to the patients' relatives, and tell them, "The moment there's any change in your loved one's condition, we'll beep you."

That's exactly what they did. The companies who contributed their pagers got a modest write-off and some good PR. Some of the hospitals got in touch with their local telecom companies and got *them* to donate free airtime for the pagers—again, with the write-off and PR fringe benefits. The next time I spoke with my conference host, she told me that in dozens of hospitals that tried this, those same critical care nurses were now spending an average of forty-five minutes on the phone every day.

From four hours to forty-five minutes, with zero cost to the hospital. Impossible—except that once you *saw* the possibility, it was easy.

Since then, more than a hundred hospitals around the nation have enacted similar programs.

>>>It's Not the Tool, It's How You Use It

Flash foresight is not always about pushing the technology envelope and finding some whizbang high-tech new way of doing something. Sometimes it is about having the imagination to use an old or existing technology in new ways.

Global positioning via satellite was developed for the military. Few would have imagined that we would all be using GPS on our phones to find the nearest Starbucks. ARPANET, the forerunner of the Internet, was designed in the 1960s primarily for military application and high-level academic research. Today we use the Internet to find movie start times and the best deals on a car, while our grade school–aged kids use it to help them do their homework.

Virtually every tool in existence offers more capacities than most of us are using, and in many cases *far* more. Here's a simple example I often use in speeches.

Imagine that your boss just handed you a 120-page document, saying you were going to meet on this subject in a few hours—and you don't have time to read it. What do you do?

Then I ask, "How many people here use Microsoft Word?"—to which most or all hands go up—followed by the question, "How many have ever used the AutoSummarize function?" And it's rare, even in a room of several thousand, to see a single hand in the air.

Here's the irony of it: using AutoSummarize, an extremely easy-to-use software feature that every person in every audience already has on their desktops, putting a short summary together would take a few seconds and two mouse clicks, and give you some good talking points for your meeting. AutoSummarize has been a feature in Word for more than a decade. We didn't need a new technology for this task, we just needed to rediscover the tools we already had. (Microsoft Word has 4,000 features; how many are you using?)

One area where this principle could do a vast amount of good is in health care, not only in the actual healing methods and techniques but also in their delivery and administration.

For example, I have shared the story of the critical care nurses and pagers with hundreds of audiences, but I can't think of any market segment that needs it more than doctors' offices. A doctor friend of mine once showed me the design of a gigantic new building they were building for his practice. The first thing I noticed was that the new design had a vastly expanded waiting room.

"Wait a minute," I said, "you're expanding the *waiting* room? Not the *healing* rooms?"

What's the real problem here? The enlarged waiting room was an attempt to solve the wrong problem. The question they needed to be asking was not "Where do we put all these waiting patients?" but "Why do we have so many people waiting?" It wasn't a space problem but a time problem, and more specifically, a *scheduling* problem.

Actually, to put it even more accurately, it was an *intelligence* problem—not the intelligence of the doctors or nurses, but the intelligence of the office itself. Instead of installing expensive fish tanks in the waiting room to keep us distracted, they should be reinventing the way they handle patient flow, and *shrinking* the waiting room, or even better, eliminating it altogether.

Typically, when you finally get back into the actual examination room, the doctor doesn't know whom he's seeing or what the problem is until he looks at your chart. Why not? We have the technology to do that. In fact, why doesn't the office's AI system already know what your symptoms are and what brought you here before you even set foot in the office? Why don't we have a menu so that when we call in (or go online) to make the appointment and describe what's wrong, they know roughly how long it will take? And let's cross-reference that with our age, because if we're ninety, we may need a little more time than if we're forty. Now the doctor's office knows who we are, why we're there, and roughly how long it will take to see us—and it knows that before we've taken off our jacket and sat down.

If Marriott can do all this with our breakfast order, why can't our doctors do it with us?

And meanwhile, even before we implement all this, why are we *still* sitting around in those waiting rooms? Doctors have been using pagers for years. Why not give them to the patients, liberate them from the waiting rooms to go shop, do errands, or at least stroll outside in the sun while they wait?

In this high-tech world, we don't always need to find high-tech solutions. Putting oil rigs on ocean floors and putting intelligent biosensors in our fields are cutting-edge high-tech solutions; giving nurses' patients' family members some corporate pager discards is a low-tech, old-tech solution. It doesn't matter whether it's high-tech, low-tech, new-tech, old-tech, or *no*-tech. It's not always the tool that makes the difference, but how we use it. It's a question of reinventing and redefining our processes.

In Chapter 4, I mentioned that the old rule "If it ain't broke, don't fix it" has been replaced by a new rule: "If it works, it's already obsolete." This is actually good news, at least for those who see and embrace it. It's very liberating to realize that the very latest, coolest, most feature-laden gizmo, software system, or office technology you just purchased was obsolete before you even touched it. You might be tempted to delay your purchase and wait for the next model—but if you do, you could wait yourself right out of business. You can't afford to wait. So what do you do? You realize that *obsolescence has become a non-issue.* While everyone else is worrying about obsolescence, you never have to spend one precious minute of your time worrying about it again.

Are the tools you're using obsolete? Of course—*everyone's* tools are. After all, the replacement device is not a pipe dream, it's in the pipeline, heading your way. The real issue is, what are you doing with the tools you have? Are you using them in ways that generate advantage? Remember: it's not the tool, it's how you use it.

Let's use flash foresight to solve a big problem before it happens, using a tool we already have.

Here is the problem: as we have more and more information to go with all our OTC drugs and remedies such as vitamins and herbs, the print is getting smaller and smaller, which means harder and harder to read, even as baby boomers get older and older. How on earth are we going to fit all that information on those little bottles?

First, notice the certainties involved here, based on the hard trends of demographics, technological acceleration, and the growth of information:

Will more and more customers in our aging society be using more and more medications? Yes. As new research turns up more and more information, will there be an increasing amount of information to fit onto each bottle? Yes. Will those baby boomer customers find it harder and harder to read this increasing amount of fine print? Yes. These are all certainties, so we know this problem is a future fact—unless we solve it before it happens.

First, let's use *go opposite.* Instead of making the fine print smaller, make it bigger. How? Instead of putting it on the bottle, take it *off* the bottle. Instead of printing it on that tiny slip of paper, display it on a screen. In other words, *skip the problem.*

But where are all these consumers going to find readily available screens? On their cell phones; everyone has one, and they carry them everywhere. How do we get all that information off the bottle onto our cell phone screens? By *using existing technologies creatively*, employing advanced bar codes or *radio frequency identification* (RFID).

Using your phone to scan the bar code on the bottle, all the information appears on your phone. Enlarge the text—no problem. Have it read to you—no problem. Or, put an RFID chip right on the bottle. RFID chips are already being used everywhere, from smart-tag tollbooths to passports to tagging animals and retail products. If Coca-Cola and Pepsi can put RFID on their bottles, why not use it to list drug ingredients, contraindications, and all the rest? Better yet, let's look a little further into the visible future and see that we'll soon add streaming audio and video to that information.

With RFID-tagged medications, you just type or say the name of the product you're standing next to, and your smartphone will read all the fine print that's relevant to you (or *all* of it, if you want)—and because your phone is tapped into the pharmacy's consumer database (which is smart enough to know who you are and every med you might be taking), you can see potential drug incompatibilities and contraindications right on your phone.

Who will implement this strategy first: Walgreens, CVS, or Wal-Mart? Or someone else? Because if it can be done, it *will* be done—and if they don't do it, someone else will.

>>>Find Your Core

In 1889 a Kyoto entrepreneur named Fusajiro Yamauchi founded a company to sell his exquisite, handmade traditional Japanese playing cards. Called *hanafuda* (literally "flower card"), each card was crafted out of bark from the mulberry tree. It was a bold gamble: card playing had a century earlier been a banned practice in Japan, and while it was no longer illegal in 1889, it was still far from a popular pastime.

However, the business caught on. Japan was in the process of hastily transforming itself from a feudal society to a modern nation, and innovation was in the air. Hanafuda began a renewed boom in popularity. Yamauchi opened a second shop in Osaka, and soon his company was flourishing. He retired a successful man in 1929, passing the business on to his descendants to run. And if that had been that, they would today either be nonexistent or, at best, unknown outside Japan.

But that was not that, because Yamauchi's little card company reinvented itself. His grandson Hiroshi visited the United States in the 1950s and managed to secure the rights to put Disney characters on his playing cards. In the 1960s he began to experiment further, creating a taxi company, a hotel chain, an instant rice company, and a TV network—none of which caught on. He kept trying. He moved into the toy market, and in the 1970s began dabbling with electronic family entertainment. In 1977 he hired a young student named Shigeru Miyamoto to help him develop some new products. If the name is not familiar to you, ask your kids: Miyamoto went on to develop such runaway best-selling games as Super Mario Bros., Donkey Kong, and The Legend of Zelda. Yamauchi is today the richest man in Japan, and his company, with a market value of more than U.S. $85 billion, is called Nintendo.

From handmade nineteenth-century playing cards to the twenty-first-century Wii may seem like a leap of light-years, and in terms of the outer form of the products, it is. But the genius of Nintendo's success is that Yamauchi and Miyamoto found a way to completely reinvent the company yet remain unerringly true to its core: Nintendo = games based on memorable characters.

What is *your* core? This is what we were asking the HVAC people. Their core is not heating and air conditioning, it is helping people manage their physical environment.

Think Zappos is about shoes? Think again. The shoes Zappos sells are just shoes—but they have completely decommoditized the way they sell them.

"We hope that ten years from now," says Zappos CEO Tony

Hsieh, "people won't even realize that we started out selling shoes online, and that when you say 'Zappos,' they'll think, 'Oh, that's the place with the absolute best customer service.' And that doesn't even have to be limited to being an online experience. We've had customers email us and ask us if we would please start an airline, or run the IRS."[5]

That is their core: not their shoes, but their approach to customer service.

An interesting example of *find your core* presented itself in early 2007, when I spoke to an audience made up of leaders in the broadcast radio industry, and AM radio in particular. They were quite depressed about their business. Many of these people started out decades ago as broadcasters and eventually bought their own stations. Now they fear they are being put out of business by digital radio and other media. They were mourning for the good old days.

When I asked them to list for me the developments they were most excited about, they couldn't name one. Instead, they ran down the list of all the things they were scared of and worried about. There was satellite radio. There were podcasts and blogs and all these new media. How could an ancient media like AM radio possibly compete?

What it boiled down to, they said, was this: *Radio is old media—and dying.*

But radio isn't dead at all. When they thought *radio,* they were thinking of the box, the device. But that's not what they do. They are not in the business of the device—they are in the business of *sponsored audio content.* That's their core.

"When you think about the good old days, the golden age of radio," I asked my audience, "what are the shining moments that come to mind?"

Because this was a crowd of older business owners, I listed FDR's fireside chats; Edward R. Murrow's WWII broadcasts; "Who's on first?" and "Only the Shadow knows."

"These are the great, classic moments of radio—and not one of them has anything to do with the *device* or the technology that drove those particular broadcasts. They are great moments of *sponsored audio content*, memorable events in sound. And here's the good news: there are many more such great moments ahead of us than there are behind us. Radio is not *old* media, it's *timeless* media that needs reinvention.

"For example, if your business is generating great moments in audio content, why not give it to people on their cell phones? What if you created a collaboration with the major cell phone carriers and made your programming available locally over people's phones? Cell phone companies know an awful lot about their individual customer profiles. You could tailor your audio content offerings to specific demographic groups and even personal interests, via menu selection—instead of broadcasting, *narrowcasting.*

"Let's talk for a moment about satellite radio. It may look threatening, but satellite radio has penetrated less than 2 percent of the market, and still hasn't made the leap from cars to homes, if it ever does. And honestly, the entire concept of satellite radio has a short shelf life anyway. With broadband wireless going in everywhere, consumers will all be going toward online streaming digital audio and video to their phones and cars.

"Instead of seeing Sirius and XM as your enemy," I suggested to the group, "think of them as your friend—because, thanks to an endless list of customized programming, they have brought the whole idea of radio back to people's minds again. So they've done you a valuable service: they have been one gigantic advertisement for the concept *radio*. Now the question is, what will that concept mean?

"In the past your business model has been based on competing with each other. That's probably not going to work anymore. You're in a position where you stand to gain by collaborating together. Collaborating in what? In finding ways to *completely reinvent and redefine radio* for the twenty-first century."

Then we talked about HD radio. At the time, HD radio had begun showing up as a feature in new cars. The most decommoditizing feature about HD was that, because it received data as well as sound signals, it could display a little ticker telling you the call letters of the station and the name of the song that's playing. Still, fewer than 1 percent of consumers polled showed any interest in actually buying an HD radio. It was just not catching on.

"That data display trick is pretty neat," I said, "but that's today. Let's look at the visible future. Instead of having to take your eyes off the road to try and *read* what's on your radio screen, why not have the radio use text-to-voice and read that scrolling text to you out loud?

"Let's say it's snowing out. Since all the snowplows are giving real-time information on road conditions to the states' highway departments, and the highway departments can put that information right out through the local radio stations—*your* stations—to the HD radios in people's cars. And thanks to the GPS in those cars, the station will know each car's exact location. When you ask your radio, 'What are the conditions ahead?' it can tell you how things look at the intersection of Calhoun and Capital, four blocks ahead. *The intersection there hasn't been salted yet,* your HD radio tells you, *but if you take a left in two blocks, on Pilgrim Drive, you should be in the clear.* Since a radio station also has a Web site, it can now be a multimedia station, not just radio. Don't think satellite or HD, think transformation of sponsored audio content.

"As far as I can see," I told the group, "the good old days are not only *not* behind us, they're actually ahead of us. We're creating the good old days right now. But you'll have to reinvent and redefine what you do, from top to bottom."

Newspapers and books are two industries that are going through much the same thing: they are both struggling to survive in the face of the digital onslaught. To the degree that they attempt to cling to their version of One Dependability Square, they will die; to the degree that they completely reinvent themselves in the context of new technology, they will survive and thrive.

Hundreds of newspapers have created online editions—but the great majority have gone out of business or continued declining anyway. Why? Because they did the equivalent of building buggy whips into automobiles—they used new technology to do old things. Most online newspaper editions have been redundant instead of complementary. They haven't given us something revolutionary, they're just giving us the same stories in digital form. Those few that have been able to stake a claim in the future have explored all sorts of new features—complementary content, interactive columns, blogged updates, tweets, narrowcasting menu choices, and the like.

E-book readers had been around for years, but digital books didn't really start to catch on until the introduction of innovations such as the Amazon Kindle and Apple iPad. Why not? Because up till that point, nobody had stepped up and actually reinvented the book. For years, an e-book was nothing more than a PDF version of the printed book. That's not really an electronic book, it's just a digitized paper book. A genuine electronic book would have interviews with the author, audio and video commentary, dynamic hyperlinks to a wide range of background information, and all sorts of other features that are impossible to include in the print book—not just a PDF version of the printed page. Once the book started being genuinely reinvented, it became freed from being linear and gained the capacity to be nonlinear as well, from display-only to interactive and participatory. And by the way, does that mean old-fashioned paper-based books are going the way of the dinosaur? Not at all—and you already know why: the *both/and* principle.

The great irony is that those who stop gazing into the rearview mirror and look clearly into the visible future, who seize the initiative and actively reinvent and redefine their field, whether it is radio, newspaper, books, or anything else, will not only command the market lead in the *new* technology but also take the lead in the *old*. Because broadcast radio, pulp newsprint, and printed-page books are not going away. The principle of *both/and* tells us that the new and the old will continue to coexist side by side—and it is those visionaries who redefine the entire market category and integrate all of its various media expressions who will lead the way and profit handsomely. (Please check out www.flashforesight.com as an example.)

>>>Be Extraordinary

A friend of mine, Lillian Montalto, has a real estate business in Massachusetts. Her husband, Bob Bohlen, has his agency in Michigan. They are both star agents with amazing sales records; combining both their best years of personal sales, the couple did a total annual business of more than half a billion dollars.

Not surprisingly, I was a little curious about just how they did that. They were not selling high-end office parks, apartment complexes, or other commercial properties; they were selling *residential* real estate. Half a billion dollars' worth, in one year?! Even if these were pretty high-end, let's say $2 million homes, that's 250 sales in a single year—one completed sale every day and a half! So one day I asked Lillian how she does what she does.

"I decided I wanted to take all the pain out of the process of finding or selling a home," she told me, "and then moving from the old house to the new. So I started thinking up creative ways I might do that."

For example, Lillian was one of the first Realtors® to set up a personal Web page for each customer, where she puts photographs of each room and the different views out each window and around the yard. She includes short video clips with narration, and highlights local attractions and places of interest for each individual family member. She takes care to manage communications with each customer in the way that particular customer prefers, whether that means face-to-face meetings, phone calls, e-mail, text messages, or whatever.

"When I was on vacation once in England," she said, "I really enjoyed riding in those English taxicabs, where passengers face each other in the backseats. I thought that would be a great way to show properties."

So she purchased an English taxi and had it shipped to the States. Now, when she drives prospective clients around, she has a driver take them to the property while she sits in a backseat across from her clients, answering their questions. Because the English taxi is unusual, people like to tell their friends about it, helping to spread the word about this wonderful agent.

When it comes time to make the actual move, she provides a moving truck free of charge. If her clients have children, she helps evaluate the school systems based on the clients' needs, and when it's time to register the kids for school, she takes care of it. If you need a cleaning service, doctor, or dentist, she finds out who is best in the area and makes recommendations. And their Web sites are in more than a dozen different languages.

These are just a few examples of the innovative things Lillian and Bob have done to give their clients an extraordinary experience. If your real estate agent did all that, would you tell your friends about her services? I sure would—and I have.

Most agents would say they couldn't afford to do all those things. This star agent realized she couldn't afford *not* to. At some point, she made a decision not to be an ordinary real estate agent. She decided to be *extraordinary.* She completely decommoditized her real estate business—and she honored her core, which was to be the best at helping people make a transition to a new life.

The principle of *find your core* applies not only to your business, your company, or your industry; it also applies to you personally. There is only one of you on the planet. Each one of us is unique. The *don't compete* principle puts each of us on a quest to be the best *me* that we can be.

This takes some directed self-discovery. I believe that we all have multiple talents, but there is one special gift in each of us, typically hidden somewhere within the talents. Many of us end up in careers where we may be using one or even several of our talents, but this will take us only so far. If you are able to create a career that allows you to tap into your true gift, and then use your talents to support your gift, there is no limit to how far you can continue to improve and excel.

>>>On Batteries and Sandwiches

Before closing this chapter, let's look at two more areas ripe for redefining and reinventing. The first is the humble battery.

As we become progressively detethered from everything through an accelerating increase in mobility, we are becoming a society that increasingly relies on batteries. The personal computer and cell phone industries have already spawned a burgeoning global appetite for more battery power—but all of that is nothing compared to what will happen as we start getting serious about reinventing the automobile as a battery-powered device.

Which is great, except for one thing. Actually, one element: lithium.

This soft, silvery element is the lightest and least dense of all the metals, traits that, combined with its intense reactivity, make it an ideal element for creating powerful batteries that don't weigh much or take up much room—increasingly valuable traits in a world of ever-increasing demands for mobility.

Lithium is the element at the core of the batteries that run our cell phones, our personal computers, and, increasingly, our cars. The Chevy Volt runs on a lithium battery; so does BMW's hybrid MINI. All the auto companies, from Mercedes and Mitsubishi to Toyota and VW, are looking to lithium to power future generations of green cars.

Unfortunately, lithium is also a comparatively rare element—and it is dwindling fast. A good 50 percent of the world's extractable reserves are located in the world's largest desert salt flats, the Salar de Uyuni region of Bolivia—a country that has been consistently resistant to seeing its lithium resources mined by foreign powers. And their own plans to process the metal are proceeding so slowly and with such modest targets, experts predict we will start seeing significant shortages as early as 2015.

"The car manufacturers will have to strike a balance between how quickly they manufacture with the supply of metal [that is, lithium]," said one mining expert in a recent *BBC News* report, "because they don't want to drive the price up to such an extent that the cars get priced out of the market." Bolivia's minister for mining, Luis Alberto Eschazu, "has a stark message for Western firms," added the report: " 'The capitalist leaders have to change.' "[6]

Lithium is a future problem that we are eventually going to have to skip. We need to reinvent the battery. This isn't a possibility: this is a certainty.*

So how do we reinvent the battery?

As with Dan Gautschi's alternative to oil, which we looked at in Chapter 5, algae may hold one answer here, too. In September 2009 researchers at the Ångström Laboratory of Sweden's Uppsala University announced their invention of a flexible, paper-thin battery constructed primarily from algae, paper, and saltwater, and using no metals whatsoever.

"We have long hoped to find some sort of constructive use for the material from algae blooms, and have now been shown this to be possible," said researcher Maria Strømme, a professor of nanotechnology and leader of the Uppsala research group that created the new battery. "This creates new possibilities for large-scale production of environmentally friendly, cost-effective, lightweight energy storage systems."[7]

The new battery is composed of extremely thin layers of conducting polymer just forty to fifty nanometers or billionths of a meter wide coating algae cellulose fibers only twenty to thirty nanometers wide that were collected into paper sheets.

"They're very easy to make," says Strømme. "You don't need advanced equipment."

The researchers are exploring new applications where batteries are not currently being used at all.

"What if you could put batteries inside wallpaper to charge

---

*As this book was going to press, the Pentagon announced the discovery of lithium reserves in the Ghazni province of eastern Afghanistan. That could be very good news—if the discovery had been in, say, Arizona or Australia rather than Afghanistan! With the Taliban retaining a powerful presence in the region, this happens to be a geographical hot spot even more politically difficult than Bolivia. Given the explosive instability of this war-torn area and near-total lack of infrastructure, this find isn't likely to have much impact on the total lithium supply for some time to come. Furthermore, exactly how vast these reserves really are remains to be determined—and substantiated. The visible future is that we are facing a clear need for an alternative to lithium batteries.

sensors in your home?" says Strømme. "If you could put this into clothes, could you couple that with detectors to analyze sweat from your body to tell if there's anything wrong?"

Strømme is quick to point out that they are not looking at the algae battery as a replacement for the lithium ion battery. Be that as it may, it certainly points in some intriguing directions.

Finally, let's look at that other area that is so ripe for redefinition and reinvention. To find it, we need look no further than our next meal.

Earlier I wrote that in the late 1800s, coal was not a problem we needed to solve but one we needed to skip, and that the same is true today of oil. But with coal and oil, at least we are generally aware that the problem exists. There are other pressing examples of the coal question that we aren't even close to skipping yet—because we haven't yet recognized them. It's hard to skip a problem if you don't see it coming in the first place. With energy, and battery-powered vehicles in specific, we have a problem with lithium. With agriculture and our food supply, it's phosphorus.

The nitrogenous substance phosphorus is an essential element of every living cell. Its name meaning literally "light-bearing element," it is a key component of DNA, RNA, ATP, and the phospholipids that form cell membranes. Phosphate rock, the predominant source of usable phosphorus, was first mined in the mid-1800s. A mainstay ingredient in the fertilizer industry, it grew during the twentieth century to become the cornerstone of modern agriculture worldwide—as essential to every aspect of our food supply as elemental phosphorus is to every living cell.

The problem with phosphorus is that, as with coal, oil, and lithium, we are using it up. As recently as 2007, some scientists were still saying we had perhaps another 300 years' worth of phosphorus reserves available. By 2009 those estimates had been revised down to *thirty* years (the experts most likely forgot to account for the billion people entering the lower middle class over the next decade who will have an increased need for a more diversified diet)—and even that figure may be optimistic.

"U.S. reserves are gone inside twenty years," says Mark

Edwards, PhD, professor of strategic marketing and sustainability at Arizona State University and award-winning author of *Crash! The Demise of Fossil Foods and the Rise of Abundance*. "And well before those reserves are depleted, phosphorus will become unaffordable to most farmers, through runaway market price increases as well as hoarding by a few phosphorus-rich countries and speculators." China, notes Edwards (whose background includes U.S. Naval Academy training in engineering, oceanography, and meteorology), recently slapped a 175 percent tariff on its phosphate rock, essentially cutting off all hope of export. Outside of China and the dwindling indigenous U.S. reserves, the world's main sources are mostly Arab countries—many of them not currently the friendliest of trading partners.

Within the next two decades, in other words, phosphorus supplies will have begun petering out, and prices will have skyrocketed to the point that food will be simply unaffordable to much of the world's population, resulting in massive starvation and civil unrest.

That is, unless we reinvent our agriculture.

Actually, it isn't just a question of phosphorus, although that is one major and dramatic symptom of the larger problem. The issue is that our entire model of agricultural production is rapidly becoming unsustainable. Our current agricultural machine, to imagine it that way, uses a massive amount of water; consumes huge amounts of fossil fuels; generates a large amount of polluting runoff; and eats up great gobs of phosphorus without recycling it.

That last point is worth examining. In the days of preindustrial agriculture, most of the phosphorus that went into crop production came back out again and reentered the production cycle, in the form of animal wastes, "green manure" cover crops, and other biodegradably recycling materials. Agrarian age phosphorus went through an average of fifty cycles, according to Edwards, before being used up. And in today's farms? Phosphorus inputs go through an average of *one* cycle. That's it.

"We're not going to get back to fifty cycles," says Edwards, "but we could get back to forty or so, and that would be enough to turn things around. But we'd have to do our agriculture totally differently."

Edwards points out that while modern, petrochemical-based agriculture is clearly not a viable path into the future, current organic farming practices are equally unsustainable, in part because growing enough green manure and vegetative wastes for organic fertilizer would take several times more arable land than is available for growing food.

"Organic and modern farmers," he adds, "are equally at risk from the vagaries of global climate change, including temperature spikes, drought, fierce storms, sea and irrigation salt invasion, erosion, rising ocean levels, and pest infestation. Organic farming often suffers from low productivity, pest and weed invasion while consuming as much freshwater as modern agriculture."

If modern, industrial age agriculture won't work, and more traditional agrarian age agriculture won't work, what do we do? We reinvent agriculture altogether.

For example, what if we created a new approach to food production that used *no* fresh water, *no* fossil fuels, generated *no* toxic runoff, and completely recycled the majority of its phosphorus? And what if we did this without taking over any of the arable land currently in production, using only marginal lands that are otherwise useless?

Impossible, right? You probably see where this is going.

Actually, we've already seen a clue to at least one potential answer, once again in our discussion of skipping the oil problem in Chapter 5. The class of organisms Dan Gautschi is using to produce a nonpetroleum oil also happens to produce an exceptionally fine grade of fertilizer—without fresh water, fossil fuels, or the need for conventionally arable land.

Algae.

There are some 4,000 different species of land plants on earth; there are 10 *million* species of algae. Some, as we saw in Chapter 5, are effective at producing an oil that can be used for fuel; many others can create excellent fertilizer. Edwards advocates a new model of food production he terms *abundant agriculture,* based largely on using algae as its primary input. Much like Gautschi's algal oil production model, it is an ingenious model that *skips* (rather than attempting to *solve*) virtually all the conventional model's defects and applies a *go opposite* strategy.

What's more, it not only addresses the issue of agricultural production, it also supplies a solution to another problem we haven't yet addressed directly in this book, but which looms as one of the largest challenges of our visible future. In fact, it's not only a future problem, it is already a clear and present danger: shortage of life-supporting water.

Drought and water rationing have already become common occurrences in some of the most agriculture-intensive areas of the world, yet we have experienced only a foretaste of the water shortages on the time horizon. Amazingly, reinvented-industry models like Edwards's and Gautschi's turn this problem into an opportunity, because algal production plants actually take in brackish and otherwise unusable water and produce clean, drinkable water as an *output*.

It is no accident that algae seem to turn up at the heart of so many of these creative, outside-the-box flash foresight solutions to some of our biggest problems. Algae are about as opposite from *corn*—the modern, cultivated, hybridized plant we have become so obsessed with in our modern food and energy systems—as an organism could be. They are, as Edwards points out, "the earth's oldest growing system." Algae were the organisms that originally transformed the earth from a toxic (from our point of view) methane-rich wasteland into an oxygen-rich environment capable of sustaining carbon-based life forms. And they can do it again—except that, as Edwards points out, "We cannot afford to wait another 400 million years for nature to act; algae will need our help."

And that sums up the reinvention imperative nicely: *We cannot afford to wait.*

You may know the popular expression, "If we do what we've always done, we'll get what we've always had." What we've always done is wait until the manure hits the fan—and *then* start crisis managing.

When do we go out and buy security systems for our homes? After we've been robbed. When do we start exercising? When the doctor finishes our checkup and says, "Hey, you're huge!" When do we start working on our relationship? As we're walking up the steps to divorce court: "Should we talk?" Yet the dangers were all plainly there to see, and so were the opportunities—if we had been looking.

This has always been a habit of human nature, but today it has become a habit we critically need to change, because there is no longer any viable reaction time. We can't afford to wait for the famine, for the crisis, for the breakdown.

Thus the question becomes, will we change from inside out, or outside in? Will we let ourselves see the opportunities and become motivated by foresight, or wait until we are seeing the crises happen before our eyes, and become motivated by hindsight? Will we try to keep living at One Dependability Square, or move to One Transformation Square?

It's time to stop mourning the "good old days" and start reinventing the new ones.

>>>CHAPTER 6 ACTION STEPS

Reinventing our business based on the visible changes taking place has always been a powerful strategy, but today it has become a continuous imperative. Reinvention is not the same as adding a twist or a new feature; once something is reinvented, it never goes back to being the way it was before.

- *Forget competing; instead,* ***leapfrog the competition*** *by redefining anything and everything about your business.*
- ***Decommoditize continuously.*** *Look for creative ways to make the mundane exceptional and transform the normal into the extraordinary.*
- ***Reinvent the old by using it in new ways.*** *Remember the critical care nurses with corporations' discarded pagers: find new ways to use existing technology creatively. It's not the tool—it's how you use it.*

Reinventing ourselves as it relates to our careers has also become an imperative if we are to thrive in this period of tech-driven transformation.

- ***Find your core.*** *Once you start to reinvent yourself around your gift and align your talents to support your gift, you will discover a career in which you can grow and keep raising the bar forever.*
- ***Be extraordinary.*** *Take the time to examine not only what you do, but how you do it. Ask yourself: "Am I imitating or innovating?" What could you do to take your business and yourself to the next level? Look at what the competition is doing, and do something else.*

>>> CHAPTER SEVEN

Direct Your Future

I am standing in my brother Jack's living room, watching my nephew Ethan map out a strategy with four friends. Oblivious to distractions and wholly absorbed in their shared task, they discuss the complex tools, techniques, and tactics each rapidly unfolding situation demands. I watch, captivated, as Ethan memorizes reams of data, variables, and contingencies: nothing is written down, yet he has assimilated far more complex information in the last twenty minutes than the typical classroom might expect of him in a day, perhaps in a week. I marvel at the fluid ease with which he and his four friends collaborate, despite the distances.

You might think those distances would form a pretty imposing barrier. After all, at this moment one of Ethan's friends is sitting in *his* living room in Russia, another in India, the third in Australia, and the fourth in South Korea. But the thousands of miles melt into nothing as the participants collaborate on their shared objectives. The five boys, some of them staying up way past their bedtimes, are playing a fully immersive, three-dimensional, photorealistic, interactive strategy game on their Xbox 360s.

Ethan is twelve years old.

Earlier, I asked him how long it has taken him to learn all the basic components and scenarios of this sophisticated game. "Oh, forty hours, I guess, maybe more," he replied. Forty hours of complex content—and no written notes. The next time you hear someone say, "Kids these days, they just can't memorize . . . they've got no attention span, all they do is sit around and play video games," picture Ethan and his globally dispersed teammates.

I think about the last few corporate teams I've consulted for, and wonder: could they muster the level of concentration, memorization, and technology-enabled collaboration demonstrated by Ethan and his team?

Now Ethan mutters a few words under his breath. He's not talking to himself: through a headset, he's audioconferencing with his team. In fact, through cordoned-off sections of the television's widescreen, they're also videoconferencing. In real time. (How often do you do *that* with your business colleagues? Ethan does it all the time, and so do his friends.)

I check my watch. Ethan is about to time travel. Not for pretend, not as part of the game. He is about to time travel *for real.*

"Time to go, buddy!" Jack calls out. Ethan looks up, sighs, tells his friends, "I hafta split," and shuts down his console. Ethan is a sharp twenty-first-century kid with a twenty-first-century mindset, about to spend his next eight hours in a twentieth-century building getting a twentieth-century education based on a nineteenth-century model. It's time to make his daily trek backward in time, from the Xbox to the ABCbox.

It's time for school.

Twelve-year-old Xiaojian is also about to time travel; like Ethan, he does it every day. About the time Ethan goes to bed tonight, Xiaojian will be getting up on the other side of the world and preparing for his daily journey, except that Xiaojian will be time traveling in the opposite direction from Ethan. When he leaves the rice paddies and soybean fields of his village for his district's newly constructed school, he will leave his agrarian past and step into a new realm of unlimited possibilities.

For Ethan, going from home to school is a journey into the past. For Xiaojian, it's an excursion into the future. This is about more than the tools and tutelage of the classroom: it is also in the attitudes and vibrant spirit of learning that surround him and permeate the atmosphere from the moment he steps into the building. At school, Xiaojian and his classmates don't just study, they study *hard*. While they may not have the technology Ethan's school has, their future is alive with opportunity, and they know it. They're eager to learn all they can, because they know the future is brimming over with potential. They have big dreams.

Ethan's classmates . . . they're not so sure about their dreams. When they look into the future, they aren't too excited about what they see. They look at their older brothers and sisters who are leaving college and going to work for insurance firms, ad agencies, and government posts and are finding themselves just as bored in their new jobs as they were in their old schools, and even less secure about where they're headed in the long term. Ethan and his friends know about layoffs, outsourcing, and offshoring, too. They hear their parents talk. They catch the headlines, and the messages behind the headlines. They're no fools.

The future looks kind of grim. Life is better on the Xbox.

Danny is twelve, too, and he has no doubt about his future. He knows exactly where he's headed: jail or the morgue, probably both.

I meet Danny on a visit to *his* time machine, which happens to be an inner-city junior high school flanked by abandoned storefronts and scruffy, broken-down apartment buildings. Approaching the building, I note the bars, wire mesh, and coating of grime that cover the windows. What kind of vision would one see looking out through that portal? I will soon find out.

Passing through the metal detector at the entrance, I get my clearance from the security guards. Metal detectors? This isn't how I remember junior high. But then, that was way back in the twentieth century.

As you know, teaching science was how my career path began,

and even today, I like to stay connected and involved with young people. The future is my passion, and it has always seemed to me that if we really want to see into the future, we need to stay close to what's happening with our nation's youth, because they are the crucible where the future is being formed. Today I'm getting a lesson in the particular kind of future being formed in the crucible of Danny's world.

During the day I have the chance to spend some time with Danny and a few of his friends. As we get to know each other, I ask them the question adults always seem to get around to asking kids: *What do you want to be when you grow up?*

"How do you see your future?" I ask Danny and his friends. "What do you see ahead of you, when you reach twenty or thirty?"

Their answers stun me: none of them expects to reach the age of twenty.

I probe further. Not long ago, Danny was witness to a drive-by shooting. Many of his buddies have knife scars; a few show me bullet wounds. These are junior high school kids in public schools in the USA. Do they care about math, science, history? Of course not. If they aren't going to see their twentieth birthday, what's the point? Today, they tell me, they've just come from a health class where the teacher went on about the dangers of promiscuity and the importance of staying away from drugs and preventing AIDS. "Safe sex!" they say with a laugh. "If you're gonna get whacked before you hit twenty, what's the difference?"

Three kids, three time machines, three snapshots of the future. Which one is most accurate? The truth is, none of them is set in stone. They each represent a soft trend, a view of the future that can still be influenced or changed. Change what future they see, and you will change what actions they take—which will change their future.

Hard trends provide accurate certainties about specific elements of the future—but combined with soft trends and our ability to influence them, how those elements play out is highly plastic. There are only seven notes in the diatonic scale, yet there is an infinite array of melodies into which they may be woven. How that future unfolds is determined to a great degree by the choices we make, and those choices are determined largely by what we see in front of us.

To a startling extent, in other words, our vision of the future is a self-fulfilling prophecy. Change your view of the future, and you *direct* your future.

In this book we've taken a broad view of our metamorphosing landscape and the kinds of transformations we can make to take fullest advantage of the possibilities in front of us. Flash foresight can yield all sorts of creative, innovative, and powerfully effective strategies. But flash foresight is about more than tools, strategies, and plans.

Flash foresight starts with seeing the certainty of hard trends, and based on that, learning how to anticipate accurately. It also lets us see soft trends, as factors we can influence to shape a better future. But it's not enough to *see hard trends and soft trends, anticipate, transform, go opposite, skip your biggest problems*, and *reinvent yourself.* These are all valuable and vital steps, but there is something larger and more embracing: we need to actively shape our own future.

Directing your future is the conscious exercise of your creative capacity to envision and rewrite your future life and career that wraps all the other flash foresight principles together.

If Martin Luther King Jr. had stood on the steps of the Lincoln Memorial on that hot August day in 1963 and declaimed, "I have a plan," he would have sounded like a politician, and nobody would remember the words. But that's not what he said.

Ethan, Xiaojian, and Danny each have different visions for the future. Imagine the choices each of them will make and the actions each will take. Our vision of the future drives our choices and our behaviors, which produce our outcomes and shape our lives. We become what we dream. Which means that if we want to know what we are becoming, we need to ask, what are we dreaming?

>>>Futureview

My friend Mitchell's life is a testament to the power of vision. Early in his adult life, while working as a streetcar tour guide in San Francisco, Mitchell went through a freak motorcycle accident that burned off parts of his fingers and left him with burns over two-thirds of his body surface. After a lengthy and painful series of operations and skin grafts, Mitchell picked himself up and moved to Colorado, where he became a successful businessman and eventually mayor of his town.

Incredibly, a few years later Mitchell was in a second life-threatening accident: while flying a small plane, its wings iced up and took him down. Now scarred and wheelchair-bound, Mitchell looked into the future and once again saw not limitations but new possibilities.

"Before I was paralyzed," he commented, "there were 10,000 things I could do. Now there are 9,000. I could dwell on the 1,000 I've lost—or on the 9,000 I have left."

Mitchell became a political activist, campaigning widely for the cause of conservation. Today he gives speeches all over the world, and devotes a good deal of his time speaking for free at prisons, inner-city schools and the like. A few years ago Mitchell sent me a picture of himself, strapped to a friend's back, in the air. They were skydiving.

Another friend, Jerry Coffee, was shot down over Vietnam and held in a cell for seven years, where he was tortured and beaten regularly. All he had was his cell and a small tin can for a toilet. "When you have everything taken away," says Jerry, "it's amazing to find how much you still have left." What Jerry had left was his faith and his capacity to envision.

In his mind, Jerry began combing through his memories. He revisited concerts he had attended, reread books he had read. At one point, he decided to reread *Moby-Dick*. He began with its famous opening, "Call me Ishmael," and then tried to remember what came next, and then what came next, and next. Like Mitchell, Jerry now travels the world inspiring people. He speaks about the prisons we so often create by the limitations we put on our view of reality. As with Mitchell, he was subjected to horrendous changes from the outside in—but made the decision to trump circumstance through the changes he made from the inside out.

The bumper sticker says, "Shit happens." Perhaps so, but humanity has an absolutely astonishing capacity to turn dung into fuel. How is it possible for people like Mitchell and Jerry to so transform their lives? Through the power of vision. Mitchell and Jerry have both cultivated the capacity to decide what they see.

This is the skill at the heart of flash foresight: the ability to project yourself into the future and then look back at your present position from the future's point of view—what I call your *futureview*.[1]

I coined the term *futureview* several decades ago to refer to the mental picture we each hold of our future existence. This is not the same thing as a goal, plan, ambition, or aspiration. Futureview is not what we *hope* for or are *trying* to create—it is the picture we actually hold, for better or for worse, of what we *expect and believe* about our future.

The reason I coined the term is that most of us are not fully aware of what that picture is. We have it—*everyone* has a futureview—but often without realizing it or examining what it looks like. But not being aware of it does not mean it doesn't control us, because it most certainly does.

Becoming aware of your own futureview puts a tremendously powerful strategic tool in your hands. It gives you the controls of your own future. Your futureview determines which actions you'll take, and which you'll avoid taking. Different futureviews create different realities.

In the same day, thousands of people buy a given company's stock, and thousands more dump it. What's the difference? There is only one: their futureview.

Danny's picture of the future is heartbreakingly clear: death, most likely by violence, while still in his teens. Based on that picture, Danny is making choices every day that virtually assure that it will come true. If he and his friends had a different picture of their own future, would they be making different choices?

You might recall from Chapter 4 the *skip it* strategy I used with junior high school kids, teaching them to write by using cassette recorders. However, that wasn't the only flash foresight strategy we used; I also showed every one of those students how to *direct their future.* On the first day of class, I showed them the grade book; next to each of their names was an A. They had never had an A; they were used to D's and F's.

"Let me explain how this works," I said. "I'm going to reveal to you all the secrets about how you can keep that A. The moment you start to lose it, I'm going to tell you, and I'll also tell you exactly what you can do to get it back. I'm going to tell you all about what's going to be on every test, and how to prepare for it so you'll pass it.

"I'm going to assume that every one of you is smart until you prove to me you're dumb. I'm also going to assume that you're honest, unless you prove that you're a liar."

The skepticism on their faces was plain to see. Still, I'd gotten their attention. Seeing an A next to their names was a new experience for them. They were listening. They weren't used to being respected; they weren't used to anyone believing in them. They were used to the opposite of those things. I was starting them off at the top, instead of at the bottom. Instead of bad kids, I declared they were good kids. There were getting a visceral experience of *go opposite.*

"I'm not going to teach you science," I added. "Instead, I'm going to turn you all into scientists. And I'll prove it to you. In one month, I'm going to bring in the principal and ask him all the same questions I'll be asking you, and you'll find that you know more than he does." A month later, that's exactly what happened.

How did it work out? By the end of the school year, they'd all gone from low and failing grades to C's, B's, and, yes, even a good number of legitimate A's. There was not a single D or F in the class.

What changed? In other classes, the teachers would say, "Okay, today we're going to do a review for the test tomorrow," and the kids would think: *Who cares?* They wouldn't have a problem until the bad grades came, anyway—and by then it would be too late to do anything about it. All I did was show them how they could solve that problem before it happened.

To them, the idea of doing well in a class like this was an impossibility. To them, the image of any of them getting an A was invisible. I just made it visible—which made it possible.

>>>Managing Futureview

Volkswagen has a vision for its future.

In 2007, just months after Toyota had officially taken the title of world's leading automaker away from GM, Volkswagen CEO Martin Winkerton announced that *his* company had set the goal of unseating Toyota within the next ten years. Its target was met with heavy skepticism; the following year VW sold a mere 6.3 million vehicles to Toyota's 9 million. Yet by the first quarter of 2009, smack in the midst of the worst months of the global recession, the German company astonished onlookers by dramatically increasing its share of the global market, and by the end of the year VW had indeed overtaken both GM and Toyota as the world's leading automaker—eight years ahead of schedule.

Volkswagen has taken great care to manage its futureview. What is GM's futureview? It's still hard to say.

As an executive, are you managing the futureview of your employees, regardless of current economic conditions? There are people working in your company right now who are already online or on the phone looking for another job. Why? Because of their futureview of working for your company. There are also people who are planning on staying. Why? Because of their futureview of working for your company.

Are you managing the futureview of your business partners, your suppliers, your investors? What about the futureview of your customers?

As a parent, are you managing the futureview of your kids? There are kids who are planning to go to college, and kids who are planning to go into drugs. What's the difference? Their futureview.

Most companies put zero effort or energy into directing their people's futureview, which means for all practical purposes, they put zero effort into directing their future. All the "strategic planning," "scenario planning," and other systematic approaches to designing an intended (read: hoped-for) future often fall short of the goal. In a world gone vertical, they typically come to *nothing.* Not without a clear focus on managing people's futureviews.

Your futureview determines the future *you*. The vision we have of our future determines our behaviors, which determine our outcomes. In a very real sense, our futureview is *everything.* And yet it is something we so seldom think about, we hardly even have the vocabulary to talk about it.

When I want to take a break, I love to take my Harley-Davidson out on the local roads and open it up. One thing that's especially great about the Harley is that there's no reverse. That's true for us, too: we can never truly regain the past, we can only go forward into the future.

The Harley's rear wheel sits behind me, powered by the engine. That's exactly what our past does: it sits behind us, and we can use the momentum of our past to drive us forward. But it's the wheel in front that we use to determine our direction. And anyone who's ever ridden a motorcycle knows this cardinal rule of the road: *You head for where you're looking.* If there's a rock in the road and you look straight at it, you'll run right over it. Stare at that looming pothole ahead, and you're ending up in that pothole.

Where you look is where you go.

Where are you looking?

>>>The Lion City

At the southern tip of the Malay peninsula in Southeast Asia, about 130 miles north of the equator, there sits an ancient city called Singapura, Malay for "lion city." Settled by the British East India Company in the early 1800s as a key trading post, the Lion City remained occupied by the British for most of the next one and a half centuries, broken only by a short Japanese occupation during World War II. Then in 1963 the city emerged from British rule to become a part of a new nation called Malaysia, along with Malaya (greater Malaysia) and the Malaysian states Sabah and Sarawak. Two years later it split off to become the independent republic of Singapore.

Along with Vatican City and Monaco, Singapore is one of the world's few contemporary examples of the city-state. It is the smallest country in Asia, and also one of the most successful. While the Lion City may be as small as a mouse, it has become the mouse that roared.

When Singapore first achieved its independence, it faced an uphill climb: how would it survive as an independent nation when it possessed virtually none of the traditional elements of national power? A tiny landmass (at 272 square miles, a bit smaller than Philadelphia) with scarcely any physical resources, Singapore consisted of a multicultural patchwork of population groups lacking any unifying sense of national identity. Its relations with its neighbors were tenuous at best; its separation from Malaysia meant it had lost access to a major common market, and the subsequent withdrawal of the British presence there eliminated some 50,000 jobs, further hobbling its nascent economy.

Visiting Singapore in the 1960s, a journalist observed, "the country seemed nothing more than a developing country fishing village—one with no territory to speak of, and no natural resources other than people." Writing nearly a half century later in 2008, however, the same journalist added, "Today, Singapore is rich, sleek and sophisticated."[2]

The tiny city-state has emerged as an exemplar of the twenty-first-century abundance economy. Singapore has been called "the most business-friendly economy in the world."[3] It boasts the world's fourth-largest foreign exchange trading center (after London, New York City, and Tokyo). It sports a world-class life sciences research center, a stunning cash balance, and a standard-setting global airline. In terms of tonnage, its port is the busiest on the planet.

Famous for being the cleanest city in the world, Singapore is also distinctly modern. For example, since 2006, a municipal wireless system has provided free wireless access to every Singaporean resident throughout the nation. The city has also established itself as a hub of medical tourism, with about 200,000 foreigners seeking medical care there each year. By 2012, Singapore projects it will serve one million foreign patients annually, creating as many as 13,000 jobs and generating some U.S. $3 billion in the process.

And then there's that airline. Ranked sixth in the world in terms of international passengers carried and the second largest carrier in the world as measured by market capitalization, Singapore International Airlines was number seventeen on *Fortune* magazine's 2007 list of Most Admired Companies. Every road-warrior executive I've talked with privately considers it *the* best airline in the world.

When Apple Computer located a production facility in Singapore in 1981, it had intended only to produce electronic boards there for later assembly into finished machines in the United States, but its experience in Singapore was so successful, it decided to produce the entire computer there.

"Apple made this decision on the basis of Singaporean workers being able to duplicate the operations of its American plant," noted *Newsweek*'s Fareed Zakaria. "But the newly trained, highly motivated Singaporean workers not only replicated the old production process but began to make improvements that further lowered costs. There developed in Singapore a culture of innovation."[4]

That *culture of innovation* is no accident, and it is the force that consistently delivers triumph after triumph in such a wide range of industries. It comes down to one thing: *vision*. From the years of its independence on, Singapore has at every turn been led by an unwavering vision of its own future.

To be fair, there are certainly circumstantial factors in Singapore's success. Its landmass, while tiny, is perfectly located at a central juncture in international shipping lanes. Its original population included a significant stratum of British-educated elite, who were able to serve as a critical source of leadership for the nation's burgeoning industrial and financial growth. Geography, demographics, and a dearth of natural resources: these were Singapore's hard trends, the given seven notes of the scale. The astonishing success story that unfolded there is the melody that vision wove from those notes.

Singapore isn't perfect; it has its problems. Critics complain that it is run by an autocratic and authoritarian government, that its progress comes only at a great expense, including the loss of significant personal and political freedoms. Perhaps. But even if that is the case, this doesn't mean that such focused progress can occur only within that particular political context. The United States has experienced similar unanimity of effort at certain moments in its history, and has made extraordinarily innovative leaps forward during those times. We could do so again; indeed, we must—and so must every other nation.

>>>A Vision for Education

In 1997 Goh Chok Tong, Singapore's prime minister, announced a vision for the nation's school system, identified with the slogan "Thinking Schools, Learning Nation." According to the Singaporean Ministry of Education:

> *This vision describes a nation of thinking and committed citizens capable of meeting the challenges of the future, and an education system geared to the needs of the twenty-first century.*
>
> *Thinking Schools will be learning organizations in every sense, constantly challenging assumptions, and seeking better ways of doing things through participation, creativity and innovation. Thinking Schools will be the cradle of thinking students as well as thinking adults, and this spirit of learning should accompany our students even after they leave school.*
>
> *A Learning Nation envisions a national culture and social environment that promotes lifelong learning in our people. The capacity of Singaporeans to continually learn, both for professional development and for personal enrichment, will determine our collective tolerance for change.*

Singapore has in the last several years actively adopted a policy of focusing all its national resources onto the singular goal of innovation: its vision is to become the "innovation nation," the planet's leader in forward thinking. And its leaders have quite intelligently put a particular emphasis on education as the pivot point in that trajectory.

Years ago, the government created a program to hold an academic contest throughout Asia to find the students who could achieve the highest academic scores. They offered the winners a free college education in Singapore.

When I was at the Ernst & Young Entrepreneur of the Year event, I asked the head of government, "The investment in those students is high; I'm sure you realize that when they graduate, they all might leave. How does that work for Singapore?"

He said, "Some will leave, but we are betting that most will fall in love with Singapore—and fall in love, too." They were betting that these young students would find someone to settle down with there. So far, the gamble has paid off.

While we've focused on Singapore as a geo-economic object lesson in the power of vision, the Lion City is just one example among many. We could just as easily have picked, say, South Korea.

In the early days of the Web's proliferation, South Korea made the decision to invest in high bandwidth to empower its citizenry and its long-standing focus on education. South Korean students routinely test at the top tier in science and math. Why? Because they *decided* to. Their vision was to be the best-educated and best-connected society in the world, and reality followed that vision.

Or we could have traveled six thousand miles westward and chosen Finland.

In a recent test-survey of about 400,000 fifteen-year-old students from fifty-seven countries, the Finnish students took first place overall. One reason is the high value Finnish culture places on reading. Asked why, even without the high-pressured push to high test scores found in, say, South Korean or Japanese culture, Finnish youth are such exceptional students, one school principal said, "We don't have oil or other riches. Knowledge is the thing Finnish people have."[5]

Like the Singaporeans, the Finns place a value on learning: it's a core part of their vision of who they are, and who they aspire to be.

And America? In that same global test survey, U.S. students placed at right about the middle of the pack, where we have been for decades now: we have become a nation of perfect C students.

In 1999 only 41 percent of U.S. eighth graders had a math teacher who had majored in mathematics at the undergraduate level or even studied the subject for teacher certification. (The international average was 71 percent.) It is hard to share a passion for a subject you are not trained or qualified to teach. And by the way, most of those 41 percent are just about to retire.

In recent tests of general knowledge in mathematics and science, U.S. twelfth graders performed well below the international average for the twenty-one participating countries. An advanced mathematics assessment was conducted with students who had taken advanced math in fifteen countries; eleven of the fifteen countries outperformed the United States, and the remaining three scored at about the same level as the United States. In other words, we and a few others were scraping along at the bottom of the barrel.

By every measure, our academic performance in the United States has reached dismal depths; but the real picture is worse than even the numbers suggest. Remember the scenarios of Xiaojian, Ethan, and Danny, and you have a fuller sense of the situation. Education is time travel—but time travel in which direction, and into what kind of reality?

One of education's perennial challenges is that it is generally the last place new technology reaches. Here's the traditional path a new technology typically takes as it works its way through society.

- An innovation originates in military/aerospace research.
- Then it shows up in kids' toys.
- Eventually it migrates to business, where it is implemented all over the world.
- And finally it shows up in education—with little funding and no instructions.

It's no accident that the latest generation of video games are capturing our kids' attention; in fact, this is the result of careful research and creative innovation. In 2002 Nintendo invested more than $140 million in research and development—about twice the amount the United States spent that same year on research and development for education for the entire nation. Nintendo (Wii), Sony (PlayStation), and Microsoft (Xbox) are in the same relationship to American formal education that iTunes and the iPod are to the Big Four record labels. Rather than resist them or rail against them, we should be embracing these technologies for the time-travel potential they represent, and using them to automate those aspects of education that are not fit for humans to teach.

Like every other institution in our society, education cannot be fixed simply by changing it; it needs to be *transformed*. As with agriculture, energy, health care, and every other sector, we need to bring digital intelligence to our educational systems. We need to *automate* education, and at the same time, *humanize* it.

My brother Jack (Ethan's dad) worked in the education division of my company for twenty-five years, and has taken our work into more than 5,000 schools. Here's an insight we have gleaned in the process: teaching a kid how to multiply numbers or diagram sentences is not a task that should be taking up our human teachers' valuable time. (We like to say that every teacher we ever saw try to teach kids what an adverb is developed a twitch in her cheek.) That sort of lesson can and should be taught via a fully immersed, three-dimensional, total engagement system—like the Xbox or Wii. They could be self-diagnostic, so that as the child improves, the level of difficulty improves with him.

Does this make teachers obsolete? Quite the opposite: it frees them to teach the higher levels of the cognitive domain—analysis, problem-solving, synthesis, and creative thinking. Normally teachers never get to that, because they're too busy being bogged down in the basics—basics that are better handled in a multimedia, fully immersed environment. We should be reserving our human teachers' valuable time for working with knowledge at least, and wisdom at best.

Let the Xbox teach kids about the parts of speech—and free the teachers to help them learn how to put those parts of speech together into something that has depth and meaning. Automate, and humanize. Let technology teach our kids how to add and subtract and do basic algebra, and then pair them with some creative human teachers to sink their teeth into using math to solve real problems—like how to balance our national budget. Free our teachers to do what it is they got into teaching to do in the first place, instead of beating their heads against the wall at the lower levels of the cognitive domain and losing their love of teaching or even leaving the profession altogether.

Even as we make education genuinely fun and engaging for our students, we can do the same for our teachers—in fact, we *must.*

Bureaucratic approaches to education are no more effective than playing catch-up to other nations' innovative automobile designs. We need a soaring vision expressed in bold parameters: for example, "By 2020, we will have 100 percent literacy, will have 100 percent high school graduation rate, and will be rated number one in science and math—globally." Concrete, measurable benchmarks that we can be excited about in the pursuit, and proud of in the attainment.

This speaks to a transformation not only in our approach to educating our youth, but to education throughout our lives and in every sector of society.

A sweeping revolution in education, not unlike Singapore's "Thinking Schools, Learning Nation," is what it will take to reinvent the American Dream and create the world that Ethan can imagine himself living in, rather than the world Danny fully expects to die in.

>>>A Vision for Jobs

Not only do we need a vision for education, we also need to extend that beyond the schoolyard and into the workplace.

In the past, job security meant you worked for thirty years for the same company. Today you can't even count on being able to work in the same *industry* for thirty years. In the face of job upheavals and dislocations, American workers are asking, "How do we get job security back?" But it's not coming back, no more so than the vacuum tubes in our radios. The new value is not in job *security*, but in job *adaptability*. To thrive in the future world, employees need to have the ability to adapt to new and different jobs.

Our present school curricula are oriented by a rearview-mirror approach. When we baby boomers were in high school, our guidance counselors would show us a list of potential careers and say, "Have your pick." Today that approach is no longer possible, because the hottest jobs of 2020 haven't been invented or even conceived of yet. We need to be preparing our kids differently: we need to be preparing them for a rapidly changing world—and the same is true of our workforce.

They say you can't teach an old dog new tricks. That may be true. Fortunately, we aren't dogs.

In the past, you could graduate from school, learn a trade or a skill, and milk it for the rest of your life. The era we live in today could not represent a greater contrast. It used to be that if you had an advanced degree, you were guaranteed gainful employment for life. Today having a PhD simply means that you used to know a lot. Today it no longer works to get our education up front in one big chunk: we need to expect our education to continue throughout our lives. Singapore's national educational policy talks about "lifelong learning" and declares that "the capacity to continually learn, both for professional development and for personal enrichment, will determine our collective tolerance for change." We would be smart to use Singapore's vision as a starting point and go beyond it. The human mind is infinitely upgradable by its owner.

In the past what we needed to survive, thrive, and excel was a well-trained workforce. Not anymore. Today a well-trained workforce produces only pain and protectionism. What we need is a workforce capable of being *reeducated* again and again.

Our unions are still functioning within the parameters of the old economy's scarcity model: their goal is to protect and defend the job, using the old definitions of retirement and security. But "employment for life" is no longer relevant: today we need to develop *employability for life.* A twenty-first-century labor union's job is not to make sure you are employed—it's to make sure you are employable.

The twenty-first-century union needs to focus not on training, but on education. The difference is that you *train* someone to do a specific task or skill, while you *educate* them to understand why they're doing that task and what the principles are behind it. Training prepares you to accomplish something in the present. Education, if it's well designed, prepares you to adapt to change and accomplish things both now and in the future.

Not long ago, a CEO of a large company told me he was reluctant to spend the money to upgrade his people's skills. "What if I do," he said, "and then they leave?"

"I see your point," I responded. "But what if you don't—and they stay?"

>>>Learn to Fail Faster

Part of living successfully in the new future is embracing a new relationship with one of our most valuable and underappreciated resources: our failures.

As a boy, I used to take the train from Wisconsin down to Texas during the summer to work on my grandfather's farm in Telephone, the little town I mentioned in Chapter 2. It was a great learning experience, and one of the greatest lessons I learned was about change and failure.

Things didn't change much in Telephone, Texas. I met my great-grandfather there just a few years before he died, near the age of one hundred. He had been a drummer boy during the Civil War. Back in 1890, the town's population was about thirty; by the outbreak of WWI it had risen to about one hundred. It rose to 280 by the time I was visiting my grampa, and slipped back again by 1990 to about 210, where it still is today.

In an environment like this, when something changes, you notice it.

One day my grampa taught me how to ride a horse. As I was barreling along, barely holding on, the horse abruptly changed direction, and I went flying. After picking myself up and dusting myself off, I made my way back to where my grampa was sitting. He looked at me and said, "Y'know, son, it's easier to ride the horse in the direction it's goin'."

A few weeks later, as we sat in the stifling Texas heat watching the motionless landscape, my grampa must have been chewing over what he'd said, because he now came out with a second piece of wisdom regarding a small project I was working on that kept failing.

"Son," he drawled, "if the horse is dead, git off."

Today, looking at the dizzying pace of technological change, this bit of advice seems more valuable than ever. The technological horses are galloping at a rapid clip, and if you miss it when they change direction, you will end up in some pretty deep dust. And the landscape is increasingly littered with dead horses—and knowing how to git off when the critter goes down is more important than ever.

The biggest problem with failure is not that it's failure, but that we tend to do it in such slow motion, dragging it out for years or even decades, that it weighs us down and prevents our forward motion.

Polaroid saw that the future was digital, but it protected and defended its analog marketplace anyway, drawing out its massive failure and assuring its ultimate demise. Kodak failed for almost a decade. Motorola did the same with its analog mobile phones and utterly lost its market dominance. The major American automakers have been failing slowly for years.

Once we learn to fail fast—to recognize failure quickly and act on it immediately—failure shifts from being a liability to being an asset. In fact, it becomes yet another trigger for flash foresight.

A good example is Dell Computers. In the late 1980s, growing at a rapid pace, the company bought as many parts as it could.

When technology abruptly changed in 1989, Dell was left with a huge inventory of obsolete memory chips, and it had to raise prices to compensate for the loss, which hurt the company's growth. In other words, the horses of technology-driven change changed direction, and Dell didn't.

But Dell learned fast: that experience led to the company's innovative approach to managing its supply process in partnership with its vendors. By the late 1990s Dell had reduced its supply chain to a less than eight-day lead, in contrast to its competitors, who maintained an inventory of preconfigured computers for more than two months out.

In the company's early days, Dell developed what it thought was a market breakthrough: a leading-edge line of computers sporting the biggest-screen laptop, the fastest processors, the best colors—the most, biggest, and best of everything. The line was called the Olympic. When it launched it at the 1989 Comdex, it was an Olympic-sized flop. It lost something on the order of $170 million on something nobody wanted.

Realizing it had failed to find out what the consumer wanted, Dell soon abandoned its retail strategy altogether and refocused on the customer-directed model of custom design that would become famous as "direct from Dell." It introduced online pricing in 1995 and started selling online in 1996, well before the rest of the herd. Defying the conventional wisdom of the day, Dell soon saw its Internet sales reach $1 million per day—and by the year 2000, $50 million per day.

In today's super-accelerated environment, we have to completely reinvent the nature of failure. Rather than something to be avoided, we need to create a positive metric for failure and seek to recognize it as close to instantaneously as possible.

It's no longer a question of whether you fail: the pace of transformation is so fast, failing is inevitable. The only question is: *How fast* are you failing? How fast do you recognize failure and regroup? Our biggest lessons come from our biggest mistakes. The organizations that are succeeding today are those that have learned how to fail *fast*—and who do not fail to learn.

>>>The Character of the New Future

Earlier we explored how we are shifting into a fundamentally different economy, one based on abundance rather than on scarcity, because of our changing relationship to information. This changing relationship also brings with it three forces that will be critical to shaping our future: *communication, collaboration,* and *trust.*

For years we have been working hard to become information age organizations. But just as with *continuous improvement* and *total quality management,* being an information age organization has become the norm and no longer provides an advantage. What we need now is to become *communication age* organizations.

What we called the *information age* was laying the foundation for the communication age we've now entered, in much the same way that the discovery and mining of raw physical resources laid the groundwork for the full flourishing of the industrial age, when those resources were shaped into all the engines and inventions of industrial technology.

The new economy we've now entered is built upon a foundation of information, mined, shaped, and crafted into its higher forms, knowledge and wisdom, and communicated globally to ever-increasing numbers of people at ever-increasing rates of speed.

Raw data, the fundamental currency of digital transactions, are in themselves useless. To be useful, data must be converted to information, that is, put literally *into formation,* structured into some useful pattern. If you had a printout of every single flight in the United States over a thirty-day period, you would have access to a great deal of random data, but it would be useless. Restructure that data so you have a list of all New York–to–LA flights in *chronological order,* and now you have information. Today, however, technology has given us access to so much information that it is becoming *less* useful, not more. (Do a Google word search on "New York flights" and you get millions of results in less than a second.)

So what does a good travel agent or online travel site do? They structure that information even further, organizing all that flight information by calendar day, by price, and by the number of legs in the trip (nonstop, one-stop, and so on)—and with your preferred airline highlighted (where you've built up the most frequent flyer miles). Now, given your meeting schedule, airline preference, and budget, you've got a solid basis for knowing which flight to book, because you have *actionable* information—in other words, *knowledge.*

Knowledge is not just better information, it is something of a distinctly higher order than information. Information is content; knowledge is content (information) *plus context.* It's the context, the meaningfully organized perspective, that gives content meaning. This is why a good storyteller puts great care into weaving the story first, before delivering the insight. Giving someone information without the context that makes it actionable (that is, that turns it into useful knowledge) is like telling someone a punch line without telling him the joke first.

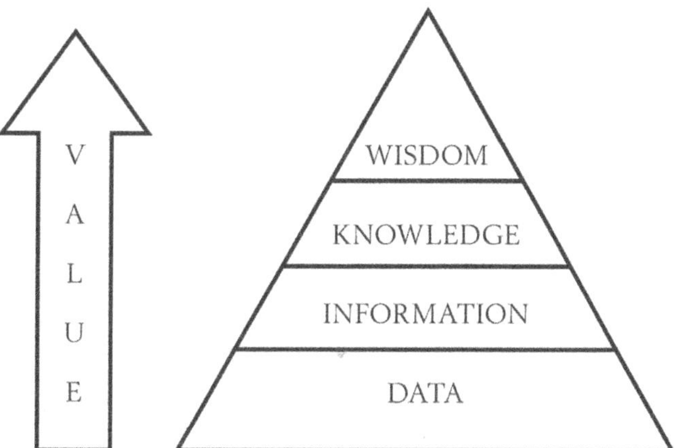

I have shared this graphic in over 2,400 speeches since the early eighties, and many have seen it in one form or another—yet few have applied it. To an extent they didn't need to, because in the past, it was optional. But in a world of transformation, it has become imperative.

Your organization or company doubtless has a database. It might even have a knowledge base. But does it have a wisdom base? It should. Because wisdom has an even higher value than knowledge.

Wisdom is the pure distilled guiding principle extracted from knowledge, set free from both content *and* context. This is why wisdom is timeless and, unlike data, information, or knowledge, can be applied anywhere, in any culture or context.

As you go up the scale, from data to information to knowledge to wisdom, value increases exponentially. (Would you rather be introduced as someone who has access to a lot of data, who has a lot of information, who is knowledgeable, or who is wise?) Therefore, the less time you spend on data and information, and the more on knowledge and wisdom, the more value you impart. Grandparents know this instinctively. When they get together with their grandkids, do they share a lot of data and information? No, they skip all that and cut right to the wisdom. (They know there's not much time!)

Before the explosion of bandwidth, processing power, and connectivity brought us all together on the Web, data and information were scarce, and you could provide value by giving people information, which was how travel agents, stockbrokers, real estate agents, and dozens of other professions made their living. Today everyone has access to the data and information: anyone can go online and see when flights are leaving, what hotel rooms are available, the current price of stocks, which auto dealer has the model you want at the best price, what medications are available and what the latest research shows about their contraindications.

Data and information are abundant and accessible, and can therefore be easily automated. So how do we add value? By operating at the higher levels of knowledge and wisdom.

For example, even though the various Internet travel services have made all that flight information amply available, I still use a travel agent to manage my complex travel schedule. Why? Because they know me so well, with all my preferences and needs, that they can work out the ideal itineraries for me far better than I would be able to, and even more important, in far less time. They add the consultative value of knowledge and wisdom to that information.

This is the difference between informing and communicating. *Informing* is one-way and static, doesn't necessarily lead to action, and tends to waste time. *Communicating* is two-way and dynamic, typically results in action, and tends to save time.

This is exactly what it means to evolve from the information age to the communication age. When you share information, you simply *inform*. When you have a two-way dialogue to establish the best result by sharing knowledge and wisdom (that is, consultative value), you have now entered the communication age.

The next time you're on the phone with someone, ask yourself this after you hang up: "What percentage of that call did I just spend giving the other person knowledge and wisdom, as opposed to giving data and information?" Giving others data and information is a waste of their time, and they know it, whether consciously or not. The time you spend giving them knowledge and wisdom *saves them time*—and they know that, too. (Business owners, take note.) This is particularly important because in today's economy, time is increasing in value. The more time I spend *informing* you, the more I'm wasting your time. The more time I spend giving you consultative advice, the more I'm saving you time and money and adding to your value—and increasing *my* value to you as well.

>>>Collaboration

The second key force shaping our future is *collaboration*. Collaboration is as different from cooperation as transformation is from change. When you and I cooperate, we are each doing our own thing as we make some accommodations for each other. When we collaborate, we are not simply making room for each other's creations, we are *cocreating* the future together.

Collaboration is a function of genuine communication. The facilitated communication environment of the Internet becomes a productive cycle that amplifies itself: communication fuels collaboration, which fuels more communication, which fuels more collaboration.

The open nature of the Internet, based as it is on standard protocols, has played a crucial role in enabling this shift to an abundance-oriented economy, as it allows any computer or other Net-enabled device, regardless of operating system, to participate in the global conversation. Likewise, a key to the growth of abundance power, in any industry or sector, is going to be the speed with which we can agree on universally shared standards. Universally accepted standards accelerate the adoption of new communication technologies and pathways, which in turn speeds growth and facilitates further collaboration.

After 9/11, we saw the American intelligence community scramble frantically to create some kind of collaborative environment, where the CIA, FBI, NSA, and dozens of other intelligence agencies could begin to communicate with one another. Up until then, they had felt relatively safe and secure operating each in their own little information fiefdoms, where they could communicate with themselves but not with one another—indeed, they saw themselves as being in hot competition with one another, and therefore it actually served (so they thought) their interests to be fairly opaque to one another. It was a classic scarcity-economy scenario.

A similar situation still exists within the health-care community. There has been a lot of cooperation between competing players in the industry, but not true collaboration. It's still protect and defend, fiefdoms and egos, legacy thinking—all the things that keep abundance from happening. The only way forward is to stop cooperating and start collaborating, bringing together all the major players—the insurance companies, hospitals, medical supply houses, and everyone else involved in every aspect of health-care delivery—to reinvent health care itself. It sounds impossible, I know—but that's exactly what Curtis Burton did in the oil industry with the creation of DeepSTAR.

>>>Trust

Not long ago, my subscription to the local newspaper expired. The paper sent me a notice, asking me to renew for $190, but I was on the road for weeks, and didn't respond to the notice. By the time I returned home, there was a message from them on my voice mail, asking if I wanted to renew for $90 instead.

I'll never trust their promotions again.

Trust is the third of these three forces that will play a major role in our future. In the communication age, trust has assumed an entirely new economic and structural significance. In an industrial economy based on physical resources, trust was important, but if it was broken, few would find out. In today's electron-based economy, if trust is broken, people tweet it to the world.

Does your phone company ever call you to say, "Hey, we have a lower rate for new customers, and since you have been a valued long-time customer, we are going to give you that lower rate as well"? No, you have to call and complain and threaten to switch to a different phone service. *Then* they'll tell you there's a lower rate. Does that make you trust them more? No, it makes you think, "How long have I been getting ripped off?"

Why do they and so many other businesses continually do things like this? They're not evil, and they're not stupid. They just aren't thinking about building trust into their business plans; they *assume* it. We can no longer afford to assume trust or to see it as a "soft" value or ancillary trait: it has become the central plank of the twenty-first-century economy. When it comes to digital relationships, trust is the new currency. I don't want to give out my credit card or buy from you if I think you're going to share my name and information with everyone. The more we dematerialize our world, the more we rely on trust. Trust is the glue that holds the Net-enabled economy together.

Digital trust is the trust that develops between people who will never see or meet each other physically. How do you create digital trust? The same way as any other kind of trust: by operating with honesty and integrity and delivering on your promises. Yet because managing trust is assumed and therefore invisible to them, many companies unwittingly break this rule constantly. How? By the way they do nearly everything, from changing prices (raising *or* lowering), hiring and firing, changing policies, even rolling out new products and services. And once you lose trust, it's very difficult to get it back.

Every time you implement any kind of change, this presents an opportunity to escalate trust, or to undermine and diminish it. Before you make the change, ask yourself, "Will this raise, maintain, or diminish trust?" If the change will lower trust, then don't do it—at least, not in that way. Find a different way to make that change so that you at least maintain your current level of trust. (And if you find someone in your organization who can raise the bar on trust, then reward them openly—because you get the behaviors you reward, and *that* is a behavior you want to see repeated.)

For example, when a company lays off thousands of employees, what does that do to the employees who still work there? It depends on how you lay them off. You can let one thousand people go and end up having everyone trust you *more*—both those who were laid off and those who are still with you. How? By giving them career counseling, reeducation, and placement support to make them more reemployable and job-adaptable.

One thing I'm absolutely certain about is that the future is all about relationships, and good relationships are all based on trust.

>>>Creating a More Human World

Earlier I mentioned that the more our technology transforms, the more human our world needs to become. This is a soft trend, a choice in front of us.

I read a news report recently about a student at a middle school in Kansas City who had developed cancer and had to undergo a program of chemotherapy. She had lost her hair, lost her appetite, grown seriously weak, and had to stay home. Going to school, she was told, was impossible.

Impossible? A local company heard about her situation and donated a broadband videoconferencing setup with a large LCD screen in the classroom and another screen in her home. Now she was able to attend classes, keep up with her schoolwork, and maintain her connection with all her friends, even while undergoing her treatment and recuperating at home. This is a beautiful example of high tech and high touch working together to create a *more* humanized, not less humanized, world.

Amid this staggering acceleration of change, to me the most fascinating thing is to notice what *hasn't* changed, isn't changing, and won't ever change. We still laugh, we still cry. We still want and need relationships. We still want our kids to have more opportunity than we had. We still take walks on the beach. We still love it when the clouds part and the sun comes out.

Our tools are transforming, faster than ever before, and they'll continue to do so faster and faster. But what will not change at all is our humanity. Human trust and one-to-one personal relationships will continue to be important; in fact, more so than ever.

And that's the truly remarkable thing about it. While technology has the potential to dehumanize, it has far greater potential to *rehumanize.* It all depends on our intention, and how much we apply that intention to what we're doing. We can change by default or by design. Change by default, and we're likely to create a future that we're not too happy about.

Here is the opportunity in front of us: to make the world not less human, but more so. To become more enlightened, not less. To make a better tomorrow, not a more chaotic tomorrow. How? By transforming the way we think about the future—the way we *see* the future and our capacity to shape it, instead of just sitting back and letting it emerge as it will.

To a degree, we've always had the power to direct our future. The future has always been a blank canvas—to an extent. But the speed of that unfolding is much faster now, and we have far more powerful tools. In the old days, when someone invented a hammer, a wheel, or a harness, word spread slowly. The change was gradual, not transformational. Today the impact of a new tool reverberates around the globe like a thunderclap.

We are in a time of technology-driven transformation; this is a given, a hard trend, a fact of future history that we cannot and will not change. It's *going* to happen; it's happening now. The transformation that is optional, the one that we *can* effect and *must* effect, is not technological but human, social, and spiritual; that is, the inner transformation.

The world is all suddenly interconnected as never before, and next year it will be even more so. As we become more and more collaborative and our lives become more and more intertwined, creating the most powerful human convergence we have ever experienced as a species, if we continue on the present course of change with the same mind-set that we had twenty, fifty, a hundred years ago, seeking twentieth-century and nineteenth-century goals with our powerful new twenty-first-century tools, we could find ourselves in very serious trouble. But if we transform ourselves along with our tools—in other words, if we loosen our grip on the old scarcity-based rules and learn to adopt the new ground rules of an abundant economy—we will find ourselves in the most thrilling, satisfying, and genuinely democratic social environment the world has ever known.

Technology can bring us together or pull us apart; it depends on how we use it. It boils down to this: *intention*, looking forward, not backward, and designing our future with conscious direction rather than by the reflexive impulse to protect and defend.

In the past, the future seemed distant and took generations to unfold. In the latter half of the twentieth century, the pace accelerated to the point where this process took only years. Then months. Now it's happening as fast as we can imagine it—and soon it will be happening faster still. With this pace of transformation comes tremendous challenge, and astonishing opportunity.

This is our moment of truth.

>>>Tomorrowlab: The Power of a Question

If you picked up this book hoping to find some answers, I hope by now you have found something of greater value: some better questions.

One day I was out in the yard and a boy from my neighborhood came walking toward me, crying.

"What's wrong, Tommy?" I asked.

He told me that his dog had died. He looked up at me through his tears and said: "Mr. Burrus, do you think there are dogs in heaven?"

What should I say? I could have given him some religious or theological answer, and it would have meant nothing to him. I could have simply said, "Absolutely! Of course!" but would that reassure him or make him feel any better? I doubted it. Because what did it really matter what *I* thought? The real question was, what did *he* think?

I looked into his eyes and said: "Tommy, would heaven be heaven without dogs?" He thought for a moment, nodded slowly, and gave a heartbreaking smile. "Thanks, Mr. Burrus."

Sometimes the best answer is a question.

Putting flash foresight to work starts with asking yourself some powerful questions. In a world filled with uncertainty, what are you certain about? What does your visible future look like? What problems are you about to have—and how can you solve them before they happen? Most important, what actions should you take now in order to have a better future?

My biggest concern is that, having learned about flash foresight, you will put this book down and go back to putting out fires and digging yourself out from the crises that started while you were reading these pages. After all, who has time to stop putting out fires and take a hard look at the visible future? Practically speaking, nobody *has* time for that; the only way it will happen is if we *make* time for it. Make an appointment with yourself; put it on the calendar.

It will take one hour per week of your time. Often, when I say this to a client, they protest, "But I don't have an hour a week!" (Of course, the reason they're in that position is that they haven't been doing this!) I urge them to look again. "After all," I point out, "the future is where you're going to spend the rest of your life. Would it be worth an hour a week to think about it?"

I call this one hour per week your *tomorrowlab.*

During that one hour, your assignment is to completely unplug from the present and plug into your future. That means disconnecting from everything—your phones, laptop, everything you're currently engaged in. This isn't just about turning off your devices; it means you need to make a commitment to stop thinking about your current problems and everything that is gnawing at you or soaking up your attention—at least for one solid hour.

Then, once you have untethered yourself from the moorings of all present-day concerns, start exploring your visible future.

What are you certain about? What are the hard trends of your future, versus the soft trends? What are the permanent, linear changes and what are the cyclical changes? How are the three digital accelerators and eight pathways of technology-driven transformation going to affect your life and work?

What are the problems you're going to have tomorrow, next week, next month? A few years down the road? What are the problems your kids, your spouse, your employees, your associates, your customers are going to have? Even better, what are the future problems of those people who are not yet your customers but *will* be if you have the solutions to their problems by the time they happen?

The first time you do this, it may take the entire hour just to unhook your attention from the problems of the present. Don't worry; just keep next week's appointment. As you keep spending one hour a week in your tomorrowlab, you will start to get your land legs in the terrain of the visible future.

Once you start seeing future certainties and playing with the various core principles—*go opposite, skip it, reinvent,* and so forth—you will start getting flash foresights, and as you do, you will find them impossible to ignore. Your mind will start working on them in the background while you go through the rest of your week, even when you're not consciously thinking about it. And the subconscious has millions of times more processing power than the conscious mind. But this will happen only if you create the undistracted time to gaze into the visible future and ask yourself better questions.

Most of the time we occupy ourselves with the questions of the moment, and these by definition tend to be questions of reaction. As we saw in the discussion of the *skip it* idea in Chapter 4, when you apply even the most brilliant minds to the wrong questions, the best you can hope to come up with are really brilliant bad answers. This is why the future seems so random and events continually surprise us, why it's so easy to see success as a crapshoot.

It's so easy to keep doing things the way we've always done. There's something weirdly reassuring about slipping back into crisis mode. It's what we know, and that makes it comfortable: a world of effort and lament driven by hindsight and happenstance. Creating your own tomorrowlab provides a door out of that cycle of reaction and disappointment.

There are a vast number of things we *could* do; there are many things we *should* do; but there are a critical few things we *must* do.

This massive global transformation will happen—it *is* happening. And it is transforming how we work, play, learn, live, and do everything. It will do more so tomorrow, and even more so next week. It will bring massive disruption for those who don't see it coming—and massive opportunity for those who do.

>>> EPILOGUE:

An Experiment

During the summer of 2009, I thought it would be interesting to conduct an entrepreneurial experiment, with myself as the guinea pig.

Over the past thirty years I've started five companies; all were profitable and two were national leaders in their first year. One of them, an experimental aircraft business, had thirty-seven national locations by the end of its first year. What is interesting about this track record is that before starting these companies, I was a science educator and had absolutely no business training, formal or informal. Moreover, as a businessperson I've never taken out a single business loan or carried any business debt. The only reason every one of these businesses was successful is that in developing and running them, I used the principles you've just read about in this book.

Still, all this took place many years *before* writing *Flash Foresight*. Why not demonstrate the principles I was writing about by actually using them to start a brand-new business, from scratch, concurrent with writing this book?

The more I thought about this idea, the more it appealed to me. As I was writing, the world was going through a historic economic crisis and the United States was in the throes of the worst recession since the 1930s. People were being laid off by the hundreds of thousands and businesses were shutting down everywhere. What's the opposite? *Starting* a new business and *hiring* people.

What a perfect time to test our principles and see if, in the midst of all this chaos, I could create something successful in a short time. I decided to put *Flash Foresight* to work even as I was writing it, and use it to start a new business with the goal of having it make a big impact and turn a significant profit by the time the book itself appeared.

>>>The Concept

Starting with certainty, I looked for a technology-driven hard trend, a relatively new development whose burgeoning future I could be certain about. There were dozens, even hundreds of possible areas to focus on; I chose *smartphones.*

Certainty, anticipation, and *transformation* all tell us this: we are experiencing a major paradigm shift in personal computing. Over the last half century we've progressed from gigantic mainframe computers and terminals, to desktops, to laptops. What's next? Our computers are now in the palms of our hands. Personal mobile platforms like smartphones and smartpads will revolutionize computing and transform business. Can we be certain about that? Yes. Given the three digital accelerators (the multiplying increase in processing power, storage, and bandwidth) and eight pathways of technology transformation (dematerialization, virtualization, mobility, product intelligence, networking, interactivity, globalization, and convergence), there is zero doubt that smartphones and smartpads are the leading edge of personal computer development, and furthermore, that each new generation of smartphones and smartpads will be successively more powerful and versatile. This is not just a change, it's a transformation.

The app revolution allows us as individuals to completely personalize our phones, and it puts the power of the multimedia

Internet in our hands at all times, whatever we're doing and wherever we go. From the mushrooming number of available apps, we can choose whichever apps we want to solve whatever problems we have. The phone company no longer tells us what our phones can and can't do. While computer programs are often expensive and tedious or complex to install and upgrade, apps are cheap and easy. The app revolution unleashes enormous power and puts it in the hands of individual users. It isn't just making certain things easier—it is transforming how we do those things.

>>>The Business

In August 2009 I filed the papers creating a new company, Visionary Apps. As we said on the company Web site:

> *[Visionary Apps] is dedicated to creating the most advanced business and personal mobile phone applications on the market.*

I got the necessary developer licenses from Apple, Microsoft, Google, Research in Motion (BlackBerry), and the others, so I could work with all the major smartphone models, although I knew right away we would start with the iPhone and go cross-platform later.

I'm not a computer programmer. I don't do graphics, Web site design, or iPhone interfaces. I needed a team. To keep start-up costs low and innovative spirit high, I looked for bright young programmers and designers, fresh out of college and hungry to be in on the early phase of a technology revolution. Rather than deal with the complications of payroll, I skipped all that and created a virtual team of independent contractors. We were able to work as a completely virtual company: one lives in Wisconsin, one in California, and one in Boston, and we used technology to link us in collaboration and production. I knew that as the company's needs grew, we would bring in others, and when the time was right, convert them into employees.

Our first big question, of course, was exactly what kind of app would our new business build? Instead of picking one type of app and jumping right into design, we first took some time to jump into the future. The rest of the app market was reacting to each development as it happened; we wanted to *anticipate*. So we started by asking the question, "A year or two from now, what will the best of the best apps look like? What will be their winning characteristics? What will set them apart from the rest?"

From this inquiry we created a set of about thirty "future benchmarks" to use as development standards that we would insist every one of our products adhered to. We wanted to know what *all* our apps would look like before we designed the first one. We wanted to create a brand, not just an app.

For example, we could see that the app market was exploding so fast, the market was already flooded with products and in the next few years would go through a winnowing-out process with the genuine cream rising to the top. A truly successful app of the future will have to have a wow factor: it will be so much fun to use that you just *have* to download it, and once you use it you'll just *have* to show your friends. These were just two of our benchmarks.

>>>The Vision

Another characteristic on our list was that we wanted to create apps that would make a genuine difference, to have a positive social impact. Given the world's need to shift from an economy of scarcity to an economy of abundance, the successful apps of the future will be agents of abundance—in other words, they will significantly improve people's lives. Here is the vision statement we put on our Web site:

> *Visionary Apps was founded . . . with a vision to improve the world we live in by utilizing the revolution of smartphone technology.*

Notice the phrase at the heart of that statement: *improve the world.* We didn't just want to make cool apps that would be fun for people and make us a profit. We wanted to make apps that could help to change the world in a positive way.

>>>The Research

The next phase was market research. With our set of future benchmarks in hand, we generated a list of one hundred different apps in many verticals. We had disease management apps, purchasing and inventory apps, and all sorts of other app ideas. Working from this list, we then used Google analytics and some other research tools to see what people were most interested in and what nobody was offering yet. We didn't want to create better versions of what others were already doing—we wanted to create something that didn't yet exist but for which there was already a large (and unfilled) need.

In all our research, one particular finding stood out. When we did a search on the strings "foreclosures" and "foreclosed homes," we found there were 120 million searches for foreclosed homes every month. That was a huge number, way bigger than most of the other opportunities we were looking at. And the number of foreclosure apps? Zero. They didn't exist. And real estate agents' MLS system for finding homes listed only a few foreclosures, so even agents couldn't find them. Perfect. Not only was there a huge market demand and no current product to fill it, but this also fulfilled our criteria of social impact.

>>>The Problem

In the summer of 2009, when we were first developing this idea, people weren't buying many homes. Home values were plummeting, the number of new foreclosures was skyrocketing, and new home construction had ground to a halt. In fact, the crashing real estate industry was a major factor in the most painful aspect—and the slowest to turn around—of the economic crisis: unemployment.

A huge number of people are involved in home construction. But it's practically impossible to start building new homes again if we already have millions of foreclosed homes we can't move. The only way to really get jobs creation going is to get all these foreclosed homes sold. If there were a way to get these properties sold, it would get the real estate industry moving again, start creating more jobs, and help turn the country's economy around.

All sorts of economic incentives had been proposed, some of them passed into law, to help first-time home buyers and others buy foreclosed homes. Well, legislation might be one way to do this—but we thought an even better way would be to give people *new tools*.

Our research told us that 60 percent of the foreclosed homes being bought were being paid for in cash, so securing bank loans wasn't a major issue here. The big problem was that most people simply didn't know how to find the foreclosed homes. There were only a few Web sites for it; those that existed charged fees to the user, had partial inventory, and provided no clear instruction on how to go about buying these properties.

What if we could create a way for people to quickly, easily, and cheaply (that is, at zero cost) find and identify foreclosed homes in their area, get good information on how to buy them, and connect with foreclosure experts right in their area to help them do it?

We decided to create an app that would allow users to find foreclosures in any given area, get all the pertinent information, and include an *intelligent guide* built right into the app that would tell them exactly how to go about buying a forclosed home and even recommend an expert who could help.

Let's pause for a moment and apply the *go opposite* principle. This app would be a great service for people who were looking for foreclosures to buy. But what about the person whose home is being foreclosed? If you ended up "under water" with a mortgage you couldn't afford and your house was foreclosed on, the chances were good you would now need to find a new place to live—and fast.

What if we created a second app that would help you shop for a new home in a price range you could afford, as quickly as possible?

And what if you couldn't afford to buy a house at the moment? Let's add a third app that would help you find an apartment or smaller house to rent right away.

Some additional online searches told us that, again, there were huge numbers of people searching for homes and rentals online. We looked in Apple's App Store and found a few dozen home and real estate apps—but they were all local, put out by individual real estate agents and covering just their own area. Another excellent place to go opposite: we needed *national* apps.

This brainstorming process and database research phase took us forty-five or fifty days. By early fall 2009 we had our product: Visionary Apps' first product launch would be a suite of national real estate apps, including one for foreclosures, one for regular homes, and one for rentals.

>>>The Money

Now came the big question: how would we make money on these apps?

Currently, the only way to make money on apps is to charge for the initial download. Some cost $2.99 to over $100, but 99¢ is by far the most popular price. With that model, once your customer buys the app, they download it and use it, and that's that. The revenue stream from that user is over. Some app creators had experimented with pop-up ads as another source of income, but according to all reports we saw, this wasn't working very well.

Our research told us that not very many businesses were really making any significant money on apps. A few had made some big money (up to $1 million), but not many—and as the number of new apps began exploding, the field was getting crowded fast.

We pondered how to price our first app. Should we make it $2.99, $3.99, $4.99? Or would that price us out of the market we wanted? Could we afford to go with a 99¢ app? With 120 million searches for foreclosed homes a month, a 99¢ app *could* do well. What was the sweet spot?

Using our *Flash Foresight* principles, we decided to skip the problem altogether and make the app free for the user. Our research showed that you could get ten times the number of users if the app was free. Instead of charging the home buyer, we decided to do the opposite: charge the people who wanted to sell to the home buyer. We could charge a fee to real estate agents for exclusive representation of all properties within a given zip code. The model we ended up creating charges $24.99 per month for each zip code. With some 42,000 zip codes, that gave us a potential of a little more than $1 million in recurring monthly revenue.

Notice what happened here: we had completely reinvented the app business. The existing income model for apps was to charge a one-time fee, period. Once your customer base reaches critical mass, the income stream stops. With our model, the income stream goes on forever.

Having reinvented the app income model, we thought about redefining it further.

Once your agent has helped you pick out a home, what do you need next? A mortgage. Could we include one mortgage company per zip code? Sure we could. Once you've bought the home, you're going to need a moving company, which meant we could also give exclusive coverage to one moving company per zip code. And if you're buying a foreclosed home, you're probably going to need a redecorator and possibly a remodeler. We put a nice list together with the idea of solving a home buyer's problems at the moment of need. If each of those entities pays $24.99 a month per zip code, we had an app that could generate as much as $60 million per year.

We can expand the revenue model in other ways, too. For example, there are seminars for real estate agents on how to sell foreclosed homes. We can make those available to our customers for a fee. There are also seminars for the public that teach about how to work auctions and actually take them to the auctions. We can charge a fee to feature auction sites on our app.

Companies that sell apps are often not that interested in putting a lot of effort into upgrades, because once you buy the app, you get the upgrades for free. There was no model for generating income with upgrades. Instead, we decided to create a model where we could continually bring in additional functionalities and features that would increase the number of leads to our paid customers and at the same time provide increasing value to the app user, thus generating more revenue with each upgrade.

>>>The Product

Our first product turned out to be a trio of products: Complete Foreclosures, Complete Homes, and Complete Rentals. We called it the Complete Realty Suite.

Complete Foreclosures lets you search more than 1.6 million foreclosure listings nationwide, with new listings appearing every time you open the app. You can search and sort listings easily by price, proximity, number of bedrooms, bathrooms, and so forth. In addition, over 800,000 preforeclosure ("short-sale") listings are updated daily.

The smartphone's GPS technology lets you quickly locate homes on the go with an interactive map, just like the maps app that comes standard with the iPhone: when you look for homes in a certain area, little pushpins drop down on the map. You can touch any pin and it will expand to show you the address, price, how many beds and baths, the year it was built, and other typical descriptive information. The app also provides pictures and satellite aerial views of each property and its neighborhood, as well as driving directions to the homes.

The app includes an intelligent Foreclosure Buying Guide that helps you navigate through the intricate process of purchasing a foreclosed home. Moreover, you can directly contact an individual foreclosure expert for that property: scroll down, and there's a picture of the person, a short description, and a phone number. Touch the phone number and it dials their cell phone, so you can talk to them on the spot. Touch their e-mail and it will send a preaddressed e-mail to the real estate agent, automatically cutting and pasting in the specific property you're interested in. Now the agent and you are both looking at the same property at the same time.

With one-click automatic e-mail you can share your listings with your spouse, family, and friends; you can also save your favorite listings for easy offline viewing later.

The application is useful to real estate agents, too, who can look through listings of preforeclosed homes (those that have been sent a notice of default) and contact their owners to see if they want help in selling them. In fact, the potential audience for the apps is broad: home buyers and sellers, real estate investors, and even economists and journalists interested in housing trends.

The other two apps, Complete Homes and Complete Rentals, are very similar in scope and feature set, allowing users to find national listings and information on real estate agents, and to search for apartments and rental homes. All are redefining how people shop for, buy, and sell homes, condos, and apartments nationwide.

>>>The Launch

Back in August '09, when I was first developing the business idea, I heard a pundit make this comment about the apps business: "If you want to start an app business, you're too late—all the best ones have already been done." That made me smile—exactly the kind of *that's impossible!* assessment I like to hear before I try to do anything.

One of the major barriers to launching successful new apps was that by this time, the App Store was already crowded with over 100,000 apps. "You'll get lost in the App Store," was one comment I heard a number of times, "and people will never find you."

That was a problem, all right—so we decided to skip it. The fact that the store was getting supercrowded wasn't our *real* problem, anyway: our real problem was finding a way to make sure people heard about our apps. So we made an early decision that every app we created would be newsworthy, so that the resulting press would bring a first wave of customers to try them. If our apps were as good as we planned, then word of mouth would do the rest.

We launched the Complete Realty Suite on Monday, February 22, 2010. That same day also saw the launch of a number of other iPhone apps, including Knife Toss, NASA Lunar Electric Simulator, Phineas and Ferb Arcade, and Brothers in Arms 2: Global Front. Guess which one made the news?

That first week the Complete Realty Suite was covered by the *Wall Street Journal* blog and then reviewed in *Forbes, BusinessWeek, Bloomberg, USA Today,* and about three dozen other major publications. *Forbes* called it "a must-have tool for serious real estate investors." Soon I was being interviewed on Fox News and other national broadcast media. By the end of the first week, it was number six on Apple's list of most-downloaded business apps, and number seventeen on the most-downloaded list of *all* apps.

Within our third week after launch, we began adding new features. We added larger pictures of the homes as well as multiple pictures, an "arrange a showing" button and a "request more information" button that included a price reduction alert, both designed to send leads to our paid real estate agents. We'll continue adding new features to raise the bar on our apps.

Even before the apps went into the Apple store, we had already signed up real estate agents all over the country. None of our real estate agents were buying just one or two zip codes; typically they bought anywhere from four to twelve apiece, and one of our early customers bought thirty. In other words, all three apps are free—but we were making money on them even before the very first download. That was another first.

One of our goals had been to completely redefine and reinvent the income model for apps. By the time of our launch we had successfully met that goal, and we were on target to be profitable in our first year. (To see an annotated timeline of the development of Visionary Apps, go to www.flashforesight.com.)

What about development beyond U.S. shores? Done. Even as I write this report in the spring of 2010, we are laying the groundwork to move into Canada, and from there into Great Britain, and onward from there to become a global company.

At this early stage, the company's entire employee base still consists of me plus one full-time employee (my vice president of marketing, Jennifer Metcalf), along with independent contractors and some strategic partners. We have contracted out various aspects of the development work to programmers and designers as needed. I expect we'll eventually bring on those two independents as salaried employees. Thus, the entire staff of Visionary Apps will be enlarged not by borrowed money, but by our customers' money.

>>> Directing Our Company's Future

The February launch in the Apple App Store was only the entry point. The apps will also be made available for other popular smartphone platforms (BlackBerry, Android, etc.). And in truth, the app revolution is not limited purely to phones. In fact, the app revolution isn't really about phones at all—it's about *personal Internet-enabled devices.* We will design our apps for iPhones and all their competitors, iPads and all their competitors, and iTV (app-driven smart TV) and all its competitors. It's a revolution of both *mobile* and *interactive fixed information.*

And not just real estate information. Early in the development process we started thinking, what if we used the same software engine and interface, but pulled in different data? We began brainstorming on the idea of other areas where we could apply the same concept. One idea that especially intrigued me was a *go opposite* concept: the realty apps would be for individuals in the private sector. What about an app for entire organizations in the military?

Even before our February launch, we began working with the military on a new type of app aimed at supporting on-site security and emergency response. Plugging into their data, rather than national real estate data, gave us an app the military could use, for example, to rapidly locate and deploy any emergency equipment they might need.

Imagine this scenario: An emergency occurs, and everyone needs to scramble *fast.* Grabbing an iPhone, you zoom in on the area in question and query where a certain type of equipment is—

and a group of pushpins comes dropping down. Touch any pin, and you can find out exactly what equipment is where.

You can also find people—in military language, *assets*. Because there are cameras on the base and facial recognition software in the system, your app can tell whether an asset is friendly or not, identified or not identified. These come down as different-colored pins: say, a green pin for a friendly, a red pin for a known enemy combatant, and a blue pin for an unknown. As these people move around and the cameras on the base follow them, you can see the corresponding pins move as well.

It wasn't hard to imagine additional applications for customs and border control, coastal ports, and other contexts.

Before even launching our first consumer product, we had completely reinvented it, and with minimal new programming and development had an entirely new app and entirely different market.

Confidentiality and secrecy requirements don't allow me to share details of the products, but I can say this: we launched our new apps for the military in April 2010, two months after introducing the Complete Realty Suite.

Having retooled our basic app concept for military use, it wasn't hard to continue to reinvent it. For example, who else might have an emergency? We all remember the shooting rampage at Virginia Tech in April 2007. One of the major issues in that terrible event was finding and distributing the right information. There was chaos—students knew something was going on, but nobody knew where to go. All they could do was duck and hide.

What if they had this app? Instead of mapping homes and foreclosures or military assets, this app would have a map of the university, and the pushpins that dropped down would show them the latest information about where the danger was happening (red pins) and the best information about where to go for safety (green pins). Every university in America could use an app like that.

Or, let's reinvent this again, and adapt this university emergency app for airports. The possibilities are endless. When we launched, here is what our Web site said about our vision for the company's future:

Visionary Apps seeks to utilize the constantly evolving smart phone, smart pad, and smart TV to bring never before seen opportunities designed to engage and empower the user in new and exciting ways in the fields of real estate, healthcare, purchasing, logistics, supply chain, sales, marketing, energy, security, and many more.

Because we used certainty based on anticipating the transforming nature of technology, because we jumped ahead by skipping over the current limitations of the app world and used every opportunity to do the opposite of what others were already doing, and because we constantly asked ourselves how we could redefine and reinvent, within some eight months we had developed a revolutionary business that was already drawing significant income and was, for all practical purposes, infinitely scalable.

Surfboards don't have engines: just position them in the right place, point them in the right direction, and keep your balance, and the pull of the wind and waves does the rest. That's exactly what we did. The reason we didn't need massive capital financing or a big staff is that we designed the concept, from the very ground up, based on where trends are going. All we had to do was put ourselves in the right place, point ourselves in the right direction, and keep our balance. The onrush of technological transformation will provide the power.

You can do that, too!

Daniel Burrus

Note: You can follow the progress of Visionary Apps and see updates on how the company is performing by going to www.flashforesight.com.

>>> ACKNOWLEDGMENTS

The lone visionary, solitary architect of innovation laboring reclusively in his ivory tower, removed from the distractions of society and sustained by inner inspiration alone . . . we've all seen this character in film and legend. He doesn't exist. He is a myth, a fabrication of the scroll and screen. The truth is that every great invention, significant innovation, or worthwhile accomplishment owes its birth and existence to the nutritive process of *collaboration*. Nowhere is this truer than in the conception, drafting, and production of a book. I owe an incalculable debt of gratitude:

To my principal collaborator, the amazing John David Mann. His gift for language and ability to breathe life into words on the page are only one facet of his contribution to *Flash Foresight*. John also brought conceptual ingenuity, fresh research, narrative ideas, and an unerring eye for detail to the project. It's no exaggeration to say that the book wouldn't exist without him.

To the incredible Margret McBride, who has held, nurtured, and believed in the vision of this book for years. Margret is more than an agent: she is also a magician, an artist, and a friend. I am also grateful for and immensely appreciative of the acute insights, unflagging spirit, and indefatigable quest for perfection from the rest of the team at the Margret McBride Literary Agency, including Donna DeGutis, Anne Bomke, and Faye Atchison.

To Hollis Heimbouch at Harper Business. Right at a moment when the publishing industry was in a panic and more uncertain about its own future than ever before, it was Hollis who caught the vision and took a chance on the idea for this book. It was also Hollis's keen grasp of the material and uncanny ability to pinpoint its weak spots that helped us polish the manuscript to a shine.

To Jennifer Metcalf, my VP of Marketing at Burrus Research, who coordinated the whole project from start to finish and contributed in a thousand and one ways, all while flawlessly managing the insanity of my travel schedule, speaking calendar, and business activities without a single one of those spinning plates ever falling to the floor.

To my wife, Sharon MacFarland Burrus, CEO of Emerita and cofounder of the nonprofit Women in Balance, who brought a vast range of experience, insights, and perspective to her reading of the manuscript in its various stages.

To my Grampa, Dad, and Mom, all of whose stories make brief appearances in these pages, and whose generous spirits inform and inspire my life and work.

And to all the pioneers, innovators, risk takers, experts, and visionaries who contributed their time, experiences, and stories as illustrations of the principles in this book: Curtis Burton at Buccaneer Energy; Mark Cironi at Green Energy Technologies; Jerry Coffee, Dr. Ben Durkee, and Matthew Christensen; Mark Edwards, author of *Crash! The Demise of Fossil Foods and the Rise of Abundance*; Dan Gautschi and Keith Meyer at Sunthenoil; Tony Hsieh at Zappos; Richard Loomis at *World Energy* magazine; John Ludike at MTN; Tryggvi Magnusson at From the Forest, LLC; Dr. Bruce McGee and George Stapleton at E-T Energy; Andrew Metz; Larry Metcalf; W Mitchell; Lillian Montalto at Lillian Montalto Signature Properties and Bob Bohlen at PreviewProperties.com; Len Sauers at Procter & Gamble; and Floyd Shelton at Superior Floor Company.

>>> *NOTES*

INTRODUCTION

1. Dale Morgen is not his real name; because a few of the inventions discussed here are in an early stage and not ready for formal announcement, we have used a pseudonym.

CHAPTER 1: START WITH CERTAINTY

1. Her name is Kathleen Casey-Kirschling, and she lives in Cherry Hill, New Jersey. Her fortieth birthday (in 1986) was recounted in *Money* magazine, and ever since then her birthdays have been regularly noted by media accounts.
2. "Social Security Hits First Wave of Boomers," *USA Today*, Oct. 8, 2007.
3. "GM: Live Green or Die," by David Welch, *BusinessWeek*, May 16, 2008.
4. "GM Shifts Focus to Small Cars in Sign of Sport Utility Demise," *New York Times*, June 4, 2008.

CHAPTER 2: ANTICIPATE

1. In fact, I recently happened to meet with a research team at Intel. I mentioned this point, and they agreed that there is no end in sight to the continuous impact of Moore's Law, because we keep innovating.

CHAPTER 3: TRANSFORM

1. These crystal ball assessments appeared in the *New York Times*, Jan. 25, 1996; *Time*, Feb. 5, 1996; *Fortune*, Feb. 19, 1996; and the *Financial Times*, July 11, 1997.
2. Miguel Helft and Ashlee Vance, "Apple Passes Microsoft as No. 1 in Tech," *New York Times*, May 26, 2010.

3. "How Apple Is Preparing for an iPod Slump," *New York Times*, April 23, 2008.
4. Daniel Burrus with Patti Thomsen, *Advances in Agriculture* (Dubuque, Iowa: Kendall/Hunt Publishing Company, 1990).
5. The iShoe is developed and marketed by iShoe, Inc., www.i-shoe.net.
6. "Self-Care Can Save Millions in Health Costs: Unnecessary Visits to ED, Other Costs Avoided," *Occupational Health Management*, November 2001.
7. "Gene Map Becomes a Luxury Item," by Amy Harmon, *New York Times*, March 4, 2008.

CHAPTER 4: TAKE YOUR BIGGEST PROBLEM—AND SKIP IT

1. "China Outpaces U.S. in Cleaner Coal-Fired Plants," by Keith Bradsher, *New York Times*, May 11, 2009.
2. "China Vies to Be World's Leader in Electric Cars," by Keith Bradsher, *New York Times*, April 2, 2009.
3. An ironic title for a putatively forward-looking journal: a more apt title might have been *Wireless*.
4. *Time*, Dec. 13, 2006.

CHAPTER 5: GO OPPOSITE

1. "The Best Service in the World," *Networking Times*, Jan./Feb. 2010.

CHAPTER 6: REDEFINE AND REINVENT

1. Elizabeth Edwards, *Resilience* (New York: Broadway Books, 2009), p. 34.
2. "Post-Maytag, Newton Looks to Smaller Businesses," by Mike Glover, *Chicago Tribune*, April 23, 2009.
3. "Xeros Washing Machine Cleans with Static and Just a Drop of Water," by Cliff Kuang, *Fast Company*, July 1, 2009.
4. "How Pigs Saved Our Bacon," by Daniel Gross, *Newsweek*, March 17, 2008.
5. John David Mann, "The Best Service in the World," *Networking Times*, Jan./Feb. 2010.
6. "Bolivia Holds Key to Electric Car Future," by Damian Kahya, BBC News, Nov. 9, 2008, http://news.bbc.co.uk/2/hi/7707847.stm.
7. "Paper-Thin Batteries Made from Algae," by Charles Q. Choi, *LiveScience*, Nov. 25, 2009.

CHAPTER 7: DIRECT YOUR FUTURE

1. Futureview® is a registered trademark of Burrus Research Associates, Inc.
2. "Singapore as Innovation Nation," by John Kao, *Huffington Post*, March 14, 2008, www.huffingtonpost.com/john-kao/singapore-as-innovation--n_b_91653.html.
3. "Singapore has been rated as the most business-friendly economy in the world. According to a World Bank–IFC report, Singapore beats previous winner New Zealand for the top spot in the 2005/2006 rankings while the United States came in third." *Singapore News*, Singapore: Channel NewsAsia, Sept. 6, 2006, cited in the Wikipedia entry for "Singapore."
4. "A Conversation with Lee Kuan Yew," by Fareed Zakaria, *Foreign Affairs*, March/April 1994.
5. "What Makes Finnish Kids So Smart?" by Ellen Gamerman, *Wall Street Journal*, Feb. 29, 2008.

INDEX

www.ingramcontent.com/pod-product-compliance
Lightning Source LLC
Chambersburg PA
CBHW030454210326
41597CB00013B/661

* 9 7 8 1 9 6 6 6 2 9 1 7 7 *